THE
BODY
SPEAKS

LORNA MARSHALL

Methuen Drama

Methuen Drama

1 3 5 7 9 10 8 6 4 2

This revised edition 2008

First published by Methuen in Great Britain in 2001

Copyright © Lorna Marshall 2001, 2008

The author has asserted her moral rights.

A CIP catalogue record for this book
is available from the British Library

Methuen Drama
A&C Black Publishers Ltd
36 Soho Square
London W1D 3QY
www.methuendrama.com

ISBN 978 1 408 10682 2

Typeset by SX Composing DTP, Rayleigh, Essex
Printed and bound in Great Britain by Caligraving Ltd, Thetford, Norfolk

By *Lorna Marshall and Yoshi Oida*

An Actor Adrift
The Invisible Actor

CONTENTS

ACKNOWLEDGEMENTS

It's hopeless. I have to acknowledge everybody I have ever worked with in Britain, France, Japan, and Australia, since they have all had an impact on my thinking. Sometimes directly, sometimes in unusual or unexpected ways. But always usefully.

In addition, much of the material in this book is obvious, or has been in currency for a long time. I have no idea where much of this material originated, and so cannot provide suitable acknowledgements. Even worse, I have 'created' many of these exercises in isolation, working through the logic on my own. And then I have often discovered afterwards that others have 'created' similar concepts. This shouldn't really be unexpected; if you have a number of people all trying to find a useful design for a wheel, quite a few will come up with a similar round shape. So if in this book you discover material that overlaps with other people's work, don't be too surprised.

But there is still a need for one special acknowledgement: Yoshi Oida. He and I have worked closely together for fifteen years, collaborating on the writing of three books, and the creation of several shows. During that time, we spent months discussing, arguing and clarifying our thoughts on performance. And on the relationship between performance and life. Without him, I would not have found my own passion for understanding these processes, or the desire to find ways to communicate whatever insight I can offer. Thank you, Yoshi. Also, a thank-you to Pamela Edwardes, without whose support and encouragement this book would never have appeared.

For this second edition I would also like to express my thanks to the Arts and Humanities Research Council of Great Britain, and to the Daiwa Anglo-Japanese Foundation. Their generous fellowship allowed me to undertake detailed research into the functioning of the human organism. This research in turn helped me to refine my thinking, and clarify various issues for this new edition.

And finally, this book is dedicated to my students. They asked the right questions. Here is the answer.

FOREWORD

by Yoshi Oida

Without Lorna, the two books I wrote – *The Invisible Actor* and *An Actor Adrift* – would never have appeared. She was able to cleverly transform and clarify my ideas for a western audience.

We wrote these books together, working through hours of discussion, and by the end of the process neither of us could tell which idea belonged to whom. At this point our writing collaboration ended, but Lorna didn't stay at the same place in her thinking. If she had, it would have been useless to write this book.

Fortunately, she is not stuck in the past, and instead has gone on to develop her own ideas and approaches.

I hope you find her as stimulating and intelligent as I do.

Paris, June 2001

PREFACE

All aspects of performance involve communication. Writers communicate their world and story through specific words and language. Directors and choreographers communicate their understanding and vision through careful selection and shaping of performers, design, light, sound and rhythm. Performers in turn communicate their comprehension of the depths and complexities of the dramatic (or comic, or abstract) journey through their bodies.

The body is also the core of all real-world human communication; probably seventy per cent of everyday conversation is body language. Your actions, your reactions, how close you sit to another person while speaking, how tightly you hold your hands, are all aspects of body language. A further twenty per cent is the music of the voice (its rhythms, pitch, volume, energy and pace), and only ten per cent the surface meaning of words. Imagine someone saying to you: 'You've got a new haircut.' The words are straightforward, but depending on how the speaker says them, and where they place their body, the phrase could mean 'You look great!', or 'What's going on in your life all of a sudden?', or 'Good. I'm glad you've finally got yourself together again' or even 'Fancy a drink?'

Performers have to take charge of this process; they need to ensure that every single physical action reflects and reinforces what they wish to communicate. Each action must be clear and accurate; a direct channel to the audience. In addition, performers who use voice and language (whether as actors or singers) must also ensure that the body forms a single unit with these elements, so that what is revealed to the audience is complete and true with no blocks, no unintended contradictions and no falseness.

This area of accurate communication is not confined to those who make their living via artistic communication. It is relevant to everyone. We all communicate, we all seek to be clearly understood.

But understanding and engaging with physical processes isn't simply a tool for 'managing effective communication'. The body's role is more fundamental and all-pervading than that. The body is the direct point of connection between our inner self and the outer world. We communicate our desires and ideas outwards through the physical activities of speech and action. We may plan and consider in the privacy of our mind, but it is the body that puts those plans into motion through spoken words, phrases, gesture and movement. In addition, we receive all our incoming information about the world via the body's sense organs; through our eyes, ears, skin, nose and tongue. It is a two-directional process; from the world through our physical senses to our inner landscape, and then from our reactions and thoughts back into the world through physical action. The body stands at the centre of this constant exchange. It is the interface between our inner life (thoughts, feelings, memory, dreams) and the outside world (other people, objects, the physical environment).

In fact, it is the sole mediator of human experience. It is our body that climbs the mountain, whispers in another's ear, trembles with excitement, notices the light change, grips the bag, tenses with fear, laughs with delight. It is our body that actually lives our life. Our mind may plan, and process, and recall, but it is the body that directly experiences the reality of the world.

And it can 'remember' this experience. If this statement seems a bit extreme, consider what often happens when you try to recall the words or tune of a song. You sit there thinking, but you cannot remember what comes next. Your conscious mind cannot provide the answer. So you just start singing out loud and, nine times out of ten, as you sing, the forgotten part of the tune just falls out of your mouth. Maybe not immediately, but as you sing your body somehow 'remembers' the tune.

In terms of training, both the central importance of the body and its role as bridge between the inner life and the outside world need to be acknowledged. The body should aim to become a more sensitive receiver for information from the world, and learn to process this information in new and more creative ways. It also needs to speak more freely, more clearly, more directly, and more vibrantly, in order to communicate the richness of the interior life to the outside world.

The first section of this book is about preparation, getting yourself ready to do the work. It focuses on becoming connected: ensuring that the world and your inner life are in clear and direct dialogue with each other via the body, and that you can fully engage with the physical, emotional and creative resources you already have.

Once this basic state of connectedness has been established, we can decide to look further. To extend our range beyond that which we already know. To develop alternative areas of freedom and control; new techniques, new styles, new physical possibilities, new imaginative processes. And when we choose to increase our range, it isn't just the anatomical structure that benefits. New ways of moving and inhabiting our bodies enrich our senses and deepen our direct experience of living. The more we allow our bodies to open and explore unfamiliar territory and the more we permit new reactions, the greater our understanding becomes. In addition, this second section looks at some of the elements that impede or promote learning, for both teachers and students.

The third section of the book is about putting the process into practice; doing the actual work in the rehearsal room, engaging with text and other people. Looking at ways to apply the body to the delicate task of working together on specific performances. And incarnating another human being.

In the fourth section we examine the process of creating and clarifying meaning for the audience. How the performer and the director can enhance understanding of situation, relationship and emotion for the onlooker. The question of style is also considered.

The four sections of the book are rather like a camera gradually moving to a wider and wider view of the scene. Initially the focus is tight; a close shot of 'I' and 'Me' as I am now. Then it moves out to

'I' and 'Me' as I could be in the future. Then a bigger picture emerges; 'Us' and what we do together as performers. Finally, the camera opens up to the entire reality; 'Us' and 'Them'; what we do to shape what the audience sees.

As you read, you may find some of the exercises in the book slightly peculiar. Because my ideas are based on the centrality of the body and its role as a bridge for experience, I work through the body and its knowledge, rather than on it. The body is seen as a medium of learning in its own right, directly contributing to our understanding, and not as an external object that 'requires proper training'. Hence, some of the exercises may seem odd or unlikely when you read them. Don't worry; they usually make sense when you actually do them with your body. In addition, since the exercises seek to integrate the entire physicality with both the inner and outer worlds, you will find very few exercises where the body or the voice or the emotions are worked in total isolation from any of the other aspects, or separately from the world around you.

I also want to encourage you to work in a way that is direct and sensory, responding to the process, rather than simply going through the exercises in a mechanical manner. I am always trying to find words that will point you in the right direction, but without telling you exactly what you 'should' experience. Everyone is different, and responds in their own unique way. Have a go and see what the exercises offer you.

This brings me to my reason for writing this book. I have worked in a wide range of performing styles and situations, including dance, classical theatre, physical theatre, performance art, opera, circus and street performance, and in spaces ranging from structures holding twelve thousand people to intimate studio theatres. I have rehearsed with text and with improvisation, both devising and interpreting. And what I have discovered through all this diversity of experience is that the deep skills of the performer are similar, irrespective of the style or the particular technical demands. The ability to be truly connected, and then to communicate with clarity and authenticity, is universal; it applies in any context, culture or medium. Good performers reach the audience, fully convincing and engaging them in the action, whether they are trapeze artists, Shakespearean actors or Butoh dancers. On stage, on film, in the street, they are all fully alive and expressive in their various physicalities. Happy to own their individual body, and to explore and employ its richness.

It makes sense to engage with your body, to 'invite it to the party' when you work. After all, it has lived, felt, experienced the world, and in turn responded through action and speech. It is you, not something separate and apart. To ignore it is to ignore the fullness of yourself and to refuse a major source of information and insight. This holds true for everyone, not just performers. Since the body provides such an easy and accessible path to development, it seems illogical to deny its importance, to turn away from what it can offer you.

PART ONE

DISCOVERY AND PREPARATION

INTRODUCTION

We all need to get acquainted with our body and its current range of possibilities, and to use what we already have to its best advantage. On the surface this would seem straightforward; just get in there and do what you know. Unfortunately, this won't really work. In an ideal world, our daily bodies would be free and effortless conduits, directly connecting our selves with the world in a constant and fluid interchange. But we don't live in an ideal world; we live in the real world – a very active and concrete world that has shaped and modified the use of the body in a number of ways. Our bodies are moulded by the requirements of daily existence, and have become selective about how they engage with the world. Not necessarily in a 'bad' way, but certainly in an unavoidable way.

Young children interact with the world directly. Their senses are alive and hungry for information, reaching out for stimulus. They also physically communicate their feelings and responses simply and immediately. When a baby has a tantrum, every particle of its being is involved in the activity. The body arches backwards, the feet drum on the floor, the fists clench and the lungs emit powerful sounds while tears stream down the infant's face. You know exactly what that baby is feeling.

But we are not babies; we are adults living in a social world that has taught us how to behave appropriately. Over the years, we have learned how we should exist and present ourselves, and how to co-exist with other people. We have become socialised. Again, this shouldn't be seen as 'a bad thing'; after all, a world full of demanding adult babies would be tiring in the extreme. But we need to understand how this process has shaped us, and how we can dismantle it when required and appropriate, because it has created limitations.

Through the process of growing up, we are taught to control and present both our physicality and the expression of our emotions. We are taught what we can do and what we can't. In physical terms, we learn how to sit, how to hold things, how close we should stand to other people, how loudly we should speak, how insistent we can be in asserting our needs. We learn what is the body of a proper 'man' or a 'woman' or even a 'rebel', according to our particular family's and social group's perception of these beings.

Similarly, according to the demands of our social web (which includes our family, class, religion, culture, job and friends), we are encouraged to manifest certain emotions, while others are discouraged, or forbidden in public. And even when a particular feeling is permitted, there will still be controls on exactly when, where, how, and how far that emotion can express itself. Anger might be socially acceptable in one family, but only if it expressed verbally. Another family might prohibit the expression of anger in any context whatsoever: it must be swallowed and denied existence. A third family might permit anger to be expressed physically as well as verbally, perhaps by smashing objects or even hitting others. Which emotions are acceptable changes according to context. In some societies, it might be vulnerability that must be hidden, while anger is socially accepted, or vice versa. But every social group has something (or many things) that must be hidden, or redirected into approved forms of expression.

This socialisation even affects private emotional choice – what we allow ourselves to feel. A person who identifies strongly with a social culture that values cool, ironic detachment will know that passionate enthusiasm will be unrewarded and even mocked by their group. Any upwellings of naïve delight will therefore be judged as being inappropriate, and the person will seek to quell them before they come to the attention of others.

As we grow up, we become more skilled at adapting to the world, quicker at learning what to do and what not to do, and better at selecting the right responses – the ones that will get us what we want from the people around us. And so we become successful adults; we fit into our particular social group fairly well; we speak, act and interrelate with others in ways that are rewarded by acceptance and approval. We create a persona that works effectively, and which we are (more or less) happy to uphold. We are reasonably comfortable being seen as 'that kind of person'. This holds true whether our society is rural Australia, Parisian art culture, or a gang of alternative bikers. We may move to another society if the one we are born into demands more adaptation than we wish to engage with, or deliberately rebel, choosing to define our identity as outsiders. But even when we look for another society where we can fit in more easily, we still adapt ourselves to that community, even the community of outsiders. We are all socialised to some extent.

This could all sound rather oppressive, even unpleasant. After all, we are not simply machines that follow programmes, or helpless victims of our circumstances. Socialisation is not imprinting; if it were, all members of the same social group would be virtual replicas of each other. But in reality, we are very diverse. We make personal, idiosyncratic choices; part of our persona is chosen, not imposed by necessity. We like being a little loud, or wearing only pale colours. No one is forcing us to conform, or punishing us when we make these choices. And our relationship with the socialisation process itself is also variable; some aspects of our cultural context we welcome, while other patterns evoke strong resistance when we encounter their demands. The persona itself also changes over time, adapting to new circumstances, and is equally capable of responding to different social contexts. How strongly we maintain our persona will depend on where we are and who we are with. Indeed, we are all unique individuals, and part of our individuality is the specific nature of our social persona; this complex structure which reflects all the diversity of our culture, class, family, as well as our idiosyncratic choices and resistances.

I have been describing socialisation as a purely external process. Certainly, our persona affects how we present ourselves, how we act, and the choices we make. It affects our external manifestation. But there is a more subtle function; it also acts as a filtering device, assessing the world around us and selecting what it considers to be relevant and useful. It affects how we perceive everything around us. It also shapes our reactions and patterns our relations with other people. In other words, it affects our thinking as well as our actions.

For example, if I am walking down my familiar street, and a large, strangely dressed man suddenly appears in front of me, my assessment of his presence will be affected by my particular socialisation. If I identify myself with a society that rewards neat, structured clothing (in order to 'not stand out'), I may assess him as weird, and possibly dangerous. But if I myself am part of a society that rewards individual eccentricity and flamboyance of clothing, I may assess him as interesting and double-check to see if I recognise him.

There is one important thing to understand about socialisation. It is a process of selection; 'this way' rather than all the 'other' ways. As you refine and adapt your persona over the years, you focus on certain possibilities and discard the rest. It is a natural and normal process, but it does involve a narrowing of experience. Imagine you have a paintbox containing every colour of the spectrum, but you decide to paint only with shades of red. Maybe red is a lucky colour in your culture and therefore you'll get better sales. Or maybe you just like red. It doesn't matter why you make the choice; the fact remains that all of your paintings are red. Meanwhile, the paintbox is still sitting there filled with unused squares of green and indigo and apricot and amethyst and emerald and gold and turquoise . . .

Unless you deliberately desocialise yourself from time to time, your persona becomes the only way for you to exist in the world. Interestingly, many of us do find ways to step outside our everyday persona. We take up unusual hobbies, learn new skills, undertake sporting activities on holiday, travel to foreign countries or even go to costume parties dressed as an alternative self. Apart from being fun, these help us to avoid becoming locked into a single way of existing and interacting. They remind us that there is a variety of ways to engage with the world.

So, what does all this have to do with performing?

Unless performers recognise how strong and all-pervading socialisation is, and see how the mechanics of the social persona affect the body, the emotions, mental processes and social reactions, it is difficult to respond to the demands of the profession. Ironically, we all spend years learning how to be well-socialised, yet if we want to perform, we have to undo this process. We must learn to relinquish everything we have spent years acquiring out there in the world. The job of communicating via performance demands the ability to access and directly express the full range and depth of human feeling, not just the aspects that we are familiar and comfortable with in our daily lives. These feelings must be able to find free release in action. Performing also demands the ability to transform ourselves into an 'Other'; someone very different, who presents him or herself in their own particular way, and has unique responses to the world and other people. Somebody whose appearance, words and habits might be alien and even horrifying to us. And we must be able to do all this under the gaze of strangers, allowing the most private moments to become public property.

Although this sounds like a gargantuan task, it isn't actually that difficult.

Firstly, in a sense we already know how to 'perform'. After all, we have lived our lives for many years, adapted to circumstance, experienced turmoil, spoken words we would give anything to call back, seen pain, known delight. We know what it is to be human. And this is the source material for performing. The only trick is being able to connect to, shape and use this richness of experience on demand. Secondly, we have all been children, so we have all known what it is like to experience the world in an unsocialised way. We have all had our senses at full engagement, we have all expressed our hungers and joys directly. And we have explored as many ways of using our bodies as our environment would allow. It isn't a case of starting from scratch. Rather, it is a question of how to retrieve what we already know and what we have already done, simply reconnecting to a more direct and fluid way of existing. I am not speaking about any kind of emotional regression, or painful self-examination; therapy is outside the scope of this book, and isn't a precondition for good performing. Nor am I advocating the rediscovery of any 'real' self. Your social persona is very much a part of your 'real' self. However, it reflects only one aspect of your potential, one framework for your relations with the world. Alternatives exist.

And we begin with the body, since this is, and has always been, the mediator between who we are and the world.

Chapter 1
CONNECTING TO THE BODY

As well as the pleasure of rediscovering your innate range of physical life, connecting to the body serves another purpose. The audience isn't telepathic; it only understands what is happening through what it sees and hears. If the script, or the director/choreographer's vision, is not fully realised in clear physical action, then the audience cannot comprehend what is going on. If your body does not truly reflect the world of the performance and the complexity of the people and ideas in that world, the audience cannot experience it.

To do this, you must be able to bring your body into free and easy contact with the emotions, other performers, the language of the text, style of presentation and, eventually, the audience. It must be fully alive, in dialogue with your inner life, and able to vividly express a chosen human reality.

But how do you this? How can you move beyond physical, emotional and mental habits established over many years, into new possibilities and a more vibrant existence?

Most people begin by undertaking training in a specific movement style, involving new techniques and forms of control. I don't recommend this. Learning a new physical language can be a marvellous and enriching experience (and I discuss this in the section on 'Extending Your Range'), but this should be undertaken only after you have established a good working relationship with your body. If you just add more technique and control to a socialised body that is working with learned habits, you simply add another layer of pattern to an already well-patterned body. Two sets of habits instead of one. Yet another 'correct' way of moving, rather than freedom of choice and exploration.

In fact, people can work very effectively with their 'daily' body, provided they are able to connect to it in fresh ways. Your everyday untrained body already has an extensive vocabulary of physicality ready to be tapped, since the basic process of growing up has provided the body with a rich store of experiences. We may not use this material very often, but it is readily available, and can be easily drawn upon. Indeed, most people are surprised at how well their bodies can actually move, once you take away preconceptions and narrow frames of reference. Reclaiming your basic physicality is a necessary starting point.

The first step in exploring your body should be awareness. Forget about what you can or can't do, as well as what you 'should' do. Instead take the time to discover how you actually move, what your patterns are and where the automatic responses reside. Then engage in dialogue with them. You might be surprised by what emerges.

AWARENESS

Most of the time, we are totally unaware of what our body is doing. Patterning takes us out of contact, and we have no sense of what is physically happening, moment by moment. The body simply follows the habitual programmes for walking, running, dish-washing, sitting, etc. that have been established over the years. It knows perfectly well how to perform these actions; it has discovered an efficient system which has now become fully auto-mated. In fact, we have worked very hard to detach our awareness from our actions. I don't want to think how I use my body when I am washing the dishes. I want the dishes to wash themselves while I get on with planning what to do next.

All of the exercises below require you to do the opposite: to bring your attention to what is happening moment by moment. To 'listen' or 'taste' what is going on as you move. Also, to discard preconceptions about what your body can and cannot do. Some things you know you can do easily – after all, they are your familiar patterns and you have been practising them for years. But there are other physical possibilities, other ways of moving. It is important to remain open to these, to avoid assuming that the unfamiliar is automatically impossible or 'wrong'.

This doesn't mean that you should suddenly decide to hurl your body into a backwards somersault. Rather, that you remain in a state of gentle curiosity. Involved in seeing what might emerge as you work, constantly asking yourself the question 'I wonder what would happen if I tried this thing . . . perhaps like this . . . ?' All of the exercises in this book require this sort of interested and generous relationship with your work and your body. In particular, the entire process is predicated on the idea of 'pleasure'; of the movement feeling good or satisfying on some level, or maybe even slightly naughty and indulgent. We often fear being judged as 'self-indulgent', and believe that anything truly worthwhile must be bought at the price of pain. When this happens, the pleasure found when working well with the body seems almost reprehensible, as if we are somehow cheating. Fine. In this work I want you 'cheat'; to see your body as source of delight, not a burden to be carried, or a problem to be solved.

As you explore the exercises, they might feel very odd or unfamiliar, surprising even, but you should never find yourself saying 'Oh dear, what have I done?' Stay tuned to the body at all times, and if it hurts, or feels somehow wrong, don't do it. If you are using willpower to force yourself onwards, stop immediately. You are working from the wrong place. In terms of emotion or personal material, your attitude is 'Nothing to prove'. No toughness or willingness to endure suffering or relive pain is required. You simply become intrigued by the possibilities within you, and so you investigate. Maybe it will work. Maybe it won't. There is only one way to find out.

GETTING THE WHOLE BODY INVOLVED

The first step is to engage the whole body. Not just hands, arms and face. Not just the features you see every morning in the bathroom mirror. You want every limb, muscle and bone in your body to be vibrantly present, and able to communicate equally well.

When we look at the anatomy of the body, certain things strike us. The single biggest bone is the upper thigh, the single biggest unit of bone is the fused mass of the pelvic basin, and there are enormous, powerful muscles attached to this region. The thigh muscles, the gluteals in our buttocks and the long and complex grouping of the abdominals. All the muscles that link leg to torso, and which enable us to stand and move. Given that very little in the body is designed by accident, there is a reason for this preponderance of heavy-duty structures below the waist. This region is the workhorse of the body, with the equipment that allows us to walk for miles, climb hills, run across rocky terrain, scale trees or clamber up slopes. Before humanity became urbanised, this is how men and women used their bodies on a daily basis, and so this is what they are designed to do. A couple of hundred years of city living, or even seven thousand years of settled agriculture, is too short a period to affect the basic design. Legs are designed for effort, to be strongly involved in our activities. That's how the body is built, and that's how it likes to work.

However, most of us underemploy our legs, and they often lack strength and flexibility. They are unused to responding to our needs, other than brief periods of walking and standing. When this happens, the top half overworks in order to compensate. For stage actors, this creates a specific problem. In its worst manifestation, the legs act as wheels that convey the upper body on to the stage, find their spot and then set up camp. The legs then switch off (usually becoming locked and rigid, like poles supporting a lookout tower) while the upper body gets on with the task of delivering the text, usually with much hand-waving. At the end of the scene, the legs wake up, turn on the motor and wheel the torso off. In this case, the upper body is asked to do all the work, while the lower limbs go to sleep.

We need to get the legs moving and linked to the upper part, so that the entire body awakens and can respond equally.

Exercise – Waking up the Legs

Using only the legs, start to explore all the possibilies of locomotion. Try to find as many ways of using the legs as possible – as many odd walks, crawls and slithers as you can. Don't stick with what you already know, or try to reproduce movement patterns you have seen elsewhere. Genuinely start from zero, as if you have no idea how these limbs operate. Ask yourself questions like, 'I wonder what would happen if I tried to move using the sides of the feet, or one foot and one knee, and backwards?'

The legs start to come alive. Now you want to join them up with the rest of the body. In this way, the entire physicality becomes equally receptive and equally able to go into action.

Exercise – Starfish

Imagine that your body is that of a starfish with five limbs. These 'limbs' are the two legs, the two arms and the head/neck 'limb', which begins between the shoulder blades. Start moving from your centre (located just below the navel) as if it is the core of the starfish's body. The movements travel outwards to all five limbs equally. So your hands and feet and hair are the five extremities of the starfish body. Try to keep the movement travelling simultaneously to all five limbs; not legs first, then arms and finally head. And never forget that the neck/head limb joins each impulse in the same way as the legs and arms. Get the feeling that every molecule of your body is saturated with the same physical reality: from the centre, right out to the extremities.

It may take some time to get the sense of moving from your centre, but as you get used to it, start playing with lots of different rhythms and tensions. Strong actions. Gentle ripples. Standing. Lying on the floor. Keep reminding yourself that the head is not a 'pilot' sitting on top of the body, but part of a longer, more flexible limb.

Here is another exercise that promotes total body awareness, while at the same time focusing on physical detail.

Exercise – Free–Responsive–Fascinating

While we are aware that the body is symmetrical from right to left (i.e. that the right side is structurally identical to the left), we sometimes forget that it is also symmetrical from top to bottom. Although they are not identical, the shoulder joints are of a similar design to the hips, while the elbows parallel the knees, and the hands and feet are based on the same skeletal pattern. We can start to explore our body, using these key joints as a starting place.

Focus on your hips and shoulders. As joints, they are designed to be *free*. To have a wide range of movement, and to be able to twist and turn to many angles. Start exploring them together, seeing their similarities and their differences.

Then focus on the knees and elbows. These are basically hinge joints, designed to respond to shifts of weight and to absorb impact. Explore their possibilities, noting the fact that they are basically only designed to bend in one direction. Do some soft jumps and gentle falls and see how they absorb your weight. Aim to make no noise when you land; this helps prevent jarring impact and makes you aware that these joints are meant to be elastically *responsive*, rather than held in rigid, locked positions. Also ensure anatomical integrity. When bending your knees, or landing from a jump, make sure the kneecaps 'ski' out over the feet. Don't let them roll inwards.

Then consider the hands and feet: many fine bones and complex joints. Although we normally specialise, letting the feet do the walking while the hands focus on fine manipulation, this is partly a matter of practice rather than absolute design function. There are people who walk on their hands and others that paint with their feet. Play with your fingers and feet as if you have never owned a set before. They are *fascinating*. See what happens when you ask your feet to clap or caress, when you try to walk on one foot and two hands, and so on. Or use unusual parts to do familiar tasks, e.g. walk on the sides of the feet, use the backs of the hands to clap.

Once you have a sense of the *free* hips and shoulders, the *responsive* knees and elbows, and the *fascinating* fingers and feet, start to work them together. Just move in whatever way you like, but keeping an awareness of these three key joint pairs. Maybe you focus on the hips for a while, and then you add the hands and feet. You haven't forgotten the elbows and knees; it's simply that you are not focusing on them at present. Then maybe you slowly flex the knees and elbows while removing your main attention from the other parts. You are constantly aware of the whole body, but making choices about which parts are in focus and which parts you have chosen to eliminate from the main action. As you explore, use lots of different rhythms and degrees of muscular tension, and remember there is no pressure to 'look good' or 'be interesting'. Do what feels fun, or intrigues you, however you like, for as long as you like.

While this kind of full-body integration work is useful for everyone, it is especially relevant for those who communicate via language. When we are keen to get our ideas across verbally, there is often too much effort concentrated in the upper body. This can lead to the 'goose/goggle/grapefruit' syndrome.

When this occurs, the head pokes forward in an effort to reach the listener ('goose'), the eyes bulge in an attempt to convey meaning and intensity ('goggle'), and the hands seem to be trying to grip something (in this case, the speaker looks as if he or she is holding invisible grapefruits). All of these are thwarted physical impulses. Inchoate desires to do 'something' to reinforce the speaker's words. And they locate themselves in the head/shoulder/hand area, because this is where the body has become used to placing many of its efforts.

Linked to this is excessive face-acting (also known as 'mugging'), where the person overworks the face, or neck-tightening. These problems are commonly described as 'tension'.

People often try to eliminate tension by simply suppressing all movement in the face, or arms, or neck. This rarely works, for two reasons. Firstly, you are still focusing all your effort in the same physical location (the face, the shoulders, etc.). Trying *not* to move one part (instead of moving it) doesn't shift the focus of effort, it simply alters the kind of effort (from doing to not-doing). You are still overworking in the same inappropriate place. Secondly, the body does not like the word 'No'! It doesn't react well to harsh negatives. 'No!' tends to block the body rather than release it.

Besides, if you try to squash the physical manifestation of tension, it rarely works. The underlying impulse tends to pop out sideways somewhere else. But you can utilise this tendency. When you want to eliminate overworked facial expressions, or any other unhelpful movement, simply send your impulse somewhere else in the body. While the body doesn't like 'No!', it doesn't mind 'Go over there'. A simple trick that Yoshi Oida mentions to get rid of unnecessary twitches is to redirect the effort into some invisible part of the body, such as the little finger or the arch of the foot. You haven't said 'No!' to the body, but you have shifted the tension to an innocuous location.

However, redirecting effort can go further than just camouflaging distracting gestures, or hiding the tension. Tension is energy seeking an outlet. A twitch or eyebrow wiggle or an unformed grope of the hand is simply a physical response to what you are feeling, or what you are trying to say. It might not be coming out of the body in a useful way, or be situated where it organically needs to be, but it is real, a genuine impulse that hasn't yet found a useful pathway to expression. And as a positive manifestation of thought and feeling, it requires management rather than harsh suppression.

There is an additional problem with aiming to eliminate tension totally. Because the body and the emotions are linked, managing to suppress the physical form of the impulse (the hand tension or face twitches) may lead you to lose connection with what you are doing and feeling. If you automatically repress all movement or physical response when emotion starts to rise, you run the risk of disconnecting from the emotion itself. In this case, your body stays 'relaxed', but it may be harder to develop emotionally. If however you are able to redirect your physical responses into other, more appropriate body parts or physical actions, the problems of unhelpful tension disappear and the work becomes richer and more vibrant. The body and the inner life stimulate and reinforce each other, rather than battling for supremacy.

Sensing exactly where and how to channel the impulse is explored later in this book, but I find that 'Go to the legs and feet' is a generally useful instruction. As a director, I often see actors 'vibrating' when they rehearse; something is happening inside, they sense they want to shift, but their legs are 'stuck' and unresponsive and so they twitch or wobble with unfocused intention. Quite often, a leg twitch or a leaning of the upper body is a manifestation of an impulse to change position or go elsewhere in the space. To move to another spot, or to get closer to someone, or further away. Because the lower body has become desensitised, you need to remind yourself of its availability. Hence, I will often give actors the instruction, 'Follow your feet'.

In addition, if you allow your lower limbs to engage with the creative process, it looks more organic, even when you are not moving around. The face neither overworks nor is it dead; in fact, it tends to join in with the action in a natural way. It is as if the impulse to communicate starts below and naturally rises upwards. But the opposite is not true. Performing that starts in the face rarely seeps down into the lower limbs. Good physical process seems to be anti-gravity. You can focus your action in the centre of the starfish, or even in the legs themselves, but start low and then let your impulses travel up and out. A second note I often give to performers is 'Get your acting "down". It's too high. Don't let it rise upwards, into your face. Get it down into your body.'

The next exercise works on keeping the whole body involved when dealing with concrete human impulses.

Exercise – Starfish with Impulse
This is the same as the previous exercise, except that you focus on physical impulse rather than pure movement. Impulse is an action or body shift that connects to something recognisably human.

You stretch out the body because it feels nice, like lying in bed on Sunday morning. You curl the whole body up in fear. You flail all of your limbs about in a pettish, childish manner. In this exercise, you are not trying to be deeply expressive or emotional, but you are aware that the actions are no longer abstract or disconnected from your experience of life. They are real. Recognisably real.

The key thought when doing this work is to 'invite the whole body to the party'. To let every cell in your body be permeated by the same feeling at exactly the same time. You worry less about initiating the action in your centre, but you still ensure that nothing has been left out. All five limbs are present and saturated by the same reality. You might not need to move much; you can use quiet, almost invisible impulses, like extreme fatigue. Or soft despair. Not much may happen, but whatever little 'happens', it happens everywhere at the same time. Or you can do ferocious 'party animal' rampaging. Whatever impulse you use, you work to ensure that it penetrates every limb as fully and as equally as possible. Every part of the body is engaged, in the same moment, sharing the same reality.

It may take a while to get the sense of every part of your body working equally, but as you continue, it usually gets easier.

Now that the entire body is starting to come alive and unify itself, we need to have a more detailed look at the head/neck area. We know that the lower body is anatomically designed to be the workhorse of the body, and that this is an ancient functional structure. But there is a different design feature in the top half of the body. As we move up the spine, the bones of the vertebrae become smaller and the muscles less bulky. By the time we reach the neck, we have seven small bones loosely held together by finer, more delicate muscles, supporting the wobbly weight of the skull. Again, there must be a reason for this structure, some reason why it has this particular design. Again, we return to our pre-settled past for the answer. In an unpredictable world, men and women had to be very alert to what was happening around them, in order to find food and avoid threat. And information came into all the senses (sight, hearing, smell) from every direction (above, below, behind). The head was the information-retrieval system, and it had to be free to swivel like a radar disc, in any direction. It was flexible in order to be alert.

Exercise – Freeing Neck and Head

Start to focus your attention on the space you are in. Look at the walls, ceiling, light fittings, etc., seeing the various shapes and forms and absorbing them visually. Then start to listen to the actual noises in the space and outside, smell the particular scents in the air. Get all of your senses tuned in to the world around and above you. Don't 'act' as if you have seen or heard something; really see and hear what is around you at that moment. If there is a sudden noise behind you, let your head turn to see what it is. And always remember that there is a world above and below you. Try to stay aware of the whole room, even when you are focusing on one object. And when something catches your eye, just walk towards it. Don't stand there and peer at it from a distance. Let your legs carry you over for a closer look. Let the head see and hear, but let the 'workhorse' move you around. Up on to your toes, down to the floor, climbing on the chair to get a better view.

In order to stay truly alert and responsive to the world around, the neck has to unlock. As you do this exercise, the head may want to come out of the shoulders and to sit in an easier, more poised manner on the neck. Again, this follows the basic design. The neck is built to be free so that the head can swivel about, taking in information.

In general, the head/neck area should not work too hard at communicating or 'getting the message across'. Instead, it should sit back in order to receive and absorb what is happening in the moment. The head is not designed to be actively 'doing things' (that is the job of the rest of the body). Its role is more passive, focused on 'receiving input'. By the way, this also affects the gaze. Many people go pop-eyed, energetically working to influence others with their eyes (the 'goggles' mentioned earlier). Instead, the gaze should relax and focus on absorbing the situation around you. Seeing and receiving information, not doing anything. It makes it easier to respond to others if you genuinely perceive what they are doing, and an overactive 'working' gaze blocks your ability to read what is happening around you.

LISTENING AND TASTING

Most of us have inherited a false view of the mind/body relationship, seeing our bodies as primitive machines controlled by the super-efficient computer of the brain. This is a false idea; body and consciousness are indivisible in practice, and the function of the mind cannot be separated from the function of the body.

In recent decades, technology has been developed that allows observers to see what is actually happening in the brain as it processes its reactions, thoughts, feelings, and perceptions. They discovered that what we call 'Mind' (including memories, emotions, reactions, imagination, as well as conscious thinking) can be witnessed scientifically as a dizzyingly rapid and complex series of connections within the brain; a supersonic firing of millions of points, following precise neural pathways. This firing then triggers chemical or electrical signals, which pass via the blood and/or nervous systems to organs and muscles. These provoke muscular shifts leading to movement, or stimulus to organs, causing further chemical alterations, including release of hormones and brain neurotransmitters. These in turn affect the brain, producing new signals in different parts of the neural network, which once again trigger a fresh thought/feeling/response. It is an endless electrical-chemical feedback loop. (If you want to follow this area further, the writings of Antonio Damasio are a good starting point. He is both a leading neuroscientist and an excellent writer.)

For the first time in history, we have clear proof that the idea of a separate mind and body is false – there is only a single interconnected entity. In fact the 'mind' and 'body' are like the palm and back of the hand; opening or closing the palm of the hand inevitably affects the back of the hand, and vice versa. Neither element leads, both respond. We regularly experience this fused cycle in our daily lives. We have an important interview or audition; we feel nervous, our pulse rate speeds up, our palms get sweaty, we need to go to the toilet, we fidget, and our thoughts run around like mice in a cage. So we decide to control our breathing – taking long, easy breaths which calm us down and restore our mental focus.

The implications of this recent discovery are vast. It means that everything is connected; how we think affects every aspect of what happens to our bodies, and what happens to our bodies influences our minds. One side of this equation has been understood for decades; innumerable researchers have shown that how we think and feel affects the physical functioning of the organism. For example, if we experience fear or stress, hormones are released which affect the heart and digestive system. Even thinking about stressful events in the past or the future can trigger this response, and these in turn have an impact on the long-term health of the system.

In the other direction, there is a certain amount of evidence that physical experiences can affect the brain and therefore the functioning of the mind. Unfortunately, the field of body-to-mind research is very young and in a state of constant change. For this reason, I don't want to make too many broad statements about what does and does not operate. Nonetheless, there are some broad trends.

There are many studies which measure the impact of general exercise programmes on cognitive functioning, particularly in the areas of depression, dementia, Alzheimer's disease, anxiety, and learning. The conclusions follow a pattern; low to moderate exercise programmes have a measurable positive effect on brain functioning (high-level programmes seem to have a slight negative effect). For example, a Swedish team recently discovered that exercising at least twice a week during midlife can significantly reduce a person's risk of developing dementia later in life (*Lancet Neurology*, October 2005). In addition, A.S. Chan, Y.C. Ho, and their associates discovered positive impact on memory as a result of both cardiovascular workouts and mind-body exercise system

(*Journal of American Geriatric Society*, 2005).

A second key area of research focuses on how specific body choices may affect emotion or response. There are studies on how particular facial expressions link to emotion; measurable changes in autonomic functioning have been noted, as well as subjective perception of altered feelings. (If you want to follow this up, look for the name of Paul Ekman and his various associates; they have published numerous articles and books in this field.) Variations in mental reaction in standing and supine positions have also been noted (Lipnicki and Byrne, 2008). Similarly, differences in breathing have been linked to differing emotional response (Berridge and Valenstien, 1991).

As yet, there hasn't been enough research to produce clear conclusions, and the exact patterns of operation, and the mechanisms involved are obscure. But the trend seems to be towards a recognition of body-to-mind impact. (If you are interested in this field, I can recommend the *Pubmed* website; it provides summaries and reviews of medical research from around the globe. Most of the studies I have mentioned can be found there, plus many others.) For performers, it isn't necessary that we understand the body-to-mind system in detail; what matters is the acknowledgement of the fundamental unity of the entity. Rather than splitting it apart, and creating false and artificial separations, we need to be aware of the innate connections.

This is why working with the body is so important to performers; not just to 'move well', or even to 'communicate well', but to be fully and deliberately alive in all the functions of the self. Your thoughts, your emotions, your reactions, your memories and your imagination can all be supported through the body and its experiences.

In daily life we are usually unaware of our self as a single, dynamic system. But we can change this situation very easily by becoming connected to our bodies, and then learning to pick up the signals that are always being transmitted. We simply need to stop disconnecting ourselves and engage in dialogue. (In many of the exercises that follow, I talk about a communication between the body and the mind. Of course, this is using the very distinction that we know to be false, but it can be useful for training purposes to work 'as if' the mind and body are separate aspects. Just remember that it is inaccurate.)

We tend to be insensitive to how information is exchanged beween our physicality and our inner realms. Sometimes, when exercising or training, we become aware of a mind-to-body link, but this is usually an external awareness. Looking at the body from the outside and instructing it, rather than sensing the subtle link between inner reality and physical action. And we rarely perceive that this can be a dialogue, rather than a one-way monologue (except when our bodies announce their discomfort through pain).

Conventional body training tends to use a 'boss/servant' relationship between the mind and the physicality. You tell your body what you want it to do, and how to do it. And then it obediently responds, as best it can.

That kind of relationship isn't generally useful. After all, my body *is* me, and it should be seen as an equal partner with my mind. While I can separate the two aspects and function on automatic pilot (as when washing the dishes), working like this all the time diminishes my awareness and sensitivity. And since it is my body that enables me to experience the world, and the world to experience me, it should be respected. Treating your body like a clumsy, unhelpful servant distances you from the reality of your own existence.

And here's another impediment. As people living at the beginning of the new millennium, we are constantly faced with negative images associated with physicality. At this moment in history, western society is not only (as we are repeatedly told in the media) incredibly unfit, but we are also living in a world that seems to see the inherited body as a generally undesirable commodity that has to be beaten and pummelled into acceptability. Many people deal with their flesh either by ignoring it and hoping it will go away, starving it into submission, reshaping it with metal instruments, or by driving it through the pain barrier until it becomes suitably obedient. And the only pleasures that such processes give these people are the sense of success in achieving a desired target or the chemical high that comes as part of the body's mechanism for dealing with pain.

By all means, continue your gym work, watch your eating, get plastic surgery, pierce and tattoo yourself, or dye your hair green, if that is what you truly want to do. Only don't despise the body you have inherited. Change it, but also delight in it.

And the first step is to learn to 'listen' to it; to 'taste' what it can offer you.

Exercise – Playtime for Hips

In this exercise, you will reverse the normal boss/servant relationship with your body. This time the body will be the master/mistress and your conscious mind will be the servant.

Lie on your back on the ground. Start by clearing your mind. You decide to avoid using any movement pattern you have learned, no matter how useful or beneficial. No yoga, Feldenkrais, or Alexander technique. Instead you start gently moving the legs and hips about while bringing your conscious awareness to that region. Start to 'listen' for any areas that want more detailed attention. Sense any muscle or joint that wants 'something' and try to give it that exact 'thing'. Maybe your lower back 'wants' to twist in order to release, or your right leg 'wants' to open out in order to stretch the inner thigh. Do exactly what the body 'wants', as far as it 'wants', and for as long as it 'wants'. And when you find the precise answer to the body's unspoken need, you can sense its gratitude, almost as if it could say 'Yes! That's it! Thank you!' Especially when that particular area has been sadly neglected.

The key point is to find and do exactly what the body wants. Don't just throw an exercise you have learned at the body and hope it works. Instead, move your legs in order to get information about what is happening in the hip/lower back region, and then once you get the information, focus your actions in order to meet the need you have uncovered.

I recommend that you avoid learned exercises since they tend to be programmatic; you start the exercise, and then you let it run while you disengage the mind. This is the opposite of what we are trying to do here. In addition, programmed exercises tend to be general; they treat all bodies in much the same fashion, and even within your own body they treat the right and left sides in exactly the same way. By 'listening' to the body, you become more specific, finding exactly which position is right for your own body, and also become able to sense and respond to differences between your two sides.

You might find yourself in some rather odd positions as you try to feel your way to the exact position/movement that satisfies the need, but that's fine. What matters is that you and your body are in dialogue with each other, as you work to release the hip, lower back and groin region.

Then do the same process in your upper back and arms ('Playtime for Shoulders'). Start from lying on your back, and begin moving your arms and shoulder blades around slowly. Roll from one side to the other, to bring your weight to bear on different parts of the upper back. Move and 'listen' to find what wants to happen, and then slither into whatever contortion creates a sensation of pleasurable release. Then finally bring your attention to the body as a whole, listening for any parts that are feeling neglected and wanting to come alive ('Playtime for the Whole Body'). In this exercise, it isn't necessary to actually move the whole body all at the same time, just extend your awareness throughout the entire structure. You might sense that the shoulders are still 'hungry', or that you want to go back to your left inner thigh. Fine, that's what you do.

It may take a while to get used to working in this way – listening and responding, rather than using specific release or stretch exercises. Persevere, and don't worry if you end up in some rather unusual shapes.

You may have noticed I give certain exercises rather silly titles. I do this for two reasons. Firstly, it helps them stick in the brain; 'Playtime for Hips' is much easier to remember than 'Body/

...nsciousness Dialogue'. Secondly, it prevents us from becoming excessively serious or over-disciplined when doing the work. Keeping things light and humorous makes it easier to relax, which in turn makes it easier to sense and respond.

The next exercise also reverses the boss/servant relationship, but you are now 'listening' across a wider band. You are not just 'listening' for what the muscles and joints require in terms of release, but for the broad spectrum of sensations the body wants to experience, including feelings that wish to emerge, or activities it wants to encounter. The focus of your attention is different; the whole organism rather than just the structural anatomy.

Exercise – Listening to the Body

Start running around the room. Then suddenly stop and, in that instant, tune into your body. Where in the room does it want to be? How does it want to be? Go to that place, and then continue questioning. What rhythm? What tension? What feel? What edge? Then do that specific thing, focusing on giving the body *exactly* what it wants. And do it for as long as the body wants. Don't ever consciously decide that you ought to change now. Let your body stay in charge of the situation. It will tell you when it is ready for something else.

Keep 'listening' all the time. Question your body. Do you want more of this? Less? Do you want to shift to something else? Yes? No? Do you want something completely different, or a slight adjustment? Your mind stays very active in your listening, but you *do* only what the body wants. If it wants to keep running round the room, or to go faster, that's what happens. If it wants to stay curled up in a corner, that's what you do. It might seem illogical, but let yourself follow the body's needs. After all, the point of this exercise is to let the body take charge, while the mind abdicates. But never tune out your awareness. Your mind remains in a state of alert 'listening', because the body's hungers could change in an instant.

Remember that the body has its own weird sense of humour. You may end up doing some very odd actions. Don't get too serious when listening, and allow yourself to surprise yourself. Also, look for 'feels' and 'sensations' as well as movements while 'listening'. Sometimes the body wants a particular sensory experience: a tension, a repetition, a point of view. It might want rhythmic rocking, or to drive the hands hard into the floor, or to lick its lips.

If you are doing this exercise in a group, ignore the other people. You do not interact with them. They are simply mobile furniture.

When people do this exercise, they often find themselves moving (or not moving) in ways they did not expect. They find they can do things they assumed were beyond them, or things that are completely inhabitual, surprising themselves. But it isn't your aim to discover 'something surprising'. Maybe your body will desire very little activity, or just to sit still. In which case, that is what you give it. The purpose of the exercise is to listen honestly, and to do exactly what the body wants. And only that specific thing: as the body dictates, not the mind.

Once you learn to truly 'listen', you have opened the gate to a two-way dialogue between the inner landscape and your body. And you should try to stay in this state of dialogue when working creatively. When you think and feel, try and sense what the body 'wants' to do in response, and let it fulfil that desire. From the 'inside' of thought and emotion, find and follow the impulse into action on the 'outside' of the body.

But equally, when you are doing physical exercises, reverse the process and work from the outside to the inside. As you make an action, try to 'listen' to what is happening inside your consciousness. What does this movement evoke in you? A feeling? A memory? A mood? An atmosphere? Or something indefinable. Something that has no name but you know is real. All are aspects of your inner landscape. After all, the mind and the body are basically the same thing, so it doesn't really matter where you start. The important thing is to listen for the link between the two aspects.

I recommend doing this every time you work with your body.

You can use this 'listening' process in class, and in training sessions, whether working through improvisation or practising set technical forms. Even the most formal, repetition-based exercises (such as those at a ballet barre) can be undertaken in this way. You don't do your '*port de bras*' mechanically, but instead look for an inner sensation that brings the movement alive. By doing so, you reinforce the habit of dialogue, and get used to being connected at all times. Even at the gym, or when swimming, take a few minutes to sense what those physical actions evoke in you.

Or you can decide consciously to create an inner dimension for the work; to do your movements or physical actions, but linking them to some imaginary process or state. You walk as if you are treading on the softest rose petals, or as if you are travelling in the wide spaces of the desert, your eyes focused on the distant horizon beyond the walls of the room. You do your stretches as if you are a cat waking and readying yourself for the hunt, alert and hungry. You lift your arms as if they are carving their way through sand, or drifting upwards of their own volition. If these images seem too poetic, find something that is more to your taste: walk as if you are going to smash your way through the walls, or imagine you are surrounded by adoring fans and flashing cameras. It doesn't much matter what you use, but find something to focus on. As Yoshi Oida noted in *The Invisible Actor*, this makes it easier to do the task. It becomes less arduous physically, and infinitely less boring.

Ownership – Connection to the Self

The previous exercise works to encourage dialogue between the body and the consciousness, but it needs to be taken one step further. Too often, physical work becomes 'correct' but empty. The body works well, moves flawlessly and maybe even presents an inner reality accurately, but you don't have the sense that there is anyone at home inside. The work is functional rather than fully 'owned'.

For performers, this is an impossible situation. Every single move they make should reflect some kind of vibrant inner reality. In a play or film, this inner reality comes from the character and their world. But even here, the actor must find a way to fully engage with that person. A way of 'owning' the other. And in performing situations where you are not playing a specific character, there still needs to be some kind of inner fire. A light behind the eyes. A sense that every action is linked to some part of a living inner landscape. And that landscape is your own human experience.

When working, we should all try to 'own' everything we do. We acknowledge a connection between what we choose to do and who we are as individuals. It is 'me' that performs – not egotistically, or self-indulgently, but genuinely and openly. I use myself, my experience, my inner landscape, my imagination, and enjoy permitting these to engage with the work. I adapt and shape what I do according to the demands of the situation, but I own every action, every shift and every nuance. I recognise my right to be fully present in everything I choose to explore.

And it is good to engage this sense of connectedness right from the start, even in the most basic exercises. In this way, there is no unnatural separation between training and the 'real thing' of performance. You are doing the 'real thing' all the time. And you don't have to do special exercises or preparation to get you connected as the first performance approaches. Instead, being fully alive and connected to what you are doing is your natural and automatic state.

Exercise – Ownership

Starfish with Self (though you can also do this work with 'Free–Responsive/Fascinating' or any other exercise that involves the whole body).

Return to the basic starfish exercise. You can either work with everyday human actions (as in 'Starfish with Impulse') or you can explore more abstract choreographic movements. Whichever you choose, start simply. You don't want complex or elaborate forms, however interesting. Straightforward actions like folding yourself into a ball or quivering all over are fine. You may hardly move at all if you are lying on the ground, softly pulsating through every limb. What matters is that every part of your body is filled with the same reality.

As you move, gradually become aware of the inner dimension. What does this action connect to? What does this movement remind me of? What is the 'feel' of this rhythm pattern? You are working towards connection, and then comes a moment of recognition. 'That's it!'; you become aware of what the movement connects to. That fast vibration of the upper body might link to a feeling of frustration, while that slow languorous stretching might remind you of lazy mornings in bed. Now for the final stage.

Once you sense the connection, lock on to it, and commit to it one hundred per cent. Clarify the outside, so that what you are doing becomes exactly and precisely 'right' for what you feel. It becomes a true expression of the inner reality. Then do the same for the inside. Own that feeling fully, recognising that 'you', the human being you are, truly understands that feeling. It is yours, consciously recognised, acknowledged, expressed openly and owned.

It doesn't matter what you connect to or what you look like. The thing that matters is that you honestly own whatever emerges. And it doesn't have to be a grand, dramatic passion. You can work with everyday feelings such as 'boredom' or 'general fed-upness'. It also needn't be very serious; you can connect to your innate sense of silliness, or embarrassment. Like the time you were just fooling around with the vacuum cleaner, treating it like a savage animal. You can work very well with that, as long as you know it is your genuine human silliness, fully owned and acknowledged.

Equally, what you connect to and own might be something much less definable than an emotion or a memory. It might be a sensation that has no name. But you can still recognise it as real and own it as part of your inner world.

By the 'inner world', I mean the full richness of your mind and experience. Everything that is human in you. That is why I tend to use words such as 'inner landscape' rather than 'thoughts' or 'feelings' when talking about what goes on in your consciousness. Your 'inner landscape' includes thoughts and feelings, but it also encompasses images, sensations, memories, dreams and indescribable impulses. It includes things we can talk about and things that have no words. Both are important and both need to be accessible to the performer. And everything needs to be able to link to the body.

So these are the basics: unifying the body (getting it all equally alive and available), then getting that body connected to your inner world, and finally owning this connection in every way. All of these aspects are equally necessary. A body that is fully 'available' in the sense that every part is working and able to move well, but which is uninhabited by an inner reality, will be technically interesting to watch, but somehow cold and sterile. Conversely, a body that is inhabited in the sense that you know something is going on inside, but where the body can't follow the impulse of that moment, will look 'clogged'. And when there is a connection between inside and outside, but it isn't fully owned, you sense a lack of commitment to what is happening. Everything must work, and everything must be connected.

Although I have outlined the exercises separately, in practice you can work on them simultaneously. So when you are doing an exercise on physical unification, remember the work on 'listening and tasting'. When you are 'listening and tasting', remind yourself that the entire body is available to you, and that you can 'own' your actions.

You won't necessarily get everything at once, but you will know what you are aiming for. Maybe you need to take things slowly, one step at a time. For example, just work with the legs for a while. When you can sense (via 'listening') that the body is starting to come alive, you begin to identify the inner dimension of those leg flicks. And then you can start to own the movements, and really commit to what they express. But don't feel obliged to hurry and get it right. There is no 'right' in this process. Work in your own way, respecting your body, curious to see what insight it may offer you. (Personally, I find it useful to do some 'starfishing' on a regular basis, since it reminds me that I am something more than a head perched on a walking machine, and to 'listen to the body' since it enables me to open the gate between my inner and outer realities. I have found that this facilitates my work, even when doing something less physical, like writing.)

Once this basic process is in place, you can choose to look at form and technique, or extend your range of movement, or explore various new styles of expression. But 'being connected' is the bedrock of your physical life, and that is why I start here. Besides, getting connected doesn't require any specific technical skills or equipment; you can explore this area whenever you want. Nor do you need special preparation; just an open relationship to your own body. In terms of training, this process is a pleasant way to engage the body and encourage it to be more alive. Working like this also introduces you to alternative ways of being physically present. New patterns, inhabitual responses. Awareness and choice, rather than automatic following of habit.

Chapter 2
IMPULSE AND RESPONSE

Once you are connected to your body and able to listen to it, another realm of possibilities emerges. In any situation, you will begin to 'hear' subtle physical reactions, and become aware of half-formed urges within your body. For example, you are listening to a political speech and you think you are processing the words calmly and dispassionately, but then you notice your jaw starting to clench. Your body is telling you something about what is really going on inside as you listen. Similarly, in a social situation, you may truly believe you are being totally open to the person sitting in front of you, until you notice that your body has crossed its arms and legs, and closed in on itself. Your body is a very poor liar.

These subtle (and sometimes not so subtle) hints are the indicators of an impulse, a desire in the body to do something concrete in response to a stimulus. The clenched jaw might be the resistance to the desire to tell the speaker to shut up. The folded arms and legs, a need to put some kind of barrier between yourself and the other person, because you find them somehow disturbing. Or simply that you are cold and ought to put on a pullover. But however subtle, all of these reactions are manifestations of impulse; the body responding to a felt need. (By the way, you will notice I am not speaking about analysing anybody else's physical patterns in order to understand their personality better. I am focusing on your own patterns. You are the one who has folded your arms, and you are the one who can best decide whether this is a response to emotional discomfort or poor heating, and then choose the next course of action. It is not easy to discern the subtleties of another individual's inner life. But if you remain honest with yourself, you are the best person to analyse your own responses.)

All of us are in a constant state of impulse and response. There are hundreds of examples. You are working at your desk and then, unexpectedly, you find yourself gazing out of the window. You see the bus waiting at the stop and start to run. It moves away and you slow down. Your nose itches, you scratch it. Or you start to scratch, see you are being observed and then unwind the gesture. And so on. All the time.

Some of our impulses are highly conscious; we are aware of what we intend to do and even prepare and rehearse our actions. You know you need to talk to your partner about household tasks, so you search for the right words and the right moment to negotiate this area. And you are aware of launching yourself into your opening words, 'I've been thinking . . .' Other impulses are literally unconscious. When you are asleep, the body chooses to shift position or roll over, without consulting your conscious mind at all. And there are semi-conscious impulses, like going to the bathroom in the middle of the night. Our body senses the impulse, responds to it, then puts us back to bed without really bringing us fully out of the sleep state. Even in waking life, we sometimes 'find' ourselves doing something specific without having made any kind of conscious decision to follow that course of action. Have you ever driven your car to work, only to find that your body has automatically taken you to your former office? Or suddenly 'discovered yourself' in the kitchen with no real idea of why you went there? Embarrassing, but not unusual.

In addition, we often feel the need to suppress direct physical responses to inner impulses. We are not sure whether they are appropriate or allowable in the particular social context, and so we squash them. When listening to the political speech, our body's impulse may be to tell the speaker to shut up. But we sense that voicing our opinion might be unhelpful and disruptive, so we refuse to follow that particular impulse. We 'decide' to 'keep our trap shut', managing the expression of an inappropriate impulse. And yet the initial impulse and the secondary management strategy have left a physical manifestation (as evidenced by the clenched jaw).

This process of assessment and redirection of impulse is often automatic. We are unaware of what we are doing. We might not even notice that the jaw is clenched, far less why. And it is the lack of awareness that limits us; if we don't know what is going on, we cannot make choices about our course of action.

But we can discover what is going on via the body. Although the impulses themselves may be unconscious, they will always create a physical manifestation or response. The reactions may be large (you leap out of your chair and pelt down the stairs), or almost invisible (your breath speeds up, or the gaze sharpens). Every tiny shift of the body reflects a change in some aspect of the inner world. Something alters inside, and the physicality responds in some way. Perhaps this is why the word 'emotion' contains the idea of 'motion', and why we say 'we were moved' by what we saw. On a deep level, we know that inner impulse links directly to movement. Changes in thought, feeling and reaction always manifest themselves physically.

This is why the ability to listen to your body is so essential. It can sense what is really going on in any situation, and can offer a physical hint about the desired course of action. Once this is clear, you can decide whether or not to follow that hint directly, or to ignore it, or to reframe the action in an alternative way.

If you are a performer, you must be in charge of this process. As well as sensing what needs to happen at any moment, you must be able to avoid the automatic and habitual management of impulse. You are able to follow any impulse immediately into direct and complete manifestation, without hesitation, fear or judgement. If an actor (playing a member of the public) feels that he wants to tell another actor (who is playing the role of the politician) to 'Shut up', it can happen. By tuning to the body, performers are able to find the exact and authentic response to the situation. Then they follow it into unfettered action, enabling real dramatic truth to manifest itself – or they modify the impulse to better serve the dramatic situation.

There are three stages in this work: sensing impulse, following impulse and modifying impulse. We have already begun the process. The exercise on 'Listening to the Body' helps you to feel what 'wants to happen', in other words, to sense the impulse that is arising in your body at that exact moment. The next step is to go with that impulse, to follow it without hesitation or conscious construction of action. Finally, only after you can fully follow impulse are you able to shape your work according to choice rather than through automatic habit.

Stage two is extremely important, and there are many approaches in improvisation and performance that recognise this fact. A number of actor-training systems focus on following impulse, and offer a range of exercises and various starting points for the work. But whichever system you use to stimulate a particular impulse, give yourself full permission to follow that impulse directly into action. Forget what you look like. Don't worry if it seems peculiar or illogical, or even slightly ridiculous or outrageous. And never try to shape your response to make it 'better' or more acceptable. To begin with, just let your impulse flow into an honest and complete response.

RESPONDING TO THE INNER WORLD

We need a starting point for our work; a stimulus that will provoke an impulse for us to follow. Many current exercises start from the inner world of thought or feeling, where the mental reality engenders a physical response. While these are effective, they actually reflect a false situation. The constantly looping exchange between world and inner reality makes it impossible to do a pure inside-to-outside exercise. What we feel is constantly (though perhaps not consciously) affected by what goes on around us. But we need to begin somewhere. So we work 'as if' such a pure possibility existed, focusing our attention inwards and then finding a response in the body.

When using the inner landscape as a starting point for an exercise, you decide to feel or think in a certain way, and then see what happens. Or you may decide to investigate a memory or an atmosphere. You ignite that inner reality, and then you listen to see what response the body offers. And this is the key point in this process; you work through the intermediary of the body. It is not 'stimulus–action', but 'stimulus–body awareness–body response–action'. The essential thing here is not to construct a response according to what you think it could or should look like, nor to illustrate that thought or idea through preselected gestures. Instead, once you have chosen a specific inner reality and engaged with it, let the mind step back, giving up its 'master/mistress' role. Try to 'listen' very openly, alert and ready to hear the body's reply.

When you were doing the earlier exercises on 'Listening to the Body', you probably noticed some kind of physical response. Maybe a clear urge to fall to the ground, or a desire to lie facing the wall, which (since you were letting the body be the one in charge) you followed. But you may have missed the subtler impulses; the desire to shift the angle of the hips, or to tighten your lips, or to alter your gaze. Small adjustments are easy to miss if your focus wanders or if you are only tuned to larger-scale shifts. As you work on responding, fine-tune your awareness. Extend your 'listening' across as wide a band as possible, sensing the tiny flickers of half-formed impulse as well as the stronger desires for clear action.

This skill is also useful for directors. As you watch your actors working on a scene, you will occasionally see the flickers appear. They usually occur when the actor is momentarily blocked; they hesitate in their speech and get locked physically. If you watch closely, you will see that they usually congregate in one part of the body. The flickers are the impulse pushing at the body, trying to move it into action. Just saying something like 'follow your feet' (as suggested in the last chapter), or 'go with your hands', or 'you don't have to stay there facing him' can be useful. A broad instruction, like saying 'go with it' helps (and is a common director's tool), but identifying the exact location of the flickers enables you to give more specific advice.

For actors in text-based work, the thoughts and feelings arise from the character's inner process in the world of the play. The character thinks X and it leads them to do Y. Dancers and physical performers may use a different approach; the inner world might be feeling-, or atmosphere-, or image-based. But again the same process applies; image X leads you to do physical response Y. So it doesn't really matter which aspect of the inner landscape you use; what matters is the process of listening to the body and following it into action.

Exercise – Responding to an Inner Reality

There are hundreds of exercises that you can do here. Since many classic improvisation exercises are based on this approach, you can use themes from other books and teachers. Consequently, I don't go into detail in this section; I am indicating broad categories for consideration, rather than giving an exhaustive list of possible exercises.

What matters here is how you do the exercise. In this work, you are *not* improvising or exploring. You are listening and following. The wrong words can send you in the wrong direction. Too often the instruction 'be free' or 'just do what you want' stymies the performer, and can lead to half-hearted wriggling about, or to the recycling of well-used habits or party tricks. The task of 'Listening and Following' is very specific. You create your inner reality, commit to it, making it alive and vibrant, and then you simply follow the tiny flickers in the body. The half-formed urge to lift your chest is picked up and given life, the chest lifting as far and as strongly as it wants, until the body (not the conscious decision-making process) decides to stop itself, or transform into something else. For example, if you work with the thought/words 'It's not fair!', you may sense something spark in your hands. Immediately go with that 'gripping/fisty' sensation, and see where it takes you.

Here are some basic categories of inner stimuli:

Thought:

When working on your own, you can use phrases such as 'It is difficult', or single lines of text. You can also use single lines of poetry, though this incorporates rhythm and sound as well. I suggest using single lines initially, since whole speeches can tend to produce a generalised and over-simplified response. Another useful starting point is a classic acting objective or intention, such as 'I want to understand what is written in this letter'. If you use thought, be careful to allow the body to find its own individual response, however quirky. Don't ask it to illustrate the thought through action – that is the game of 'Charades', not direct physical response.

Emotion:

The next chapter focuses on this area in detail, but you can start basic work now. You can trigger impulse via choosing a specific emotional note such as joy or frustration. I find that the more complex emotions often lead to more interesting responses, e.g. joyful anticipation, frustrated despair, bitterness, naïve nervousness.

Exercise – Working from Emotion

Create an atmosphere of bitterness (or whatever) in the space. Connect to that source feeling in whatever way works best for you, and then let the room echo with bitterness. Follow your body, and let that bitterness into the space and air. Let it be seen. As you work, let it grow and develop as it wants. Let it change and alter moment by moment, but keep it alive and flowing outwards through your body into space. Also, no cleverness, or false expressivity. It's simply real, here and now.

Memory and Created Memory:

Real memory is fairly straightforward, e.g. the 'feel' of your first day at school, remembering the atmosphere, the noise, the objects, your emotions, how big or small things were, your reactions to other people. You recall these concrete details to help you re-create that 'feel' in your mind now. You do not attempt to tell the story, but to find a direct physical manifestation of that specific 'feel'. Remember, your body is creating the response to the memory, not your mind.

I would like to emphasise that this isn't regression in order to do therapy, but association in order to elicit a specific reality in the body. The memory itself is relatively unimportant; it doesn't require detailed examination. What matters is evoking it and then passing it directly into the body. In fact, I recommend not using memories that are too personally charged for this work. If something is 'hot', in the sense that the repercussions are still with you today, you will find it difficult to explore and use creatively. Memories that are 'cool' are more useful; you can evoke and examine them with curiosity and interest rather than fear or anger.

Created memory links to your imagination and empathy. You can create false memories that are as rich and detailed as real memory. You evoke the exact place, the hour, the temperature, and the sounds of that moment. This is why I call this exercise 'created memory' rather than 'imagination'; it isn't just an idea or image. It has the same degree of detail and specificity as a real memory. It has denseness and texture. It also involves the senses.

For example, imagine you are walking down a country lane. It is dusk and the sky is clear. It is summer and it hasn't rained for two weeks. The scent of dust is in the air, and you are alone. Suddenly a cloud of butterflies erupts from the bush in front of you. They flutter all around you, some of them landing briefly on your skin. And then they vanish. Become that moment.

When doing this, beware of mime or storytelling. You do not want to illustrate the events as they unfold. You want to evoke this 'memory', let it seep into your consciousness, discover what it connects to, and what manifestation it desires in your body.

The paradox with created memory is that it is totally unreal (in the sense that you have never directly experienced it), yet you give it the immediacy of actual lived truth. It can offer great freedom, since you cannot measure (and perhaps judge) your response against your real memory. It is always fascinating to go beyond that which we have personally experienced and make a leap of empathic identification. To truly connect with an alternative moment or mode of existence. And performance specifically demands the ability to incarnate a reality that may be totally alien to our lives.

How else could we portray Medea? Or Hellboy?

These kinds of exercises can also work in more abstract ways. Japanese Butoh dance incorporates this approach into its methodology, using odd or even paradoxical 'memory' (such as being dead) as a stimulus to creation and embodiment.

Image:

Again, a thousand possibilities. Photos can be useful starting points, since they are often extremely powerful. And paintings. Jacques Lecoq taught an exercise whereby a group of students had to study the work of a painter. They then created, rehearsed and finally presented a physical evocation of the artist's 'painted world'. Not the personal history of the artist, not the viewer's response, but the reality of the work re-created in another medium.

Sensation:

Lecoq also had a number of exercises that worked on a sensory basis. These used pure sensory information such as light, colour and materials. Or something more complex like the four elements of earth, air, fire and water. In all cases, it was necessary to transform directly into the sensory reality. To discover a physical way to manifest fire, rather than describe it. For your body to create a direct correspondence to 'green'. It was also important to be very specific when doing this work; water slopping in a basin has a different quality from water crashing on a beach in the form of surf.

As you work, stay aware that the whole body is available for transformation. Remind yourself of the exercises you did in the first chapter.

Obviously, the danger with this type of work is that it can tip over into the kind of unstructured indulgence that is every student's nightmare ('I am a tree, feeling the loss of my leaves'). You must remember that your task is to find ways of letting an inner reality connect to your body. You are not doing the exercise in order to empathise with the painful trials of vegetation, but to train your ability to pass an inner reality into direct physical action. Any kind of inner reality; it doesn't matter what starting point you use, as long as it clear and specific. And you work with focus, to find a precise and real counterpart in your body. In which case, why not a tree?

RESPONDING TO THE OUTSIDE WORLD

Turn your focus away from your interior world and relocate it in your physical environment.

Our bodies constantly respond to the outside world, though we are generally unaware of it. That is why we can walk down a busy street without bumping into anything or anybody. When you think about it, this is amazing. Lamp-posts, uneven paving, gutters. And mobile objects: cars, bikes and buses. So many people, constantly moving, and at different speeds. How on earth do we process all of this information and chart a path through this ever-changing maze of bodies? It very rarely goes wrong. When it does, we suddenly have to negotiate the process 'manually', through one of those little pedestrian dances we all encounter ('I'm going to bump into you, so I'll move to my right. You've moved to your left. We're still going to bump into each other, so I'll move to my left,' and so on).

In the same way, how you hold your body when you are outside in the open air is different from how you hold it indoors.

Exercise – Respond to the Room via Listening to the Body
This exercise is very similar to the earlier 'Listening to the Body' and operates in the same way. The added dimension is a more concrete awareness of the space and objects around you. You are not just looking for what your body wants to do with itself, but also what it wants to do in relation to the physical environment. It is now finding the 'wanted' action in a real and tangible world.

Stand somewhere. Perceive the room with all your senses. The shape, the noises, the light, the textures, the air itself. Extend your awareness above, below and behind you, as well as in front.

Now tune to your body. Is this where it wants to be? Does it want to stand, or sit, or lie down? Where exactly does your body want to go? What does it want to touch? A curtain catches your attention. Does your body want to touch that curtain? And does it want to touch with the hands, or would it prefer to rub its face against the velvet? You continue to listen. Is your body happy to stay with this activity? Or does something else enter your perceptions and shift you to another impulse? Perhaps a sound or a smell presents itself and your hips engage with this fresh information. Or the bumps on the floor create a response in your feet. Stay aware, and listen for when the body wants to change. Follow the flickers that arise in the moment.

You are aware of everything in the room, but some things are more important than others. Some things catch the attention of your body and involve you immediately. They might hold you for a long time or be of only passing interest. Follow what your body truly wants.

As I said earlier, responding isn't the same as exploring, playing or improvising. When you are 'playing' with a surface, or 'exploring' the space, you tend to put yourself in charge. In the same way, when you 'improvise', you often find that you maintain a functional, normal relationship with the world. Floors are for walking, chairs are for sitting, curtains are for opening. Your conscious intelligence and learned experience are still 'master/mistress' of the situation. Responding puts the space in charge. It affects you. You yield and it changes you.

You work to keep your responses open. You have no idea what you will feel or what you might be led to do. Perhaps something very simple and obvious. Perhaps something more unusual. For example, a line on the floor might lead your body to walk along it, as if it were a tightrope. Or it might produce a 'long thin' physical sensation, which leads you to stretch your arms and legs wide. Or a tight and held emotional response, which in turn might provoke a thin, high moan in your voice. Who knows? Find out.

In daily life the body constantly reacts to space, and the strength of this response should never be underestimated. For example, if you see a precipice in front of you, the body will not let you get too near. If you want to peer over the edge, you must forcibly override the body's instinctive response. And you can feel the battle between your will and your body.

Performers and directors need to become aware of this exact syndrome, since it affects staging and rehearsal. If the stage has a sharp drop-off, the actors' bodies will automatically adjust to keep a certain safe distance. If you want to get a particular part of the action right to the edge, you will have to give a strong and specific instruction to that effect. You will have to override the instinctive 'keep back' response.

And if the stage has a drop-off but the rehearsal room is flat, you may have another problem. You can mark the edge of the stage with tape and tell the actors there is a drop-off, but their bodies will perceive a nice, flat surface with a line of inoffensive tape. That is the true physical reality existing in the space. And so they will happily go right up to the edge of the stage (as marked by the tape). Their bodies know it is perfectly safe. But when you transfer the production to the actual space, the performers' bodies react to the new reality in front of them. The action retreats to a safe distance, throwing the staging into disarray.

Because your bodies respond to the actual physical environment, your rehearsal space should replicate the reality of your performing space. Then the physical environment of rehearsing is the same as that of performing, and there is no alarming transition. And make this tangible. Don't just tell the performers that 'this is a six-foot drop-off'; put some kind of definite barrier there (a row of chairs will do). Then their bodies will know that there is a 'thing' in front of them. Something that could have a real physical impact on them. Their bodies will adjust accordingly. Visual information (tape) isn't sufficient. It has no volume, or tangible existence.

The exercise 'Responding to Space' can be very useful when moving into a performing space for the first time, or when touring from venue to venue. Even fifteen minutes of simply allowing the body to become acquainted with this new environment can create a sense of ease and familiarity. The body becomes comfortable in the space and understands its problems, possibilities, and quirks. Too often performers look as if they are shrinking away from the walls, or as if they have been parachuted into alien territory. This is easy to fix.

The same logic holds with objects. Work with the real props if possible. You handle a heavy earthenware mug differently from how you handle a crystal wine glass. Sitting on a solid bench is a different process from folding yourself into a canvas deck chair. If the real objects are not available in rehearsal, get something of similar shape, size and, very importantly, weight. I know this sounds terribly obvious, but I constantly see actors rehearsing with mimed objects, or flimsy substitutes. Paper cups instead of real glasses. And then they are surprised at how unwieldy the real objects seem at the dress rehearsal, and how awkward they feel handling them.

RESPONDING TO OBJECTS

In daily life, we tend to consider objects in a purely functional way; chairs are for sitting on (or occasionally standing on, when you can't reach the top shelf). We take them for granted. In our minds, object equals function. Yet the body reacts differently; it will spontaneously adapt itself to the object. How you sit depends on which type of chair you are offered. A rickety chair will evoke tentative perching, while a big, solid armchair will enable you to fall and slump. And you can carry the body's ability to respond to objects into conscious process.

You can do this work in two ways. The first involves suspending your normal functional knowledge of the object, and simply responding to it as a baby would. You move it around, shifting it, playing with it, seeing what noises it produces, how it operates. There is a very famous clown act based on this approach: the 'How do you put up a deckchair?' routine. In order to find the problems and illogicalities of deckchair behaviour, the performer has to spend time investigating all of the possibilities of the object. All the ways it can move, how it reacts to pressure at different points, how it balances, how it falls.

Or you can do the same kind of work I have already outlined, where you find a direct, less 'logical' body response.

Exercise – Responding to Objects

Take an object, such as a chair. Place it in a specific position. To begin with, avoid the position that corresponds to its function. Don't stand it on its legs, because that is how chairs appear normally. Tune your body to this object via your senses, especially sight and touch. But remember, touch doesn't automatically mean the hands. Your whole body is capable of touch. Don't forget the sense of smell either. In theory, taste is also available, but in practice most rehearsal rooms are uninviting to this sense. Recognise that it exists; there are cases where you can engage it. And then just tune in and respond. Your body can find unexpected ways to engage with this object. Maybe it will want to curl itself around the legs, or drape itself over the seat. Maybe it will keep a distance while visually echoing the shape and outline. Maybe it will become an organism with which you form an emotional relationship. All are possible. Follow the body.

RESPONDING TO ANYTHING (LIGHT, MUSIC)

It is possible to apply the responding process to a range of phenomena, investigating music, light and sound in a physical way. Responding to music is not the exactly the same as choreography or dancing. You are not interpreting it, or looking for moves that correspond to the musical quality or atmosphere. Nor are you treating it as a sound environment in which you do your work, or which frames your artistic statement. All of these are valid and valuable approaches, but they are not 'responding'. Responding is more a case of letting the music connect to you directly and seeing what aspect of your physical life it ignites. You are not thinking in terms of steps or learned styles of dance, but rather a naive receptivity to the life embedded within in your anatomy. You can physically respond to music without any knowledge of dance.

Having said that, many dancers and choreographers do employ this approach. They instinctively respond to the music, and then combine the 'feel' of what they discovered with more formal methods and specific technical languages. The distinction between responding and choreography isn't that important in practice, except that it helps you refine your focus when you are working.

Exercise – Responding to Music

Put a piece of music on the CD player. Use an external source of music rather than an MP3 player – that way you don't have to worry about the earplugs falling out. Also choose music that does not directly link specific dance styles. In particular, avoid currently fashionable dance music. When you go to a club to dance and you move to that music, your objective is something other than detailed investigation of responding process. Social dancing is one thing, investigating is another.

As you listen to this music, let it move you directly. You don't look for 'steps' or any kind of formalised movement. If it just makes you walk, or sit down, that's fine. It might shift your breathing, or alter the tension in your muscles, or shape your body into a specific posture. Resist the pressure of the rhythm; don't get trapped by the beat. You might want to synchronise with the rhythm at certain times, but that is a specific response, not an automatic reaction. Keep going, and keep 'listening' to your body rather than to the music itself. Your body might want to shift response or radically change before the music does. This is one of the differences between dancing and responding; in responding, the body follows its own desires as evoked by the music. It does not follow the patterns and structures inherent in the score.

All of the previous exercises are based on the idea of a fixed and unchanging physical world to which your body responds in a one-way process. But what if those elements respond to you? When this occurs, you have a dialogue. Your 'partner' (the thing that affects you, triggering impulse and response) could be the floor, the set, the light, even the air itself. For example, you move, and the floor makes a sound. That sound then affects you, changing your physical response, which produces a different sound, and so on. Anything can become a partner.

In the same way, if you are working with live musicians, or a good sound or lighting operator, you can develop a creative partnership. They offer, you respond, and your response in turn triggers a counter-response from them. I will go into more detail about the responding exchange process in Part Two, but it is worth reminding you here that our performing 'partners' are not always co-actors or dancers. They might be an improvisational musician or a technician; someone who, with their particular creative language and equipment, is 'present' in a real but less visible way.

A final word. People change all the time. When doing pure listening and responding work, don't expect to stand still. You might use the same image or object as a trigger for investigation three days in a row, and you are most likely to find three different responses. As you work today, what happened yesterday no longer feels appropriate. Today, some other aspect of your self responds.

USING AND REFINING IMPULSE

Through all this work, you become more highly tuned to impulse. You can quickly sense what wants to happen and go immediately into action with it. In fact, you have become so tuned to the process that there may be very little conscious awareness involved any longer. Occasionally you will have to tune your attention to the body, looking for the 'flickers' and the 'hungers', but commonly you simply find yourself moving directly into action. You have no clear idea of why that movement came to your body, but you know it somehow 'feels right'.

As I mentioned earlier, I avoid the phrase 'Do what you want'. It is too general and can leave the body confused as to what it is supposed to achieve. The body often flails around, trying to be interesting, rather than gradually homing in on an exact response to a particular image or thought or performing partner. It also focuses on 'you' and what 'you' want, rather than responding to a demand located outside you. As a performer, you don't do 'what you want', you do 'exactly what is required in the performing situation'. In other words, you respond rather than construct.

What we have explored so far is a useful starting point. The basic skill of 'free and full response to impulse' is becoming established. You have stepped outside your normal habits of appropriate behaviour, and are able to go immediately into action according to what is required from the situation. Like a child, you do exactly 'what wants to happen', fully, without hesitation. The stimulus and the response are symmetrical; nothing impedes or modifies the flow between impulse and action. Now we can explore impulses in greater detail.

FURTHER WORK

You can use this impulse work to practise other skills. For example, your sense of timing is linked to the ability to feel the shape and duration of specific impulses.

Exercise   Sensing the Shape of Impulse
Start working with any kind of impulse, listening and allowing your body to respond directly. Just keep going, following impulse after impulse. After a while, it should start to flow freely, one impulse leading organically to another. You may also begin to sense that impulses are like waves, rising, following their trajectory and then disappearing. And as one impulse ends, another tends to rise. Even if one impulse ends, and there is no clear new impulse arising, don't panic. Just wait in a state of receptivity, tuned to your body. As one of my directing friends

said to her actors, 'Just wait there. Something will come along. It always does.'

Once you are freely following impulse, start to tune more finely to the exact nature of each individual impulse, and the physical response it requires. How far does this one want to go, how long does it need to continue, what is the exact energy, or duration, or rhythm it wants? Follow this urge without hesitation or impatience until it ends of its own accord. And a feeling of satisfaction arises when you have completely and precisely expressed an impulse. A voice inside you says 'Yes! I liked that. It was exactly right.'

You will notice that the impulses themselves vary enormously. Some require you to fling your body around the room, some require stillness. Some require that the entire body is engaged while others locate themselves in a specific part of your anatomy. Some need to go on and on and on, way past the point where your logical brain would have ended the action, while others are over in an instant. You are discovering the precise life and nature of the impulse.

You will also become aware of the difference between a strong impulse that is blocked, and a small impulse that doesn't require a huge expression. The flicker of blocked response feels very different from a tiny impulse that has had its full and complete life. The second one leaves you with a little glow of pleasure, rather than a sense of confused frustration.

This 'responding to impulse' work is actually simpler than it appears in print. As a child, you were in a constant state of direct response; you found the spinach bitter, so you spat it out. You sat glued to the window for ages, watching the raindrops meander down the pane. Then suddenly that ended, and you ran to the kitchen. No child is aware that they are in a state of organic responding, and as adults we have lost the instinctive connection, but there is no mystery here. We all know (from our early years) how to follow impulse. And the feeling of pleasure and satisfaction I mention above is no hard-won transcendent state. When you are hot and thirsty, cool water feels exactly right. Immediate recognition. Pleasure and satisfaction. (As you may notice, the pleasure principle underlies every aspect of my work. It is a safety net that prevents injury, physical and emotional. It is a motivating force to keep working, and encourages the persistence required for real learning. It stimulates deep exploration. It also links to audience response; a performer who takes no pleasure in their work is rarely attractive to the onlooker.)

Another skill you can practise via impulse work is 'Staying out there'. Too often, we go in and out of action. We make an offer, do our bit, and then retreat back into non-awareness. You can see it happen on stage; actors do their speech and then they switch off their attention, except for the monitor that is listening for the cue for their next line. Horrible, and completely unnatural. Because when things actually matter in real life, we 'stay out there'; we speak our thoughts, and then switch our attention to the other person in order to see the impact of what we just said. We wait in a state of receptivity until something happens to create a new response within us.

Exercise – Staying Out There with Impulse
Start listening to your body and following impulse. When the first impulse ends, stay exactly where you are. Don't change your body position, or alter your gaze. Keep the same emotional note in place. Wait. And see what arises from there. Then follow the new impulse until 'it ends you', and remain where it deposits you. And so on. Never 'step back' to where you began.

If the impulse ends and you don't 'stay out there' where it 'lands' you, there is a tendency to return to your initial starting place; the same emotional/physical point in yourself. But the fact that you are initiating each stage of your work from an identical place every time affects the discovery process. It is as if you move from A to B, then back to A again. From there you might move from A to C, or from A to D. But you will not make the journey from A to B to C to D, and you will never discover the leap from B to R and from R to Z.

To help you 'stay out there', avoid management gestures. These include brushing your hair back, or hitching up your trousers, or even returning to a particular stance when the impulse ends. Such gestures disrupt the flow of impulse and response. While you wait for the next impulse to appear you are in a state of suspension; nothing changes, nothing retreats, your mind simply holds a question mark.

Becoming aware of impulse and response enables you to connect to the truth of your own reactions. You find yourself in a situation and you can sense what the body wants to do and where it wants to go. You can sense when something requires 'more' from you, or when something has truly ended, and you need to let it go and simply wait for the next impulse to arise. You remain in the moment, fully connected to your inner landscape, sensing how far you need to go; or alternatively, how long you need to wait, alert and receptive. And from here, you can make choices about which course of action to follow.

MAKING CHOICES

As performers, we must adapt our responses to the demands of the dramatic situation, including character, technical requirements and stylistic approach. We always sense and follow impulse (that is fundamental), but the way it expresses itself can be altered and modified. And the nature of the modification is determined by the performing context. It is not simply the manifestation of our own personal 'blocks', or habitual patterns belonging to our social persona. It is the character that hunches her shoulders in fear, not the actor. This is a conscious choice, not an embedded habit. We sense the prime impulse (fear), but we choose the most effective physical response for that situation. We are able to modify our response on demand.

Exercise – Modifying the Impulse
Start working with any kind of impulse, listening to and following your body. You can use the basic listening exercise

detailed in the first chapter, or you can use any of the above systems. It doesn't matter what you use, or even if you shift between systems (starting with the space, then if this triggers a memory, following that, and then discovering that a particular emotion arises in turn). Or just drifting from response to response without any clear idea of why or what you are responding to. How you begin isn't important. Just follow what feels alive, what is intriguing at this exact moment. Don't over-control or work too hard at it.

Now start to make choices about how you will manage the expression of that impulse. The three categories I suggest are 'follow', 'resist' and 'provoke'. 'Follow' is straightforward; you just do what feels right. When 'resisting', you say to yourself, 'No. I won't follow that. I'll stay exactly where I am. I resist being changed.' You don't actively suppress the new impulse; you just hold it in suspension. Resistance can be either stillness (not going into action), or staying with your current course of action (refusing the impulse to shift). Finally, there is 'provocation', where you follow the impulse but twist the form of expression, where you say to yourself, 'No. I know what wants to happen here, but I'll do something else instead.' In this case, you can choose a different course of action (to run forward rather than following the impulse to retreat). Or make a small adjustment – there is an impulse to raise the arm, but you decide to initiate the lift through the elbow rather than the wrist as you normally do.

Whichever response you choose, remember that it is a response; you sense the impulse and then decide exactly how you want to deal with it. You are not trying to create interesting movements or construct reactions, simply making choices in the moment.

We all know that living as adults involves something more than following impulse. We are required to select and modify our responses according to the demands of situation and the social context. But it is more pleasant to make considered, useful choices, rather than blindly reacting out of habit. Next time you notice a clear physical hint arising in your body, pause for a moment, sense what it links to, and then ask yourself what you want to do with it. Let it go? Follow it into action? Or perhaps reframe the impulse. In fact, we do this regularly in daily life; we encounter an irritating bully and we reframe our reaction as a joking comment rather than a slap in the face. The body lets you know something is happening, and pausing gives you the opportunity to assess your options.

Chapter 3 EMOTION

Working with emotions is often seen as a daunting task, like approaching a jungle full of lurking animals all ready to tear you apart. But this is a false fear. After all, we 'feel' every single day of our lives. We are very experienced in 'feeling' all sorts of feelings. And although we encounter very strong emotions from time to time, it is rare that they become truly unmanageable. Emotions are more like weather; sometimes it rains, sometimes it snows, sometimes it is sunny. Emotions are as strong and as changeable as weather; while it rains, the water just keeps falling from the sky. Then it is over, and the clouds move away. And like weather, problems tend to occur when something gets locked in and cannot make way for another reality. Too much rain causes floods. Too much sun causes drought.

The other reason we sometimes fear emotional work is the kind of the material we use to trigger the chosen emotion, especially when we use personal life experiences as an approach. Emotionally resonant ('hot') memories can be a valuable stimulus, as long as they are not too 'hot'. When that happens, they can impede the process of communication. The reliving (or the managing) of the feeling becomes more important than exploring, and the performer becomes enmeshed in the emotion rather than finding a way for the audience to experience it. You can work just as effectively with 'warm' memories, or 'cool' ones.

Or use no memories at all. Emotion, like any impulse, can be triggered just as effectively by image, or empathy, or sensation, or pure imagination. What matters is that the emotion is real and usable, not what you employ to evoke it. Besides, the real difficulty with emotion is not the feeling itself but the process of expressing that feeling. What am I allowed to show? How far can I/should I reveal it? Here? With these people?

I have already spoken about how socialisation shapes and modifies the way emotion appears in daily life. Young children directly express most of their feelings, adults do not. As an adult, you may have a clear emotional impulse, but what is felt on the inside may be held back and not permitted to pass into any kind of direct physical manifestation. In which case, we say the emotion is blocked. Or if it is allowed to go into manifestation, it may be displaced into other patterns (the feeling of anger becomes diverted into pernickety point-scoring, instead of a major tantrum).

In most public situations, we put on masks that hide our emotions from other people. We don't actually want everybody to know what is happening inside, and so we ensure that our feelings and reactions are less readable to others. Sometimes the feelings leak out from behind the mask, and then someone might ask 'Are you all right?' But we don't intend them to see what is actually going on. Full and easy release of emotion in the presence of other people tends to occur only when we feel totally safe.

Occasionally, the emotion we are feeling is so strong that the mask can no longer hide it. It crashes through the cover-up layer, and we don't care any more who sees and hears us. But this is rare, and usually embarrassing for all parties. In fact, there is nothing wrong with a mask; it makes it easier for all of us to survive our daily life in a world of strangers. But performers must be able to drop the mask at will. They must invite strangers (the audience) into their private world, and fully reveal what is happening there.

In terms of managing this process, we first need to retrieve the ability to let the emotion fully into the body, rather than automatically holding it back. Later, we can modify our impulse (for example, according to the 'blocks' and 'displacements' of the character we are playing). But the first step is to dismantle our own.

We often recognise feelings of holding back or being blocked. We feel something definite inside, but we can sense that it isn't going anywhere. We feel stuck and frustrated. Usually, we try to tackle this problem from the inside, by increasing the emotional charge in the hope of smashing our way through the blocks. This is hard work, emotionally draining and very hit-and-miss, since big feelings can't always be turned on at will.

There is an easier way; work with the body. The problem with emotional expression is not the feeling itself, but its physical manifestation. The channels of emotion in the body (not the mind) are dammed up. Rather than trying to dynamite the dam by 'pushing' from the inside, just find where the channels are and open them. You worry less about the strength of the emotion, and instead focus your attention on finding a physical handle that can release the emotion into the body. Once the gate between the body and the mind is open, whatever is felt (even a tiny shift of feeling) flows straight into response and action.

SENSING THE CHANNELS OF EMOTION

The work you have done on impulse has already opened many of the blocked channels of emotional expression. Following impulse requires that you sense what wants to happen, and then immediately allow yourself to do that exact thing. Some of the impulses you were following were emotional. The next step is exploring this area in more detail, and finding exactly where the channels of emotions are, especially the less familiar ones.

Exercise – Sensing Emotion in the Body

Stand facing the wall in a neutral position. Stand tall. The body is free, the hands hanging easily by your sides, the face is forward (not down) and the eyes are open. By whatever means work for you, generate a real emotion. It doesn't matter what you use, as long as it is real. Possibilities include anger, joy, despair, confusion, determination, pleasurable anticipation, nervous anticipation, boredom, frustration and certainty. Continue to build whichever feeling you choose, but don't move. Stay still. Don't release the emotion through action of any kind. This can feel very frustrating, but don't worry. The frustration is an inevitable by-product of the exercise. Stay with it.

As the feeling manifests, observe what is happening to the body. You may notice that certain parts of the body want to shift in response to the emotion. Observe these details. Lots of details. For example, what wants to happen to the breath? Does it want to rise into the chest, or descend into the belly? Does it want to get faster, slower, deeper, or more shallow? Next, what wants to happen to the gaze? More focused or less, tunnel vision or hazy? And so on. Do you sense that the body as a whole wants to take up more space or less, to get taller or smaller, to get heavier or lighter, to twist or remain straight forward or cave in? Does the body want to speed up or slow down? And the texture of the body: does it feel more brittle, or softer, or harder? What about the individual muscles? What wants to happen to the muscles of the face, the neck, the shoulders, the spine, the buttocks, the belly, the knees, the toes, the hands? Do the feet feel solid on the ground, or do you feel light? Do the feet want to be wider apart or closer together, turn in or turn out? If you like, you can let these 'wants' into the body a fraction, to observe better, or to prevent the emotion evaporating. You are not trying to maintain a fixed neutral position, but equally, don't fully release the body into action. Keep it in for the moment. Any physical shifts should be virtually invisible to an onlooker.

As you work, you will notice subtle shifts throughout the entire body. Changes in the gaze, the rhythm, the breath and zones of tension and release. Mentally note them. Then do exactly the same exercise with other emotions.

As you go through each of these feelings, you will discover a range of different and distinct patterns in the body. Each emotion has a definite idea of where it wants to go, and how it wants to manifest in various places throughout the body. Maybe just a tiny shift in the weight, or a sharpening of the gaze, or a clenching of the buttocks, or a feeling that the whole body becomes soft, slow and heavy. Every feeling links to a number of physical details. Each detail can be seen as an available channel for that emotion, and the totality forms a kind of map.

You are likely to find that every map is unique. The map for anger and the map for despair are distinctly different. From time to time, you may find an overlap; maybe two different feelings affect the shoulders in the same way. This is fine; just keep looking for all the other factors (breath, gaze, rhythm, feet, weight, etc.). You should find plenty of differences. One more thing: your map is unique to your own body. While many people discover certain similarities in physical response, you are not looking for any kind of 'right' or universal template. In this work, it is essential to investigate without preconception, and to accept the felt truth of your body, rather than to search for 'the one right way'.

This exercise demonstrates one fundamental fact. Emotion is actually experienced in the body, not the mind. The mind can trigger emotion, but it is the flesh that feels it. When you suddenly get good news, it is the breath that alters to produce shrieks of joy or laughter, the feet that start jumping around, the eyes that open and brighten, and the hands that start waving around. And that is why we need to get the body engaged when working with emotion; it is the real site of our emotional lives. Disengaging or ignoring the body while attempting to connect to emotion is pointless, and totally counterproductive. Hence sitting on your backside while thinking about emotions rarely works.

In the next exercise, we start to let the emotions flow through the physical channels we have identified.

Exercise – Allowing Emotion into Action

Start at the wall again. Build any emotion you like, and observe, without moving, where the feeling wants to go throughout your body. When you are happy that every part of the body is sensitised to the feeling, go into action. Start to do a simple physical task. This needs to be a real task, using real objects in the real space, e.g. getting dressed, shifting the furniture, writing a letter, etc. Don't mime. Go about the task while ensuring that you keep all of the details you have observed alive. As you walk, walk with the feet of the feeling, and at the specific rhythm that the feeling requires. Keep the sense of expansiveness or retreat going. Maintain the texture of the whole body. Touch the objects with the emotion's hands, and look at the world with its gaze. Breathe its breath. Follow the sense of urgency, or non-urgency, in every molecule. Let the emotion ride your flesh all the way through. Keep all of the channels open.

Stay tuned to your body. As you do the task, sense where in the room the body feels most comfortable. Sitting in the corner? Lying on the floor in the centre? As you handle the objects, let your hands be as rough or as gentle or as precise as they want to be. The main thing you should concentrate on is letting the feeling pass into your flesh, via the channels you have identified, and then doing tasks that enable the flesh to interact with the physical world. If you feel that you are starting to lose contact with the feeling, don't worry – just remember all of the physical details that you discovered, and find another task. Do the task with the rhythm, weight, body texture, gaze, breath, etc. of the emotion, and you will soon get back in contact.

As you work, you may find that thoughts emerge, or even that the emotion seems to shift itself. Fine. Don't consciously attempt to show how angry or sad you are. You don't need to. The exact way you sit down in the chair, or how you pick up your shoes reveals to the audience precisely what is going on inside you. You betray your feelings to the onlooker, through how you perform ordinary everyday actions. All you are doing is letting the emotions flow outwards through all of the channels of the body, and then letting that body impact on the physical world. Doing the task enables you to reveal how you feel, without needing to signal to the audience through a chosen gesture.

I will strangle the next actress I see who skips around the stage to demonstrate that 'she is happy'!

In fact, there are two common traps that performers fall into when working with emotions. Firstly, trying to find signals to show the audience what they are feeling, i.e. constructing expressions and gestures such as the aforementioned skipping. It is like holding up a sign which says 'Do you see that I am feeling happy?' At the other extreme is the performer who is clearly feeling a great deal but whose body is inert. Something is felt but it cannot find its physical counterpart. The emotion is locked in, unable to permeate the body or propel it into natural action. In this case, it is very hard for the audience to guess exactly what is going on. This is why the idea of a task is useful; it gives the performer concrete activities that enable the inner life to be revealed. It becomes a kind of script, and it is how the actor physically responds to each moment of the task that betrays what is happening inside.

With this work, the right kind of 'accidents' happen. Once, when I was teaching this exercise, an actor decided to put on his boots while his body was in the grip of rage. As his angry hands tugged at his shoelace, it broke. And this 'accident' made him even angrier. Back to the boot he went, trying to get what was left of his lace to do the job. Again he tugged with his (now furious) hands, and again the lace broke. At which point he grabbed the boot and hurled it at the wall. The 'accidents' that the emotion channelling through his body had provoked gave his feeling of anger further stimulus. In turn, this spiralled naturally into a strong action. But if he had simply chosen to throw the boot as a gesture to indicate anger, it would have looked contrived. What happened emerged organically out of his body's physical contact with the world, and so it looked (and was) real. (By the way, this is partly why bad days just keep getting worse. You fumble your keys, you trip over the mat and then you drop your favourite dish. This isn't necessarily the universe giving you a hard time. More likely the emotion in your flesh interacting with the physical world in a consistent way.)

The important thing with this exercise is to keep all of the channels, everywhere in the body, open and active, all of the time, while you get on with your task. In this way, the emotion doesn't get blocked in our interior, but constantly flows out through the body and into the world. It finds its natural expressive form, and can be read by co-performers and audience. As you work, keep reminding yourself: 'Out. Get it out. Out.' But always do it through the various specific channels you have identified while facing the wall. Not through a constructed gesture, or a single body part (e.g. the face). Use all of the channels, especially the more unfamiliar ones. Specifically remind the legs to keep passing the emotion out, since it is the legs which will carry the body around the room. In this way, as you allow the emotion to shift the body in space, a sense of placement starts to emerge. You discover where in the room your body feels comfortable with that feeling, if it needs to stand or sit, in the centre or in a corner. And when it needs to move elsewhere. Then just follow the body; it will tell you where it wants to go and what it wants to do.

Exercise – Another Emotion

Do the previous exercise again, but use a different emotion. Go into the task, starting with the same focus as last time. As you work, see what differences emerge. See how your hands touch the objects this time, and how in turn the objects respond to your hands. See where you want to sit, and exactly how. See what thoughts emerge. What are the urgencies, the priorities of this body? And so on.

Although the task is the same, you will probably find that it needs to be done in a different way. Your thoughts will be different. And your reactions. Then try a third emotion.

In all of this work, it is very important to allow yourself to surprise yourself. Don't over-control the exercise, or plan anything in advance. Just stay with the physical details and the task, and see what emerges. You may think that your 'confusion' will look a particular way, but when you actually let it into the body, it might take a completely different direction. Permit yourself to discover what is actually happening, rather than limiting yourself by an idea of what 'ought' to occur. There isn't a universal pattern for confusion that you have to discover. While there are certain deep emotional forms that are shared by all humans (and this is how we recognise another person's distress), the details of how an emotion manifests itself varies from person to person. And for this work, it is the details that matter. Lots of individual, precise details. If a twitch in your right knee is part of your personal channel pattern for confusion, use it. Trust what your body discovers. Don't go for one or two broad patterns that you think will convey your feelings. Don't try to find an appropriate acting gesture. That way lies cliché.

This is the reason why I say 'don't move' while you are generating your emotion at the wall. If you immediately release the emotion into action, you are likely to head into cliché, or your habitual physical response to that feeling. And this response has already been shaped by and for the social context. It is 'selected' and 'learned', and therefore limited. Your body innately has a far greater range of physical responses available. When you hold the body back, you prevent the emotion releasing itself through its habitual pathways. Yet the urge keeps trying to find a way out. As it seeks an outlet, you become aware of the multiplicity of emotional channels that are available to you, many of which are normally overshadowed by habitual responses.

Remember that it is the process of listening to the body, reminding all the various channels to stay open, and following the body into action that is important here. Working to maintain the emotion is less necessary, since once the process is initiated, it will tend to sustain itself.

Exercise – Emotion and Words

Move into speech. You could take the phrase 'O for a muse of fire', or any other line that can be linked to various feelings, such as 'He hath a daily beauty in his life that makes me ugly', or 'Take note, take note, O world, to be direct and honest is not safe'. (These last two lines are from *Othello*, and are good to work with since they have a personal quality, as well as being relatively 'open'.)

Using this phrase, speak from where you are emotionally. How you speak the words becomes the sound dimension of performance, letting the audience hear where you are, in the same way that watching how you do your task is the visual dimension of your inner reality. Don't think about how to make the line interesting, just let it come out as it needs to come out, in that moment, from where you are in yourself. Maybe the phrase will emerge as a self-knowing laugh, or a frustrated interjection, or a cry for help. It doesn't matter. Let that particular body find its voice, and speak out of its situation.

It is important when doing this work to use text (the chosen language of a writer), rather than improvising your own words. Using your own real words to communicate your own real situation is fairly straightforward, and does not require any kind of transformation. To speak someone else's words within that situation requires that you shift to their language patterns while remaining connected to your own truth. While you are not playing the character who uses these words within the script, you are not permitting yourself to return to your native tongue. Instead, you are working to retain the sense of 'otherness'.

This exercise enables you to sense that the words arise out of the situation; they are not imposed on top of it. The body speaks out of its reality, and that body has a voice which then finds words for that exact moment. It is important that *how* you speak emerges from the body and its situation, not from the conscious intelligence and its decision-making process. In other words, you discover that a despair-shaped body says 'O, for a muse of fire' in a very particular way, rather than the mind deciding that since your body has been shaped by despair, a despairing tone of voice would be a good way of speaking. It is very rarely that straightforward.

In addition, as you do this work, you are likely to discover that feelings and thoughts are constantly shifting, constantly transforming themselves.

Exercise – Life of the Emotion
Do the basic exercise again, with any emotion you like. As you go about your task, observe specifically how your inner life unfolds and develops over time. Because you are working physically, your body will start to feed back into your feelings, which in turn may shift and evolve. As you do this exercise, you might find you need to sit down for a while, but then sense that the hips need to

change position. Let them. Follow even the tiniest hints of what your body wants to do. This will enable you to remain in contact with your inner life, while also enabling you to create believable physical responses.

Also observe if the prime emotion shifts and transmutes from time to time. Maybe as you sort through your papers with an angry body, frustration starts to emerge, and then maybe a note of despair appears as you find yourself thinking 'I'll never get this done'.

This is the natural life of the emotion, which must not be confused with blocking or social displacement. And the easiest way to stay aware of this is to keep listening to the body and follow the flickers as they emerge. Emotions naturally grow and shift, retreat and advance, become inward and then surge outward. This aspect is very important to recognise. Trying to maintain a constant state of identical feeling is difficult, since it is not how we actually experience our inner life. Next time you are near someone who is having an argument, observe how the tactics and reactions constantly shift.

In fact, trying to find or maintain a constant state of emotion is the enemy of good acting. What matters is to stay in the moment and respond to exactly what emerges here and now. Searching for any single, unchanging, eternally appropriate state is a waste of effort. Life doesn't follow 'state', and since performance follows life, resisting organic change just creates problems.

In a sense, these emotion exercises are slightly artificial, since they demand that you arbitrarily choose and create a particular emotion without reference to context. Actors working with script have a clear blueprint for their emotions and reactions. But the rest of us have to begin somewhere, so we 'decide to feel' something. You can use anything at all as a starting point. It doesn't have to be a grand passion, even the sense of general 'fed-upness' that your journey from home generated is fine. What matters is the process of getting that reality into the body, letting it manifest physically and then carrying it into visible action in the space.

When you decide to end your exploration of a particular emotion, stand up and start moving very actively. Because the direct connection between the body and the consciousness is so strong, you will have to work hard to disengage the previous reality. Do this via the body. Move everything, and deliberately break the rhythms and textures you have been using. Change which muscles you are using in the face, and blink the eyes to alter the gaze. Keep doing this until you feel the emotional matrix depart.

On the other hand, the very strength of this connection can prove useful. Once you have identified the exact and specific physical patterns that are associated with that emotion in your body, you can employ them to help trigger or sustain the emotion. You use them to work from the outside in. If you know that your 'anger map' involves flattening the hands, sharpening the gaze, tightening the buttocks, speeding up the breath, allowing the texture of the body to become somehow 'steel-like', and anchoring the feet solidly on the ground, then activating this map will bring you closer to what you want to feel. And when you want to feel calm, trigger the 'calm map' in all its detail.

The key is accuracy and fidelity to your own map of emotions. For example, the cliché gesture for anger is clenching the fist. It is a cliché because in reality, many people do clench their fists when they are angry. Fine. But if your personal matrix for anger does not involve fist-clenching, it won't work for you. If your personal anger manifests as a tense, open palm, that is what you use. And the greater the number of details you use, the easier it becomes to trigger an inner reply.

Actors, particularly non-western actors, have been using this technique for years, probably centuries. They know that if you trigger the physical manifestation, the emotion or inner reality will tend to follow. That is why it doesn't really matter whether you start from the inside or the outside; as long as you stay connected to the body, they will simply flow into each other and keep on flowing as a constant, mutual feedback loop.

Once you have an awareness of multiple channels for the expression of a specific emotion, you can also choose which to activate, and how. For example, with genuine anger, your throat may tighten and your breath become impeded. This is unhelpful in terms of speaking, so you choose to maintain an open throat and connected breathing, and then to channel your reactions into other body details which are equally true but unproblematic, e.g. a feeling that your feet want to pace, and your elbows, shoulders and ribs become wider.

In addition, the constriction in your throat may be a learned response, rather than one of your instinctive channels of anger. A child in the middle of a raging tantrum does not constrict the voice or tighten the throat; the sound flows freely and strongly out. It may be unable to find the words it needs to describe exactly what it feels and wants, leading it to become incoherent with rage. But the sound quality is fine. It may be that much of our vocal restriction is habitual and imposed. Just as we are told to 'sit still and don't fidget', we are taught to lower our voices from a young age. 'Don't shout. Sssh!' is a command heard in supermarkets across the world. So, when working with strong emotions like anger, let the impulses flow freely through all the other channels of your body, but keep the throat released so that you can experience the same degree of vocal ease and power as a child.

USING THE SELF

A question sometimes gets asked when I am teaching. 'Isn't this emotional work dangerous? It looks very strong. Really quite mad.' The answer is, 'No, it isn't.'

There are four reasons for this answer. Firstly, the work looks stronger than it actually is. The actor is concentrating on keeping the channels fully open in order to let every particle of feeling enter the world through direct manifestation. What is seen is equivalent to what is felt. But in real life, what we see in the body is usually much less than what is actually happening inside. The mask is in place. And since all of us (including the audience) understands how the masking mechanism operates, onlookers will read more behind the action than the actor currently feels.

Secondly, with this technique, there is no violent destruction of the mask (which could be dangerous); it is simply laid aside for a time. The key factor in this process is that it is physical, not psychological. We work on freeing the body and allowing it to manifest emotion, not on the emotion itself.

Thirdly, I do not believe that accessing emotions is dangerous for a normal, well-adjusted person. As I said at the start of the chapter, we are very experienced managers of emotion. And remember, as a child you encountered very strong emotions on a daily basis; you passed from rage to delight to frustration in a matter of moments. Nobody would suggest that the richness of a child's emotional life is abnormal. Tiring to deal with, perhaps, but definitely normal.

Finally, in this work you are fully in charge of the process. In real life, an event happens and the emotion occurs as a response to that event. But we cannot really control what events occur in our world, and so the nature of our emotional life is equally beyond control. We can decide to avoid certain situations that we know trigger unwelcome feelings, or we can manage our physical reactions, but we can't order the world to do what we want, when we want. Here, we can. In this exercise, you choose what you wish to encounter and manifest. And you choose how far it goes and when it ends. That being so, it becomes rather good fun to play with your emotions.

For the purposes of this book, it isn't necessary to probe your inner life in depth, or to examine who you are as a person. Instead, try simply to acknowledge the extraordinary depth and range of your inner reality, own it and connect to it. If anything feels too uncomfortable when doing these exercises, just leave it alone. The aim is to enable you to get physically connected, not to disturb your inner realms. And besides, even if one area feels a bit uncomfortable and you decide to leave it alone for the moment, it doesn't matter; there's plenty of other territory to explore. Territory we want to explore and claim for ourselves without apology.

But this question of emotional freedom hides a fairly big can of worms, which we need to untangle before we feel we have the right to use our inner landscape with authority. Firstly, 'madness'. In our daily lives, there are certain emotions, under certain conditions, that are acceptable to show other people. Other emotions are out of bounds in front of onlookers. A 'mad' person is someone who transgresses those boundaries, who shows things in public that are unacceptable. But the key thing here is that they do so unknowingly. Performers similarly transgress the boundary of socially acceptable public behaviour, but they do so consciously, in the service of the performance. A good performer is saying and doing in public what might normally be unacceptable. And that is the core of their work.

Performance exists in the realm of the 'extra-ordinary'. It includes the 'ordinary' (that which we see in normal public contexts), but it also goes beyond, into the 'extra-ordinary' (that which is not normally revealed). And the majority of dramatic writing and performance specifically deals with the 'extra-ordinary'; fundamental human situations and dilemmas that are real but rarely acknowledged in daily social interaction. This is one of the satisfactions that audiences seek. To encounter something on stage or screen that they recognise as true from their life; to be able to say 'Oh, I know that. That's it exactly.' Good performers reveal a private truth in a public situation. So, both the 'mad' and the actor do the same thing, but from two totally opposed perspectives. One is unconscious, the other is chosen and carefully shaped.

Learning to manifest a wide range of emotions in public is central to a performer's training. At first, it may feel uncomfortable, showing what you normally only release when you are alone. Or even what you don't permit yourself to release even when you are alone. The voices of 'what is socially acceptable' can even control our behaviour in private. But we must go beyond this limitation in our work.

Another impediment to claiming our emotional territory is the general attitude towards this kind of work. There are a lot of misconceptions about the processes related to performing in the general community. It is often suggested (in the media) that performers are childishly self-indulgent, or weird, edgy, unbalanced individuals, preferably neurotic. Wrong. As in any profession, there are people who have difficulties, but most performers are fairly well-balanced. They have to be, since the job requires an ability to deal with criticism, rejection, uncomfortable venues and sheer hard work. Plus a willingness to negotiate effectively with co-professionals (you can only afford to be a prima donna when you reach the top). It is too hard a profession to sustain if you aren't reasonably competent and focused as a person. In addition, performing is a job, and most professionals reserve their theatrics and their energy for the work. Connecting to emotions is a technical skill requiring awareness and control, and the rehearsal schedule doesn't leave much space for self-indulgence. Most performers are normal, well-socialised beings, no more deranged or difficult than the next person. But 'normal, ordinary, hard-working performers' don't make for exciting news or salacious articles.

CLAIMING THE TERRITORY

Sometimes a student will say 'I don't have that feeling' or 'My character wouldn't do that'. The only thing you need to remember here is that every single person on this planet has the capacity for every human emotion. What makes us different is what triggers the emotion, how far it takes us and what it leads us to do. In terms of character, it isn't a case of 'He wouldn't be angry', but rather, 'What triggers his anger, what does it do to him, and how far and in what way can it come into the world?'

However, although we all embrace the entire emotional spectrum, we don't experience it in the same way. For example, you yourself might not have the full-blown fear of difference that manifests itself as racial hatred, but you probably do have a tiny grain of discomfort with the unfamiliar. That's what you connect to in yourself in order to make real and believable the racist killer that you are portraying. Even a tiny grain is enough, as long as you own that grain as real and work to find a valid physical life for it.

In terms of our own explorations, we should permit ourselves to claim our entire emotional territory, even feelings that we choose not to reveal in daily life. Those reactions lie dormant for most of the time, but we know exactly where they are situated, and what they feel like. They are part of what makes us human, and when we decide to work, we switch gear. We open up the entire territory, the full range of our personal knowledge and experience, working simply as humans, rather than within the narrow parameters of our socialised being.

Chapter 4
VOICE AND WORDS

In daily life, we generally speak and move simultaneously. We think or feel, an impulse appears, and we 'act' on it. The words emerge from our mouths in the same instant that our body shifts. Sometimes these verbal/physical statements emerge directly, without any kind of censorship, either conscious or unconscious. What we feel, we reveal completely, through our words and our gestures. And these manifestations don't have to be big; even tiny vocal hesitations or subtle shifts in the angle of the head reveal and confirm meaning to the onlooker.

At other times we 'mask' what we say, veiling our body's reactions, and carefully choosing appropriate language. But whether open or masked, there is always a direct and integrated connection between body and speech.

In performance, the opposite frequently occurs. Actors often look as if their bodies and their words are living in different realities. Such actors look awkward on stage, as if they have forgotten how to be human. The words of the text seem to suggest that great passion is driving the character, but the actor just stands there and twitches. They look uncomfortable in the space, as if they can't work out where to stand, or how to shift position when the communication changes. The words and the gestures are unconnected; they often have problematic hands that never quite know what to do with themselves (hence the perennial popularity of cigarettes and glasses).

Good performers are hardly noticeable; everything that they say and do looks natural and inevitable. How they move and the quality of their voice just seems right; right for the character, right for the feeling or relationship, right for the words of the text. If the scene requires stillness, they are motionless without effort, channelling their impulses into language. If it requires ferocious violence, they can convince the audience that there is genuine danger in that moment, real anger behind their words (although their colleagues know that there is no possibility of things actually getting out of control). Equally, they can work minimally for the camera without ever losing the vitality of their body and its ability to convey meaning. Their words and actions always reflect a shared reality, no matter which play, or what style they are using.

So what goes wrong?

In most drama schools, you work on the voice and the body as separate skills. This is necessary, since the technical demands of training require a very detailed focus. You need to analyse the mechanics of breath, alignment, articulation, physical placement, etc., in order to fully understand the complex processes involved. You also need to train specific muscles so that you can manage and sustain effective performance. What sometimes gets forgotten (in the mind of the student) is that after you have pulled these elements apart, you have to put them back together again. When you perform, what you say must integrate with what you do.

In order to facilitate this process, you need to practise the skill of integration as part of your preparatory work. You can't wait for the night of the show and hope that somehow it will all fall into place by itself. But linking the voice and the body is more than simply adding one to the other; it is remembering that the body, the voice, the impulse and the choice of words are all a single unit. And the easiest way to access and employ this connection is via the body. After all, it has been using its breath and vocal muscles to form words in response to thought and feeling for years. It is very skilled at doing so. Use this knowledge.

CONNECTING TO VOICE

As a performer, you need to be able to connect yourself fully with the music of speech, as well as understanding the exact meaning of all your words and phrases. Many students seem hesitant to really pronounce the sounds and rhythms the writer has created; they mumble, or reduce the words to blandness, rather than letting the richness of the word-music exist and affect them. As Yoshi Oida once said, good writers create more than meanings; they create sound, energy and rhythm patterns which the actor must acknowledge and use. We need to become more sensitive to these, and let them connect to the body.

In the book *The Invisible Actor*, there is an exercise based on the vowel sounds A, O, U, E, I. This exercise can be extended into physically connecting to sound.

Exercise – A, O, U, E, I

The sounds are A (pronounced 'aaah' as in 'car'), O (pronounced 'aw' as in 'jaw'), U (pronounced 'oo' as in 'hoot'), E (pronounced 'eh' as in 'led'), I (pronounced 'ee' as in 'need').

Start with the sound 'ah' and intone it out loud, pitching it where it is most comfortable in your voice. There should be no sense of effort when making the sound. Don't aim for volume or 'interesting' vocal qualities. Just easy and comfortable. As if you could continue all day.

Continue making the sound, and when you can keep producing it without effort, focus on the body. Start to move around the space, following your feet, trying to find where in the room your body wants to be. Near the window? Facing the wall? Tucked into a corner? Gazing at the ceiling? When you get a sense of where the body wants to be, start looking for details. Sitting, kneeling or squatting? If kneeling, on one knee or two? And how far apart should the knees be? And the hands? Do they want to touch anything? And the gaze? Where does that want to be? And the muscles? Do the hands want to grip firmly, or lie at rest? As you investigate, keep producing the sound 'ah'. Gradually, you will home in on a specific body shape, placed in a specific location.

And when you find that exact place, something happens. The voice and the body suddenly 'lock' together, and the sound becomes more resonant and seemingly effortless. It is like trying to fit a plug into an electrical socket with your eyes closed. You 'fiddle around' for a while, trying to sense where the socket is, which way you need to turn the plug, and then suddenly you find it and the plug just slides in. It is the same with the voice and body. When you find the corresponding physical reality for the sound, it feels right; it just 'clicks into place'. You know it connects and it feels truly pleasurable to vocalise from that place. Trust this feeling of connection: it links to your actor's instinct.

Then you repeat the exercise with the other four sounds, looking for the exact physical counterpart to the sound. Each vowel might require a totally different place in the room, another body shape, a different point of focus for the eyes. Follow your body till you find what works. And remember, there is no standard form here. Your 'ah' might be leaning against the wall, gazing at the ceiling, while someone else's 'ah' requires the body to grip the chair and close the eyes. What matters is that each version 'rings true' and is connected.

When I talk about instinct and connection, remember that I am not referring to some mystical sixth sense. Simply a recognition of accuracy and appropriateness that bypasses words. Like drinking cool water. You might find your own way of identifying it, but a 'click of rightness', an inner 'Yes!', a laugh that signals 'Got it!' are all reliable indicators of work that is heading in the right direction. In addition, instant connection seldom happens. It usually takes a little time to emerge. Don't worry, just keep 'fiddling about', trying this, adjusting that, shifting here, till you feel that you are getting 'warmer', closer to your goal.

CONNECTING TO LANGUAGE

Everyone's body knows how to produce speech naturally and easily; after all, it has been doing so for years. Every time we open our mouths, we construct and perform 'text'. Thought and feeling create an impulse to speak, and then words emerge and coalesce into phrases. We can tap and harness this practical experience, and use it to connect to text created by a writer; to enable us to own another person's speech, in the same way we 'own' our personal vocabulary.

Take a page of writing. Look at it. What do you see? Thoughts? Feelings? No. The first thing your brain sees through your eyes is a series of small black marks on a white sheet. They are all about the same size, they run together in horizontal lines with occasional breaks, and they go on and on and on in much the same way, all down the page. This is 'text'.

Of course, text is an essential guide to thought and feeling (and reaction and response). It also provides a blueprint for speech, but it isn't the physical process of moving thought and feeling into language. Reading lines on a page and speaking thoughts out loud are very different actions. They engage the body differently (speech involves breath and muscular activity) and involve different parts of the brain. We must find ways to turn printed text into believable speech. Text is like a map; it outlines the shape and every detail of the landscape. But a map is not the same as the living geography of mountain and river and meandering road. And actors must use the map of the text to re-create the landscape itself, not just hold the map up and say, 'Here it is!'.

It is important to acknowledge this fact, otherwise you run the risk of turning speech into 'audible text'. When this occurs, you literally 'speak lines' of words, ploughing on down the page, ignoring changes of thought and maintaining a similar level of engagement with every new phrase. Sensing that this feels false, you may then impose artificial variation; arbitrary shifts in volume, or pitch, or speed, in order to avoid monotony of delivery. Or you might recite the words and then try to camouflage the absence of true connection with a wash of emotion or generalised intensity. But neither response is organic. An organic response can only occur when the changes in the voice and emotion reflect the changes in the inner landscape, and where the body shifts automatically in response.

In order to turn written text into speech, we must understand how the body actually produces spoken language. The first step is to physically remember how we speak.

When people talk, they construct their speech in blocks of language; this, then that, then another this, then that. Not 'Word word word word word word word word. Word word word word word word.' You have a thought/image/feeling that you wish to communicate, so you reach into your pool of language and haul out a unit that reflects (more or less) the reality you are trying to convey. Then you add another unit to clarify, and then another to clarify further. 'Yesterday, I went to the shops to buy some new curtains' isn't an elegant sentence, but it shows how we build our communications step by step.

(Context) Yesterday, (What happened?) I went (Where?) to the shops (Why?) to buy (What?) some new curtains.

There are five 'blocks' of thought, varying from one to three words, within this speech, although there is only one comma and one full stop. Punctuation marks reflect some of the steps in forming communication, but they don't pick up every individual building block of language. And it is the accumulation of these blocks that creates speech. In my daily life, I am not conscious of this process; I do it instinctively. And since the body understands this instinctive process, I can use it to sense speech structure, rather than simply reading the text with my eyes and attempting to isolate these blocks intellectually.

Exercise – Walking to Find Natural Shifts in Language
This takes its inspiration from one of Cicely Berry's exercises (outlined in her excellent book *The Actor and his Text*), but it proceeds in a different direction. Her exercise (described on page 106 of the book) uses punctuation marks as a guide to sensing the

movement in a piece of text. But since a unit of language is not exactly the same as a phrase (as outlined by punctuation), I have adapted her exercise so that it focuses on the more basic language blocks.

Hold your speech in your hand and start reading it aloud, very simply and naturally. Forget about interpretation, character, accent or rhythm. Just speak the words. Not slowly, or fast. Not loudly, but not under your breath either. Normally. And as you open your mouth, start walking. Words and feet start together.

As you walk and speak, tune into your body. When your words go from one language block to another, when they go from 'this' to 'that', the body subtly registers this shift. It feels like a kind of hiccup. (Or, as one of my students so wonderfully phrased it, 'It's like driving along in a car, and then suddenly running over a small, furry animal.')

It isn't a huge sensation, but as you listen to the body, you will start to feel it react every time it moves from one language block to another. Once you are tuned into your body, you will feel slightly 'off', almost uncomfortable, whenever you 'run over' a shift from one block to another.

Now we can use the body to clarify further this sense of shifting from block to block, defining it more clearly for ourselves.

Start walking and talking. Every time you sense a shift 'hiccup', you stop (both walking and talking), turn on the spot to face another direction, and then start walking and talking again, from where you left off in the text. The voice and the feet start at the same time and they both stop together. No walking without talking, or continuing to talk once your feet have stopped. No talking while you are turning to face the new direction. Wait till you have turned and then recommence your walking and talking.

A kind of dance emerges, with you walking (and talking), stopping, turning, moving and speaking again, stopping once more, turning to another direction, and continuing. You might find that you stop and turn after one word, or after five or six. It doesn't matter. It is up to your body to decide, not your brain.

Listen to your body.

When you are not sure if a shift has occurred or not, try it both ways. Stop and turn where you sense there may be a shift, and then try it again, walking (and talking) through the moment. Whichever feels right, whichever feels 'nicer' to say, is the one you accept. You are looking for your own body's way of producing speech, using its personal knowledge and experience, not some externally imposed programme, or any 'right way' to create language blocks. When I did the following speech from *Othello*, I discovered a certain pattern of stopping/turning/speaking, and then I marked each shift from block to block with a slash (/).

Act 2, scene 1

DESDEMONA: O/heavy ignorance/, thou praisest/the worst/best/. But/what praise/ couldst thou bestow/ on a deserving woman/indeed/? One/ that in the authority/of her merit/ did justly/put on/ the vouch/ of very malice itself?

I would emphasise that this would be my body's way of deconstructing the text; your body might find a slightly different pattern. For example, you might put a slash between 'One that' and 'in the authority', rather than after 'One', as I have done. It doesn't really matter, as long as it feels 'right', and natural. Also, don't worry if this breakdown looks odd, even illogical, on the page. What matters is that it feels comfortable and familiar to the body, and easy to speak.

It is surprising what emerges from this exercise. People often find they understand much better what they are actually saying. In the same way, any lack of comprehension of the literal meaning of the words tends to make itself evident. By sensitising yourself to the natural shifts in the language (as your body recognises them), you break it up into real speech units. Blocks that reflect how communication and meaning is built up moment by moment. You prevent yourself running the words into each other, driving through the speech in an attempt to reach the end.

This process doesn't need huge amounts of training. I have done it with inexperienced teenagers, working on Shakepearean text which they found difficult to comprehend on the page. Nonetheless, they were able to feel the shifts in the body and sense the language blocks almost immediately. Their minds might not have understood what everything meant, but their bodies could recognise the deep structure of the language.

When working with language, people sometimes feel it is odd to use the body. Surely the brain is a more appropriate tool for analysis? Of course the brain is useful, but never forget that it is the body that actually goes about the business of uttering and articulating on a daily basis. It has its own source of knowledge.

At this point, I would like to reassure you: this is an exercise in finding a link between your own body's way of speaking and the words of the writer, not a direction for performance. It is a very basic, preliminary exploration and does not involve interpretation, style or character. These come later. Nor would you ever perform the speech this way, marking each shift so concretely. But having defined each shift with your body, you will understand better how the speech constructs itself moment by moment. You are beginning to produce speech, which is a familiar daily habit, rather than simply reciting text (which is an unusual, rather 'exotic' activity).

As well as enabling you to locate the blocks of speech/thought in the writing, this exercise reinforces the connection between the voice and the body. The natural organic pattern is for impulse to manifest itself equally and simultaneously in speech and movement. And it helps to underline the connection. This is why you must speak out loud and be on your feet. It is as if the feet and the mouth are directly connected. Only speak when you are moving. When you stop moving, stop speaking.

OWNING THE WORDS

In order to speak language with true conviction, you must fully own it. To do this, you must know what you are talking about. Yet I constantly encounter people who don't understand what they are saying. This occurs on two levels. Sometimes you literally don't know what you are saying. If you are unclear about the exact meaning of a word, get a dictionary. This is an obvious statement, but you cannot possibly speak truthfully if you are uncertain about the precise sense of what you are saying. The second problem occurs when actors do not personally 'know' what they are saying. They may 'understand' the words they are using (they comprehend what has been written), but they do not know how these phrases connect to their own individual experience of living. They do not own the writer's words with the same authority as they own their personal language.

In real life, we are fully connected to every word and phrase we use. We know what they mean to us (even if this isn't always the correct, dictionary meaning) and we are happy and comfortable with this vocabulary and turn of phrase. Otherwise, we wouldn't use them. Patterns of language are very personal. One person might like simple, blunt language, while another individual prefers more roundabout ways of alluding to particular subjects. X is comfortable using swear words, while Y would find it extremely difficult and unpleasant to utter such phrases. The words we use and don't use are a part of our character; they are a reflection of who we are.

There is a lovely scene in *Othello* where Desdemona refers to this fact. In Act 4, scene 2, she says:

'I cannot say whore; it does abhor me now I speak the word.'

And earlier in the same scene, she refers to Othello's naming of her as 'whore' with the following (wonderfully convoluted) avoidance of the 'W-word'. Also note Emilia's bald and direct statement of facts.

IAGO : What name, fair lady?
DESDEMONA: Such as she said my lord did say I was.
EMILIA: He called her whore . . .

Completely different words and music from the two women, although they are actually saying the same thing.

For this reason, when we are using someone else's language we have to bring it inside ourselves, linking it to our experience, so that it becomes as easy and comfortable as our own language. Then we can use the writer's words with certainty and confidence, instead of scrabbling after this new language, and trying to paste it on top of our own native tongue.

DEEP CONNECTING

All of us are connected to our personal language and vocabulary. We know what these words and phrases mean to us, and they all have a long history of use in our bodies. They are also linked to pleasure; the words we choose to utter are ones we like and are comfortable using. None of us speaks words that we dislike unless forced to do so. But a writer's words and phrases tend to be more or less alien; some blocks of language are shared, but they are strung together in ways that are not familiar to our bodies, or the writer will put word against word in a way we have never encountered or used. Yet we have to find a way to bring this alien tongue inside our experience, to enable this language to have history in our body, and to actively enjoy using it.

Exercise – Deep Connecting to Language Units
Go back to the language units you have discovered through 'Walking for Shifts'. See what the first unit is, memorise those few words, and then put the book down. You must not do this exercise with the book in your hand. Speak the phrase out loud, and tune in to the body. Keep repeating the phrase and start to follow the body's hungers. Where does it want to be in the room? Touching what? Gazing where? Tense or relaxed? At a certain point, you will feel the 'click' of connection.

It might be logical – you are handling real currency when you say the unit 'money' – but even so, you won't sense the moment of connection until you find *exactly* how your body wants to handle that money. One of my Dutch students was investigating the word 'gelt' (which is Dutch for 'money'). She kept saying the word, while trying different ways of dealing with it – counting it out, gripping a purse – but when she started running coins through her fingers, something happened. The word suddenly resonated, and this shift was immediately audible. Both she and I heard it. Even though I didn't know the meaning of the word she was working on (since I don't speak Dutch), I knew she had found a real connection.

Sometimes the connection is strange, seemingly illogical. My body wants to curl up and clench its fists while gazing at the rubbish bin when it says the unit 'no revelations'. I have no idea why. It doesn't make logical sense. This is an example of how the brain recognises connection through alternative pathways. When you go to that physical place, your body somehow recognises the truth of that reality.

The priority is to sense when you are speaking with authentic connection and when you are speaking falsely. To put it rather crudely, to turn on your 'bullshit meter'. You can tell when you are speaking 'bullshit'; it feels fake and horrible (and people often pull faces or groan aloud when they sense they are speaking 'bullshit'). It feels very different from the pleasure of connection. And from the outside, you can hear the sound of authentic connection. (You may have noticed this when listening to productions in foreign languages. In some plays and films, you know that the actors really mean whatever it is they are talking about. They are revealing truth, moment by moment, and you believe them, even if you find the language incomprehensible. The recognition of connection lies deeper than an understanding of the literal meaning of the words.)

This approach also gives the language a felt experience in your body. The words now have a tangible reality, and a history of physical existence. I was teaching in Utrecht a few years ago, using *Othello* as a base for work. An actor was investigating one of Iago's monologues, and he quickly realised that there were many words and turns of phrase to do with sex. He had already understood this intellectually, but until he physically engaged with these words over and over again, he didn't know what it actually felt like to be so driven by one single need. He allowed himself to physically connect to each phrase and word (when required, he used the floor as a safe and non-personal means to release his impulses). By using his own body as a conduit to understanding, he began to directly experience the reality of Iago's character, and how this man's thoughts and words constantly circled back to specific physical sensations. Also, he discoved that Iago was a man comfortable using such language and imagery in his speech. These words came easily to his lips. In this way, he was able to sense how to move away from his own reality, and enter Iago's world. And Iago's world became present in the actor's body.

Here is one of Iago's speeches, with the sexually charged words printed in capitals. Notice also how physical the language is ('hand' is used twice, as are 'lips' and 'breath').

Act 2, scene 1
IAGO: LECHERY, by this hand; an index and obscure prologue to the history of LUST and FOUL THOUGHTS; They met so near WITH THEIR LIPS that their breaths EMBRACED together. VILLAINOUS THOUGHTS, Rodrigo: when these MUTUALITIES so marshall the way, hard at hand comes the master and MAIN EXERCISE; TH'INCORPORATE CONCLUSION . . .

We all know that a good writer will reinforce certain themes in a character or speech through the choice of vocabulary. And many of these can be picked up through reading the text, but this is not the same as connecting to and claiming this reality via the body. Recognition is not the same as ownership.

This process does not belittle the actor's intelligence or analytical skills. Quite the reverse. Actors need to be intelligent, but they need to be intelligent with their entire brain, not just one small part. When we think about thought, or try consciously to plan or analyse, we tend to think in words. 'What will I do now?', 'Where did that come from?', 'If she thinks she's going to get away with that, she's wrong!'

But the verbalising brain is only a tiny fraction of our capacity to observe, remember, draw conclusions, understand reality, etc. Much of our understanding in daily life is non-verbal; the brain uses imagery, colour, memory, association and physical response to process information. You see something in the street, and for some reason a long-lost memory flashes in front of your eyes. Your brain has made a connection and has articulated that connection through an image from your past. The words appear later, as you wonder why that memory emerged. Or you may hear certain music and your body suddenly relaxes. You are thinking about tomorrow quite calmly (so you believe), but then you discover that your shoulders have tightened and your mouth has hardened. Your conscious brain believes that everything is under control, but your body is telling you that things aren't that simple. All of these manifestations are examples of the non-verbal intelligence pro-cessing information. Intelligently and efficiently, but bypassing language. And the body is able to access this area of knowledge and experience. This is why 'inviting your body to the party' is so important; it enables you to engage the entire brain more effectively. Not simply to move better, but to be able to think better.

Most of the connecting exercises use the speech block as the basic unit for work, but you will sometimes find that certain phrases seem somehow 'too big' for the body to manage. In this case, you may have to connect to the words on an individual basis. Writers like Shakespeare often rub words up against each other in unusual ways, e.g. Berowne's description of himself as 'love's whip' (*Love's Labour's Lost*, Act 3, scene 1). Most people would never juxtapose these two resonant words together, and you probably need to work in more detail to own such an unfamiliar turn of phrase. You would say the word 'love', and fully own that, then proceed to investigate 'whip', before putting them back into the block 'love's whip'.

Indeed, whenever you are doing connecting work and your body seems unable to link to a particular unit, it is a good idea to break it down into smaller units or individual words. Nine times out of ten, when the body goes all 'fuzzy' and can't find a response, it is because the block is too big for it to manage.

POINTS OF VIEW

While it may seem superficially similar to 'Deep Connecting', the following exercise is actually very different. Here, you observe where the writer has shifted 'viewpoint' in the speech, coming at the material from another angle, like a camera switching from distance to close-up, or cutting to focus on another image. And then you find a way to incorporate those viewpoints into your body.

> *Exercise* – Discovering Points of View
> Look at the following speech by Medvienko in Act 1 of Chekhov's play *The Seagull:*

MEDVIENKO: There's no ground for making a distinction between spirit and matter, because spirit might consist of a combination of material atoms. But you know, someone ought to write a play describing how our sort of people live – I mean, we teachers – and get it produced somewhere. It's a hard life, a very hard life.

> Read the speech aloud, standing somewhere in the space. As soon as you sense that the writer has shifted direction, or seems to be coming from another angle, change your position. Turn to face another direction, moving both feet crisply. It doesn't matter what angle you change to. What matters is that you make a clear and definite alteration in your stance. Taking this text again, I would change as follows:

MEDVIENKO: There's no ground for making a distinction between spirit and matter,/CHANGE/ because spirit might consist of a combination of material atoms. /CHANGE/ But you know, /CHANGE/someone ought to write a play describing how our sort of people live – /CHANGE/ I mean, we teachers – /CHANGE/ and get it produced somewhere. /CHANGE/

It's a hard life, a very hard life.

To clarify the nature of the changes I might give them names, such as:

MEDVIENKO: There's no ground for making a distinction between spirit and matter, /GENERAL PHILOSOPHY/ because spirit might consist of a combination of material atoms./CLOSE-UP IMAGE OF SPIRIT/ But you know, /SHIFT FROM FOCUS ON YOU HERE TO SOMEONE OUTSIDE /someone ought to write a play describing how our sort of people live /SUGGESTED COURSE OF ACTION/ – I mean, we teachers – /DETAILED FOCUS ON ME AND MY GROUP/ and get it produced somewhere. /SUGGESTED COURSE OF ACTION/ It's a hard life, a very hard life. /COMMENT ON LIVING (repeated twice).

The sorts of things you should look for are changes in subject matter, differences in tense (past, present or future), new degrees of inclusion (the world, this country, our community, my family, me), places where the character quotes another character or a text, and where the character alters from discussing generalities and moves into talking about self, or about another person. Notice shifts between 'I', 'you' and 'it'. Repetitions of the same phrase are also interesting.

Don't worry about what it all means. Simply mark where the writer has altered the point of view, rather like a camera zooming in or out, or coming at the subject from a different angle. Think visually rather than analytically.

Here is another example, from *Twelfth Night*, Act 2, scene 2:

VIOLA: I left no ring with her (DESCRIPTION OF ACTION/PAST TENSE/ME). What means this lady? (QUESTION FOCUSED ON HER) Fortune forbid my outside have not charmed her! (BACK TO ME/SPECULATION) She made good view of me (BACK TO OLIVIA/PAST TENSE/DESCRIPTION OF ACTIONS), indeed so much, that sure, methought her eyes had lost her tongue (BACK TO ME/INTERPRETATION OF ACTIONS), For she did speak in starts distractedly (OVER TO HER AGAIN/DESCRIPTION OF ACTIONS).

> You could, of course, do this work mentally, just by reading and analysing, but you will miss the dimension of energy. By physically shifting the body every time the point of view changes, you can feel how energetically (or otherwise) the character is thinking.
>
> You then do a simplified version of the physical connecting work with points of view. Start with your first point of view. Find where you need to be physically, and which tone of voice and emotional note suits it. Then, when you are happy that it resonates and feels good to say, leave it. Start to connect to the next point of view, forgetting what you have just done on the previous one. Don't let them run together. The physical reality and emotional tone may vary greatly from viewpoint to viewpoint. That's fine.

I find that 'Points of View' work is particularly useful when the actor doesn't have a lot of rehearsal time (the 'deep connecting' work isn't a fast process). It is also an excellent way of learning lines, and avoids the pitfall of learning your speech as a series of consecutive words (lines of text), rather than as recognisable communication. It (and the 'Walking for Shifts') can also help you disentangle a complex piece of writing. It also works for opera singers: treat your libretto as a text and do the 'Points of View' process, speaking rather than singing the units.

However, there are two principles that you must adhere to when working in this way. Firstly, keep the units totally separate. Do not let the feeling from one unit carry over into the next. This is one reason why I suggest putting the book down, rather than keeping it in your hand as you investigate. You work on one unit, connect to it, then go back to where you placed the book, learn the next unit, put the book back, walk away from it and then start connecting to the new unit. Each unit has its own unique physical/emotional/vocal reality.

Secondly, work from who you are (the actor) rather than who you think you need to become (the character). The words may give you insight into the character (and this is one reason not to impose any ideas in advance: you need to stay open to the information the writer has provided, rather than imposing a preconception), but the aim of all these various exercises is to bring the writer's language into your body, so that you can use it with the same degree of ease and authority as you use your own. It is as if you 'swallow' the writer's words, so that they can become a part of your own language pool. Then, when you start working with them, they are yours, no longer an alien tongue.

None of this work is designed to replace your normal text work; rather, it provides an additional, deeper layer of connection and ownership. It is like bedrock, sitting under and supporting your technical structures. At no point do you attempt to re-create it in performance. You never think about your own language when you are speaking in daily life; you simply use it. It is the same with this work. You connect to the writer's language, it is now inside you, and then you forget about it.

Whenever you are working with a theatrical text or vocal score, get up on your feet as quickly as possible. If you simply read text silently in your head while sitting in a chair, you will only contact the very surface of the writing. If you read out loud without preconception about how it should sound, you will discover all sorts of hidden patterns and meanings emerging through the dimension of sound and rhythm. If you then keep your body free to respond to this sound and meaning (by standing in a clear space as you speak), you will discover further patterns emerging.

When I direct, the first read-through always takes place on our feet, rather than sitting in chairs. Right from the beginning, I prefer actors' bodies to be involved in the investigative process. At this stage, the actors don't worry about doing anything physically; they just get on with the reading. But if something does want to happen, the body is free to follow, not locked into a chair. As you speak, you see the other characters in front of you. Instinctively, you might turn towards them as you speak, or you may even start to move away. As a director watching from the outside, this is most instructive, since certain relations and reactions make themselves known through the actors' bodies.

CHANGING THE CONTEXT

In the previous exercises, we worked from the inside to the outside. You spoke the words and then found the appropriate physical and vocal response. But it is possible to work the other way round, while still retaining full authenticity. And you need to be able to work both ways; directors do. Some directors want you to follow impulse into action. In this way, the staging emerges from the actors' choices. Others have extremely clear ideas about what they want to see, and they give precise instructions. When a director gives a specific note, such as 'do the speech from that chair', the actor has to shift the inner reality so that it justifies the particular position. So that sitting in the chair becomes the right place; where you need to be in order to speak. In both cases the body is fully connected to the inner life. With director A, the actor's body responds to the impulse; with director B, the actor finds which impulse corresponds to the demands of the physical reality. Both approaches use true inner-outer connection, and can produce equally believable performances.

Exercise – Sitting/Standing/Lying

Take four or five lines from your speech. You will speak them in exactly the same way as in the earlier 'Deep Connecting' or 'Points of View' exercises, proceeding from moment to moment, and finding a personal connection to each unit before moving on to the next. No hurry. But you have less freedom of physicality. You must do those lines either sitting in a chair, or lying on the floor with some part of your anatomy in contact with the wall while your head remains on the ground, or standing somewhere in the room. That's it. No choice.

Start with sitting. You sit in a chair and begin speaking the first unit while listening for the click of connection. As the words leave your mouth, you 'fiddle about' with your feelings and your voice, and you also make minor adjustments to your body. You are sitting in the chair. Yes. But how? Upright or slouching? Relaxed, or gripping the seat? Where are your legs? Your hands? Where do you need to focus your gaze? You must remain in the chair, but in exactly which position? And what emotional place do you speak from? Is it assertive, or vulnerable, or humorous? And your voice? Louder? More personal in tone? Whispered? You are looking for the place where your body lines up with your voice, feelings and the words you are speaking. You keep juggling the three available elements (vocal music, emotional springboard, precise physical position) until they line up with the two fixed elements (director's instruction, the words of the text).

When the first unit satisfies you, continue through the speech, continually adjusting, and adapting yourself until it feels comfortable and easy to say. Since no speech stays exactly the same, all the way through, allow yourself to keep changing in order to stay connected to what you are saying. Don't force unnatural changes, but sense where and how you have to shift in order to remain true to your words.

Then do the same work in the other two positions: standing and lying on the ground. You may be surprised to see the range of possible interpretations that emerge. Lying on the ground might produce 'pillow talk', while standing and speaking create an angrier need to make people understand what is happening. Stay open.

As well as giving you a way of responding creatively to strict instructions, this exercise also helps you sense the myriad possibilities of the text. You start to realise that there is more than one authentic interpretation. In fact, I would say there are a thousand possible 'right' interpretations of any speech, and only one wrong one. The right ones are fully connected and sound human, and the wrong one is 'bullshit'.

This approach can also help you deal with directors who ask for utter immobility while speaking the words, or when you want to eliminate distracting gestures. Actors and singers are often required to remain still while speaking or singing. This is a stylistic choice, which helps the audience focus on the sound element and the word imagery.

However, standing immobile while speaking to another is not a natural reaction. Vocalising through words is strongly active (you are doing something concrete, e.g. changing another being's thinking or responses through your words), and in active states the body will instinctively wish to engage, in this case by reinforcing the communication via gesture. Stillness is more naturally associated with receiving and processing of information – watch a cat observing its prey, or a child sitting in front of an absorbing television programme. Even then, total stillness does not last for long. Only as long as the prime focus is on receiving information through the senses, or processing information through intense thought. When the balance tilts towards actions, the body engages.

While it is necessary for performers to be comfortable using stillness while vocalising, it is equally important for directors and teachers to realise that this is a learned skill and not an innate ability.

So how do you do it? You use the principles outlined above; shifting your emotional foundation to a place that aligns easily with stillness. And there is one point of emotional origin that meets this criterion: certainty. When we speak with utter conviction, simply revealing the truth of what we know, we rarely need more than our words. They become our weapons; the channel through which we drive our certain knowledge. So, if you require 'stillness while speaking', try shifting your emotional bedrock to 'certainty' and go from there. But be careful; you are not doing the speech with an overall tone of certainty. Rather, you are certain about the truth of every single thing you reveal, whether it is funny, or vulnerable, or irritating, or simply information. But to speak from certainty, you must truly know what you are saying. Which brings us back to ownership.

Your body can speak words in many ways, revealing countless different realities through language. We know how it feels when we communicate well – vibrant, lively, true. Every part of ourselves is engaged. But too often we fear unfamiliar language, or feel that words must be handled reverently, or believe that they are someone else's area of competence. We fail to claim words as our own. And then we miss the opportunity to encounter someone else's reality, through the direct physical experience of their unique language.

And now that you have words, you can begin to communicate. But remember, people constantly adapt what they say and how they say it, according to what they sense is happening to the listener as they speak.

So, what does this mean?

It means that it is very difficult for anyone to work out exactly how they will communicate via words if they are shut up in their own little room, away from the reality of other people. The detailed interpretation of a scene, or how you actually speak to another person, will depend on the context, and how they respond. It is very difficult to plan in advance, and attempting to do so can impede your freedom to react truthfully. The exercises I have outlined above are preparatory. They enable you to connect with the writer's world, and to own fully his or her words with the same authority as your own personal vocabulary. Then you can play.

PART TWO

EXTENDING YOUR RANGE

Chapter 5 HABITS

I have already mentioned how socialisation has shaped and modified us; how the requirements of our society, our class, our family, our job, together with our preferences and tastes, have created a social persona which enables us to function more or less successfully within our chosen world.

In practice, this persona operates through patterns and habits. This is how we move and speak. This is how we dress. This is how we respond to strangers. Over time, these patterns become more and more deeply embedded, until they become fully automatic. We learn to put on the proper body 'costume' for our culture, family, gender and class, partly in response to direct instruction ('Don't sit with your legs apart like that!') and partly through our own desire to fit in.

It seems that this process begins very young. Up until the age of about three or four, it isn't too noticeable. Most children at this age move well, using their body in an anatomically sound fashion. They follow the imperative of their bodies' needs, and actively feed their hunger to engage with the world. There is a minimum of physical shaping. If you look at this age group in a range of different cultures, you will see that the children move in much the same way. They haven't yet taken on their national body 'costume', although they will probably have the beginnings of the 'family body' and the 'gender body'. And eventually, these learned patterns of the persona will determine the physical range of the body.

Even patterns, such as a stoop, that you assume are genetic because your father and grandfather had the same pattern, are often learned and inherited through subconscious imitation. My jaw swings to one side, and for years I believed that it was genetic since my mother has the same pattern. Then, one day, I was looking through the family photo album and noticed that my jaw was normal until about the age of five. A few pages further on I came across a number of photos of me at the age of six or so, where I was smiling in a deliberately lopsided way. It was a conscious, exaggerated copy of my mother, and, as a result, I have 'inherited' her jaw.

As we grow, our bodies select a particular pattern of use, so our muscles develop (or don't develop) accordingly. We literally sculpt our own bodies. When you were a child, your muscle use was fairly balanced; most muscles were equally developed, or rather, equally undeveloped. As you grew up and began learning to move 'appropriately', certain muscles came into prominence while others learned to disengage. Any formal movement training you under-took in a sport, martial art or dance style further selected particular muscles and patterns of use. As a consequence, in adulthood most of us have certain muscles that are strongly developed and in regular use, while others are rarely engaged. The patterns of habitual use are engraved in our muscles, tendons, ligaments and joints. They are equally strongly engraved in our brains.

The phrase 'stuck in a rut' is literally correct. This is how the brain functions; the first time you undertake an action it creates a trail of neuron connections in your brain. If you repeat that same action, the firing sequence in the brain follows the same trail. But in fact the trail is more like a groove, since every time you repeat the action the groove gets deeper, and each repetition carves it more strongly. And this groove is not neutral; once it has become established, similar but unrelated choices will slip sideways and fall into the existing track. If you have ever skied on snow you will know this behaviour; if there are already grooves carved by previous skiers, your skis will tend to slide into them, and unless you make an conscious effort to lift them out, the skis will continue their journey in the ruts already carved. And so make them even deeper. In scientific terms, this is defined as Hebb's axiom: neurons that fire together, will wire together. (If you want to pursue this area of brain and behaviour, I recommend *The Developing Mind*, by Daniel J. Siegel.)

This is why changing habitual patterns is so difficult; they are literally carved into our brain, and each repetition makes the pattern even stronger. And once a pattern of thinking or action becomes a habit, we follow it without thought or awareness. But in fact there is nothing wrong with having 'ruts in the brain'. A habit is simply an easy way for the brain/body entity to function, one that allows the conscious mind to disengage. And this is very useful in many areas of human activity. A ballet dancer does not want to discover how to do an arabesque each night on stage; she wants to know that her leg will rise to the correct height and that the upper body will counterbalance without any conscious control. The movement needs to become habitual in order to free the brain for other activities.

You can see the same thing when learning to drive a car. At first you are faced with a bewildering array of technology and procedures, all of which have to be done in a strict order. Clutch in, engine on, gear chosen, accelerator, handbrake off, and so on. But gradually, over time, the confusion diminishes and it becomes easy – a habit that frees your mind to observe the ebb and flow of traffic, and the insistence of red lights. And when driving is truly habitual you can even sing along with the radio while doing all of the above.

The problem lies in being unaware of the function of habits. If you don't recognise how powerful and all-pervading they are, you become their prisoner. You become the sum of your habits, rather than a responsive and constantly developing individual. Ideally, you want to be able to choose whether to follow a habit or not. And you want to have a broad vocabulary of experiences. You want more than ten patterns you can choose to follow (or not). You want a thousand.

Freeing yourself from imprisonment by patterns is a two-fold action; firstly, we must refrain from repeating the old, unwanted pattern (stop carving the groove any deeper), and then we need to divert our actions into a search for new patterns. You must de-rut and then re-rut.

Chapter 6
GOING FURTHER

We have examined the first stage of body ownership (connecting to the full range of your present body) in the previous section, and for many people this is enough. After all, disengaging yourself from automatic patterns and exploring the various untried possibilities is pretty exciting. But there generally comes a point when you want something more.

As a performer you want a highly articulate body that can keep pace with bigger, stronger and wilder impulses. Your inner landscape demands a hyper-slow drift across the stage; you need to be able to drift without wobbling. You have a ferocious impulse to leap and turn. For five minutes. While speaking. It would be nice if your body were capable of responding to this desire. And this is why we need to work on extending our range of physical possibilities beyond those that exist in our current body.

But 'going further' isn't simply a matter of increasing the physical skills of strength, stamina or flexibility. It also implies enriching and extending your knowledge and vocabulary of experiences. As I said in the introduction, your body is you. It is the bridge between your self and the world. Tasting new ways of inhabiting this essential being can only enrich your existence. And learning new ways of moving doesn't only give you a broader physical vocabulary, it engages the brain in fresh experiences and carves completely new trails through your neurological landscape.

There are many different ways to expand our physical/mental horizons, but one of the simplest is to train in selected movement styles.

As well as providing new sensations and physical stimulus,

formal movement training can also be very helpful in rebalancing the muscles of the body. Muscles that are too tight can be lengthened, while weak ones can be strengthened. This in turn can prevent injury and long-term damage, and even ameliorate pain. But when you do this, please remember that *how* you train is very important. Probably more important than which style you choose.

GETTING STARTED

First of all, be honest. You are doing this work to extend your range, not to demonstrate your existing skills and competence. This seems an obvious statement, but many people choose new styles because they fit with what already exists, rather than going where there is an absence of competence. In other words, you need to train in areas where you can't do the work, rather than in the areas where you can. So you need to be clear about what you need, and then look for the techniques that allow you to focus on that territory.

Secondly, be aware that there is quite a big gap between the way we habitually use our body in daily existence, and a way of moving that is determined by our anatomical design. As well as socialisation, our personal experience of life (our occupations, the sports we play, our relationship with our body, the impact of various events, old injuries, etc.) has added another layer of shaping to the physicality. All of these various patterns are so deeply embedded in our bodies that they feel 'natural' and 'easy', so that when you start moving in inhabitual ways, it can feel very odd and alien. Even uncomfortable or disturbing for a while.

But the body likes moving and, in a sense, it wants to experience new possibilities. Just accept that it might feel very peculiar at first.

As you engage in this process, please respect the body and its limitations. Physical training can be wonderful, provided that it acknowledges the realities of your personal anatomy, and causes no injury. Try to remember that it is your own unique body that you are training, with its specific anatomical structure, learned habits of use and particular experience. Listen to the body and never force it to the point of damage. If you are in any doubt about your health or the advisability of a particular style, check with your doctor. And always remember the 'pleasure safety net'; if what you are doing doesn't enhance, intrigue, amuse or delight you on some level, don't do it. Despite what you may have been told, physical suffering is not useful.

OUR NATURAL PHYSICAL CAPACITY

One key element in effective training is understanding the basic design of the body and how to use it effectively. If you comprehend and respect the anatomical integrity of your body, you will be able to develop physically with minimal risk of injury.

BONES

When we normally think about our bodies, we tend to focus on the visible: the skin, the fat, and the general shape of our outline. We forget about the invisible components which are the real basics: the bones, the muscles, and the connective tissue. Learning to respect and utilise these structures correctly is half the battle in terms of fully developing our physical capacity. Begin with the bones.

The skeleton is the framework of the body; without it, our bodies would simply collapse into puddles of organs, tendons and muscle. It enables us to stand upright, resisting gravity. We all know this to be true, but what does it mean in terms of that dreaded word 'posture'? Quite simply, when we normally talk about 'correcting our posture', we talk about our muscles. We are told to 'pull your shoulders back', or 'hold your stomach in'. These are actions of the muscles and have very little impact on the skeleton. And yet it is the skeleton that enables us to stand upright in an easy, relaxed manner.

What this means in practice is getting the bones stacked properly one on top of another, so that the muscles have only a minimum of work to do in order to keep you upright. Imagine a stack of bricks.

If they are piled up haphazardly, some sticking out on one side while the rest protrude on the other, the structure is very unstable. Even a small amount of pressure on the top will make it collapse. And if you are determined to prevent it from collapsing, you have to keep using your hands to shore it up. The body is the same. Most of us do not 'stack' our pelvis on top of our legs, our ribs on top of our pelvis, our shoulders on top of our ribs, our neck on top of our shoulders and finally our head on top of our neck. Bits keep sticking out, and we have to use our muscles as 'hands' to keep the whole thing upright. Far too much hard work. Let the skeleton carry the load. This is what it is designed to do.

Once the skeleton is balanced properly, the muscles can release and focus on their appointed task: moving the limbs around.

Exercise – Sensing Placement

Stand with your feet about five to seven inches apart. Find the place where your weight is equally distributed on both feet, and neither too far forward or back. To check this, take your weight right forward so that your heels lift off the ground quite easily. Then move your weight backward, so that the balls of your feet can detach from the floor. Now move your weight to a central place, where neither the heels nor the balls of the feet can be lifted. That's where you need to be. Already you might find that this position feels odd or unfamiliar. That's fine; many people habitually carry their weight mainly one way or another. Just observe how it feels.

One thing you may notice is that this position involves less muscle tension. When your body goes too far in any direction, the muscles start to work to grip the body and thus prevent it from tipping over. Try taking your weight as far as you can to the front and then to the back. Observe how hard the different muscles have to work. The central place is where no muscle works strongly; they can all relax a bit because the body weight is now directly over the feet, and the bones of the leg are carrying the load. In this position, you can also unlock the knees more easily.

This partial relaxation of the leg muscles might make you feel a bit peculiar. If your muscles have got used to working very hard to keep you upright, it may feel rather wobbly and insecure to release them. Don't worry: the bones are still there; they'll keep you upright.

> Now, feel your spine lengthening from behind. Imagine someone has a fingertip tucked under the base of your skull, gently lifting your head and upper back towards the ceiling. At the same time, another imaginary hand is stroking your tailbone downwards. As your upper back lifts and your sacrum drops, you may feel some space appearing in your middle back. This is good, but don't feel impelled to exaggerate this position. You don't want your pelvis to tip itself too far forward, or for the neck to be excessively 'pulled up'. Just a gentle awareness of a long, open, flexible spine.

In this position, you become aware of the air between your hips and the ribs, and between the shoulder girdle and the back of the skull. The shoulders themselves are wide, as if they are moving outwards. Your legs are soft but strong. Your head is poised on top of a long but relaxed neck, and your arms extend outwards from broad shoulders, ready to touch and handle the world.

You will notice that when I talk about adjustments, I refer to sensations rather than to any 'correct position' for the head or pelvis. Seeking to maintain a 'correct position' at all times tends to lead to rigidity, tension and fear of shifting. This is most unhelpful, since the body is designed to move, rather than being held in place. It also *likes* moving. Even the most anatomically correct posture is unhelpful if it is rigidly imposed and excessively maintained. For example, your head is poised on a long neck, but this isn't a fixed position. Instead, the head remains alert and able to turn easily in any direction. The 'aligned' posture can also shift in an instant to a fierce crouch, or a quick moment of salsa. In addition, physical rigidity stops the body from responding to whatever is happening in the moment, either in terms of emotion or outside events. It is therefore poison, and to be avoided as much as possible.

Sometimes technical work on anatomical alignment can become

mechanical, and feel imposed on the body. To prevent this, try to find a positive image, linking the aligned body to your imagination. For example, you discover that technically you need to open out the upper chest/base of neck region, since your neck pokes forward. You could imagine that you are walking along a beautiful beach with warm sun on your chest. Or that you are wearing a stunning diamond necklace. Both of these images tend to help you maintain an open neck and shoulder area. Or, in order to move effort down into your lower body, you might imagine you are a panther in human form, prowling the forest. This reinforces the sense of moving from your centre on flexible, powerful legs. And so on.

The key element is to choose an image that you truly like and which feels pleasurable to explore. That way, the body will want to reinforce this new system of moving. If you think the image is ridiculous, or it is meaningless to you, it won't work. The link needs to be positive, so that the mind associates the new position with pleasure. In that way it will want to repeat it. Again and again.

It is only through repetition that a new trail can be formed in the brain. In order to claim new territory, you must repeat it, over and over until it engraves itself on your neurological landscape. But repetition can very easily become boring and dutiful, especially when imposed from outside rather than initiated by the individual. This is why the pleasure element in my work is so important; only through repetition will real change and ownership occur, and this is far easier to do if you find pleasure in the physical doing of the task.

Of course, following efficient anatomical alignment isn't the only system you use when working the body, or even when standing. If you are performing and doing character or expressive work, you can deliberately choose to destabilise your form. But this is the basic, anatomically easy way to stand, one that requires a minimum of muscular effort to maintain. It's nice to know where that is, and what it feels like. In addition, it is a good starting place for creative decisions, since you can feel very precisely how any chosen changes affect the body.

Understanding and following the inborn anatomical structure is the basis of both the Alexander and Feldenkrais techniques, and if you wish to go further in this area, both techniques are excellent and worth exploring.

THE CENTRE

This word is used frequently in many contexts ('get centred', 'find your centre'), but what do we actually mean by 'the centre'? In Asian theatre and martial-art forms, it refers to the core of the body's energies and is physically located in the lower abdomen. Curiously enough, this is also the site for the body's structural centre of gravity, which is the focus of our body's weight, in relation to the gravity force coming from the planet. Working with our physical centre of gravity means we fall over less.

Exercise – Moving from the Centre

Pat your tummy just below the belly button. This gives you the physical sense of your centre. Now imagine that this area is a globe that simply floats and glides around the room. You don't walk forward; the globe floats forward. And backward, and sideways. It suddenly changes direction, it rises, it descends. You just sit your torso on top of your centre and let it carry you about, while your legs seem almost soft and invisible. They are flexible and responsive, shifting easily, but remaining under the centre. You can use your arms and hands. If you want to fall softly against the wall, they can catch your weight, or they can assist your centre as you roll over. But it is always the centre that moves your body through space. As you get familiar with this sensation, let the centre get more adventurous. Run, tumble, jump, turn, but always with the centre making the move.

You will probably find that you have a greater sense of ease and stability. You are working less hard, while being able to shift and turn more efficiently, because you are working with, rather than against, the body's basic design. If you doubt this, try the next exercise.

Exercise – Moving against the Centre

Stand still, and then deliberately 'go off centre' by tilting your body forward from the waist. See how the muscles react. Then start running around the space, keeping the chest ahead of the pelvis. Change direction, rise and descend, exactly as you did in the previous exercise. See what happens.

Doing the 'wrong' version usually makes the effects of non-centred body use very clear, emotionally as well as physically.

When you work from the centre, you are also bringing the lower half of the body into engagement and action, stimulating it and reminding it that it is part of the performing equipment. The head remains free, poised lightly on the neck, alert and receptive. Not only to reduce tension, but to engage responsively to the world around us. Practise this feeling of 'effort down/skull alert' in daily life. It will take a lot of the strain off your muscles and bones, since this way of moving is anatomically efficient and minimises unnecessary effort. All healthy young children use their bodies like this as a matter of course.

MUSCLES AND CONNECTIVE TISSUES

Most muscle-focused systems work on three areas: strength, flexibility and stamina, and this is where many of the injuries and problems arise. Whether you are engaged in dance, yoga, sports or the martial arts, it is worth taking some time to understand how these actually operate.

When we talk about muscles, we tend to talk about them as single entities. We do strength work on our abdominals, or stretch our hamstrings. In a sense, this is a false isolation. Muscles tend to work in pairs, one muscle tightening while its opposite number stretches. As your bicep tightens in order to bring your forearm towards your shoulder, your tricep (underneath your upper arm) lengthens. And then vice versa; when you straighten the arm out, it is your tricep that tightens while your bicep lengthens. In order to tighten the bicep fully, the tricep must be fully flexible. So you are actually working against the body's muscle function if you only do strength work (i.e. exercises based on tightening) without any kind of flexibility training. Ideally, every muscle in your body would be equally balanced, having equal strength and flexibility. But very few of us fit this profile. Most of us have a lot of slack muscles with very little strength, and an equal number of overtight, overworked muscles with minimal flexibility.

Strength:
The first step in strength training is deciding what outcome you desire. Do you want to increase the strength of specific muscles in order to improve sports performance? If so, which sport? The muscle use required by different sports varies enormously. Or are you working aesthetically, sculpting the muscles into a particular form because you like that look? Again, a different process.

My aim as a teacher is to promote greater freedom of physicality and responsiveness, primarily for non-dance performers, and so my strength-training programme is directed towards that goal. Accordingly, I focus on leg and spine activity combined with upper-body freedom. The strength exercises I recommend are mainly for the legs, as well as some work on the postural support muscles. I tend to ignore the upper body, shoulders and neck in terms of strength work, since I am trying to disengage those (usually overactive and tense) areas. And I don't care what your pectorals look like.

When you are working on your own, find systems that are tailored to your exact needs. All performers need leg and back strength, so dance and certain soft martial-art forms like t'ai chi and aikido are useful. Acrobatic performers will also need to work on upper back, arms and abdominals, though this is often included in the skill-specific training. Yoga is an excellent system, since it develops the entire musculature of the body, employing both strength and flexibility work, and also links the breath and the mind to the process (as do the soft martial arts). And remember, because muscles tend to work in opposing pairs, you cannot do effective strength work without also focusing on flexibility.

Flexibility:

The first thing to recognise is that flexibility training concentrates mainly on muscles and not connective tissue. While it is possible to stretch tendons and ligaments, it is not desirable to make them too loose. The function of a ligament is to hold the bones together; excessively stretched ligaments can lead to unstable joints, which in turn are more prone to injury. And tendons are designed to be a strong anchor between a muscle and a bone. For example, the Achilles tendon at the heel starts its life as muscle in the calf, gradually transforming into stiffer tendon tissue until it welds itself on to the heel bone. It is very strong, and only slightly elastic. Tendons do need some flexibility in order to accommodate the comings and goings of the muscle, and to absorb unexpected shocks. And if they have been injured, you must gently stretch them until they regain their full elasticity. But their basic responsive strength should not be compromised. For this reason, most flexibility work should focus on the muscles themselves, and not overload or stress ligaments and tendons.

Stretching:

Many people stretch badly, and for the wrong reasons. Certainly there is a 'health and safety' reason for stretching; a tight muscle is more likely to tear under pressure. But more importantly, you are literally unable to move, and therefore unable to experience what it means to engage fully with your body, until you loosen the corset (or straitjacket) of held, overtight muscles. Stretching should be an essential part of your body work, but it needs to be undertaken correctly. Many people stretch in the wrong way, at the wrong time, or use techniques that are actively counterproductive. A classic book on this subject is *Stretching* by Bob Anderson, and many of the ideas in this section come from his work. However, there are plenty of other excellent books on the market, usually in the sports medicine section.

Basically, there are two kinds of stretching: maintenance stretching, to ensure that your existing physicality remains flexible (and to prevent the muscles getting progressively tighter as you work); and developmental stretching, where you are gradually altering the muscle balance in the body so that tight muscles lengthen and become more flexible. Again, I recommend yoga for both kinds of flexibility training, since it is very adaptable. People of any age, any condition and any level of skill can do this work and benefit equally.

First of all, when to stretch? People often think that they should leap out of bed first thing in the morning and plunge straight into a strong stretching routine in order to wake up. This is a bad choice. While you have been sleeping, the muscles have gone into a state of semi-connectedness. You move about in bed from time to time, but not very actively and you tend to have limited awareness of what your body is doing. In addition, because you have been horizontal, the muscles have not been working at weight-bearing. All of this is fine, and indeed is the reason we go to bed, but if you suddenly demand that the body move into a state of high activity and strong action, you can create problems and risk injuring yourself. In addition, your ability to be acutely sensitive and aware of what is happening inside your body might be limited. Many of us are zombies on waking. This doesn't mean that you should not stretch in the morning, only that you should wait till the body has had a chance to wake up before beginning. Even a gentle potter around the kitchen is useful.

This brings us to the first key point: it is a good idea to mobilise the body before stretching it. Mobilisation means undemanding physical activity, which nonetheless gets most of the body moving and the blood flowing into the muscles. It makes stretching easier and reduces the risk of injury.

A quick digression. In many sports and performance practice, people have the habit of doing stretch work as part of their warm-up. This is fine and useful, but you should also stretch *after* your activity. Playing your sport, or even standing on stage for long periods of time, will cause certain muscles to tighten, and these need to be stretched out afterwards in order to regain their flexibility. You can feel this necessity in the legs (especially the hamstrings and calf muscles) and the back (usually the lower back, shoulders and neck region).

How Not to Stretch:

Firstly, don't bounce. This method actually prevents your muscles from stretching and can lead to injury. While gentle pulsing can help you mobilise the muscles prior to stretching, strong ballistic bouncing is counterproductive to flexibility work. There is a reflex in the muscles called the 'stretch reflex' (although it would be more accurate to name it the 'anti-stretch reflex'), and this activates when a muscle senses that it is being asked to stretch too far. The reflex is triggered and the muscle pulls up short to prevent the stretch from going any further. This contraction causes the muscle to bounce back. The very process by which the body bounces up and down is a process designed to prevent stretching. You cannot stretch through bouncing. The stretch reflex won't let you.

But sometimes the stretch reflex isn't strong enough to 'catch' a really strong throw of a limb and bounce it back into the safety zone. And so the muscle hits its limit of flexibility and then goes beyond, into tearing. This occurs when you are working ballistically (forcefully throwing the weight of your leg, arm, head or entire body in a particular direction like a ball). When you strongly launch a weight into space, its momentum will carry it onwards. It takes a lot of work to halt such a launch, more than many muscles can provide either consciously through effort, or unconsciously through the stretch reflex. If you throw a limb hard or fast, you may go past the physical limit of the muscle, into rip-and-tear territory. Beware of fast, high kicks; the hamstring muscle can be most unforgiving.

A simple test to ensure that you are not working ballistically is to use the principle of reversibility. You should be able to stop any movement easily and send it into reverse. You don't fling your arms open (ballistic), you release them into the air at a normal rhythm that can be arrested at any moment. In this way, you are effectively mobilising your body, not bouncing it around in a doomed attempt at stretching – an attempt that might cause injury rather than increased flexibility.

There are effective stretching systems that avoid bouncing. Most of these involve slow sustained work in specific positions. The principle behind them is to take a given muscle into a position of stretch and then to let it extend further from that place. The two key concepts in this work are time and gentleness. Muscles have their own timetable for releasing, relaxing and allowing themselves to be stretched. Forcing through this timetable will only cause resistance and possible injury. A better procedure is as follows. Go to a position of stretch where you can feel that the muscle is gently lengthening. Stay there for at least twenty to thirty seconds. If you only want to do maintenance stretching, that's enough. Move on to the next position. If you want to do development stretching, stay in the position. After the initial twenty to thirty seconds, deepen the position slightly to increase the stretch, and stay there for a further thirty seconds or even longer. At no time force the stretch to the point of agony. Your breathing should remain easy, and it often helps to actively breathe into the stretch. Ignore the phrase 'no pain, no gain'.

The Role of Pain:

Pain is a signal that something is going wrong, and you must never ignore it. If you are having to use will-power to force yourself through a pain barrier, or your breathing is getting restricted by the effort, chances are that you have gone too far. Listen to the body, and remember that real physical change comes slowly, little by little, in months rather than weeks. If you try to force things, you are more likely to end up with tissue damage, which in turn puts you back to square one in terms of training and is very disheartening. Listen and gently persist.

By the way, when I talk about pain, I am referring to the sharp 'uh-oh' phenomena, or the hot, grinding sensation of overworked joints. A certain level of 'mild discomfort' as muscles start to move and discover that they are alive is inevitable and causes no problems. It isn't very difficult to sense the difference between the pain of damage and the mild discomfort of the body waking up. The latter occurs when you are taking the body into new territory, outside its normal range of reactions and abilities. When you 'listen' in this place, the sensation is more 'How interesting! I don't believe these muscles have worked quite so hard in a long time,' or

'Hmmm. I didn't think my leg would actually go there. Fascinating.' And the day after, you may feel it. But you will never 'hear' things like 'Go! More! I can do it! I can! Stick with it!' or 'Oh! I wish it would end! Please!' These are not useful in the long term.

The key technique for safeguarding your body while continuing to develop is 'listening'. Your body will tell you what it finds dangerous, provided you stay tuned to what exactly is going on, moment by moment. This is why I tend not to use paired stretches, or any kind of flexibility work where someone else pushes your body. Unless that person is highly skilled, they will not be able to sense what is happening in your body as well as you yourself can. You are the best person to judge what is effective, and what is too much.

I am asking you to see your body in a new light. Many physical training systems emphasise breaking through the pain barrier in order to achieve a specific outcome. This approach fails to recognise the realities of the human body, often creating new physical problems. It also is based on outdated ideas of demonstrating toughness, or pain as validation of experience ('If it hurts, it's worth more'). We will examine this philosophy in more detail in the next section.

As you work with the body, keep focused on the feeling of what is actually happening at the present moment, not what you hope to achieve. In general, the entire concept of external outcomes or goals is unhelpful, especially a single, targeted goal, such as trying to put your head on your knees. Person A (who was born naturally supple, or has done a lot of flexibility training) may get their head on their knees with no effort at all, while person B (who has a different genetic structure, or has done a lot of high-impact running sports) tears muscles and sets up huge tension in the neck in a futile attempt to achieve this goal. So when you work, never aim for a particular outcome (e.g. getting the head on the knees), but simply engage in the process (stretching the hamstrings to their natural limit).

In addition, forcing the body in an insensitive way takes us further and further away from where we need to be as performers and human beings. The body becomes something we manipulate and drive, rather than an aspect of our self that we are pleased to explore and develop. We can't work with cowed, obedient flesh that has learned to be silent; we need alive, vibrant bodies that are our partners in creativity.

Stamina:

The phrase 'stamina work' conjures up the image of a sweating, groaning body using the last remnants of willpower to force aching muscles the final few miles or repetitions at the gym. Utterly repulsive. Why on earth would you want to punish your body in this way? Especially if you are becoming quite fond of your physicality, and are starting to listen to the interesting things it has to say. Nonetheless, there are benefits that can come from endurance training or work in a gym, plus pleasures based on a sense of mastery and progress. And the chemical high of endorphin release. But too often it becomes mechanical and disconnecting, rather than enabling and enlarging.

What do we really mean by stamina? And how do we develop it without needing to grit our teeth?

'Stamina' implies physical work to promote heart and lung fitness. Movement activity where the heart rate is slightly raised and the lungs engage more actively in order to bring air into the body. This is also described as 'aerobic' training, and such work can be easily undertaken. Obvious activities such as walking and cycling develop your aerobic capacity, as can swimming. Swimming is particularly useful, since you use a variety of muscles while the joints are fully supported by the water. It is therefore a safe way to develop stamina, and less stressful to older, untrained or injured bodies. For this very reason, I don't recommend running. The jarring impact of the feet hitting the ground again and again can create problems in the knees and lower back, as well as excessively tight hamstrings and calf muscles. I realise that proper shoes and technical awareness (plus stretching out the muscles after running) can ameliorate these problems, and if you really enjoy running, please continue. But if you are just starting out, try an easier system first. And remember to do flexibility work as well.

Whichever system you follow, try to make it a pleasure rather than a duty. Choose an activity you enjoy, and then do it aerobically. This isn't hard. Aerobic activity simply raises the level of heart/lung work above the habitual and keeps it there for ten to twenty minutes. That's all. Nothing fancy. You can do aerobic walking, housecleaning or dancing along to your iPod. Just work harder than usual, so that you can feel the breathing become more pronounced, and stay there for a while. Never work too hard and go into strained breathing. This is quite counterproductive for the body. How do you tell? If you can keep chatting while working (or humming along to the music), you are working at the correct level. If you haven't got enough breath to speak, or are gasping the words out, you have gone too far. Ease back. You want to get your breathing going and keep moving, but without triggering an unhelpful response, or needing horrendous amounts of willpower to sustain you.

Even as little as ten minutes is valuable. We sometimes feel that aerobic training is a huge undertaking involving serious commitment, special equipment and organised activity. The magnitude of this task often puts people off. Instead, just walk energetically round the park with a friend, chatting all the way. Put on a good CD and just dance your way right to the end (this is my favourite). Or even cavort like a maniac at a club (though the air quality in such an environment might create other problems). But enjoy it. Do not listen to the 'inner voice' that tells you 'training is only effective when it feels like hard work/suffering'. Enjoyment does not prevent or impede effective training.

EXPERIENCING THE UNFAMILIAR/NEW PHYSICAL SENSATIONS

If you train in a performing institution, you will probably be taught new ways of using the body – perhaps styles that you would never have studied by choice, such as acrobatics, or period dance, or Laban. This is one of the benefits of such schools, since the curriculum demands that you move beyond your normal physical habits, and encourages you to explore new movement styles. In this way, the body directly experiences unfamiliar patterns, and so increases its range of physical responses. You can (and should) continue this process when you are on your own.

One simple exercise is to take the ordinary activities of daily life and deliberately approach them in a fresh way. For example, one day I was cooking some soup, and as usual I was stirring the pot with my right hand. So I thought, let's try stirring with the left hand, just to see how it feels. It was obviously less efficient than the habitual way, but I persevered. After all, the soup wasn't going to be damaged by clumsy stirring, and it didn't matter if it took a bit longer. Then I noticed that the whole balance of my body altered. My weight shifted to the other leg, my chest rotated towards the other side, and even my head leaned in the opposite direction. Something as simple as stirring soup with my right hand had huge implications for the rest of my body.

Another way to give your body new sensations is via training systems. But which one should you choose to study?

This is an individual choice, and as I said at the beginning of this section, one that demands complete honesty with yourself. When you work with the body, you probably recognise certain recurring patterns. Your body likes slow movement, or lots of hand gestures, or it dislikes crawling around the floor. Fine. But to extend your range you must deliberately choose to work with the areas of unfamiliarity and discomfort. If you are naturally fast, explore the slow sustained technique of t'ai chi. If your body prefers slow, heavy work, take up tap dancing. If you like lots of free rolling around the floor, study period dance. If you don't like free rolling around the floor, participate in contact improvisation. And so on.

There are a number of excellent training systems which are readily available. Feldenkrais and Alexander technique are especially useful for physical awareness, and yoga and t'ai chi are good for strength and flexibility, and also train you to link the breath to action. Laban is particularly helpful for performers, since it encourages awareness of time and space as well as of the body itself.

Kendo and fencing both employ physical attack and leg strength, plus full commitment to impulse. Dance is good for strength, co-ordination and presentation. Then there are all the various sub-styles within dance: contemporary, jazz, tap, flamenco, ball-room, historical, salsa, and so on. Each style emphasises and develops a particular area of physical expression, elaborating it into a precise and articulate code. Simply work out what you personally need to enhance in your body and then find the form that focuses on that area. In addition to the styles I have already mentioned, here are some other possibilities: tango (leg strength, poise and precision), African dance (lower body strength, flexibility and rhythm), ballet (control, awareness of placement, flow), mime (isolation, precision, clarity of action), Indian dance (detail, precision and rhythm), Irish dance (leg speed, upper body control).

When you start learning a new movement language, it can be quite daunting, since you will be working in a style for which you have little natural aptitude. It won't come easily, and you won't be the star pupil (at least at the outset). This can be hard, since we all like to be good at what we do. We like to be praised, and an inability to achieve something successfully can sometimes feel like personal failure. Just remember why you are doing this work and who you are doing it for. You are doing it for yourself in order to extend your range. You are studying flamenco to increase the poise of the body, and to deepen your sense of rhythm. Or you decide to experience this style of activity because it looks like fun. In neither case are you trying to impress anyone with your innate gypsy passion, as demonstrated by your ability to go longer and harder than anyone else.

I apologise in advance to the dedicated practitioners of these arts for any suggestion that their styles are limited to the elements I have noted here. Each of these traditions is much deeper and more complex than described, and demands great integrity and dedication. I have simply noted particular strengths in each style so that people wishing to extend their range in a certain direction know where to begin. But beware: although you start training simply to support your work as a performer, or to extend your range of physical experience, you might develop a real passion for the style. They are complex and engrossing: who knows how far you will go? One of my ex-students started studying tango to increase his skills. He is now a professional tango dancer.

Chapter 7 WHAT STOPS US WORKING?

My work began from a very simple question: why is it so difficult to reproduce vibrant, humanly authentic life in performance? We all know how to think and feel and speak and move, we do it every day of our lives. Leaving aside questions of technique and stylistic presentation, why does it take so much training and hard work to reproduce this existence on demand?

As I started to think and observe, I realised that the problem was complex, and that it was not confined to the performer's process; it was much more far-reaching. Looking at the human requirements for good performers, I noted certain key criteria; they need to be physically and emotionally alive, open and responsive to others, thinking and feeling with great authenticity and expressive freedom. At the same time, they must be fully aware of the need to choose the appropriate response, according to the situation, relationship, demands of the context and audience reaction. To be fully alive, without fear or self-indulgence. To be free but totally aware of how each action affects other people, and to be able to manage this process effectively. Then I realised that this was a pretty clear description of how most of us would like to live our lives. Everybody (not just performers) should have the ability to respond like this if the circumstances are appropriate. Gradually, I began to perceive how certain factors operate, and how they create unnecessary limitations for all of us.

Many of the issues in this chapter have already been alluded to in earlier sections, but it is worth examining their mechanism in detail.

CULTURAL ATTITUDE TO THE BODY

As was mentioned in Part One, we live in an era that is both desperately unphysical and full of body loathing. We tend to assume that as our society becomes more complex and we develop a clearer technology of the body, we are more physically attuned than our ancestors. Wrong. We may know more about how the body works, but we actually use it less. And we use it in an incredibly narrow range of physicality, which seems to become even narrower as we grow older.

By the time we are adults, the range can be as limited as: walk, sit, lie, drive, watch live events or filmed performances and, occasionally, if we are lucky, something additional. A sport, hill walking, or dancing in a club. Some of us may undertake physical training of some sort, but this can become a joyless duty rather than physical delight. Our bodies are undeveloped and underexperienced, and are rarely perceived as a source of pleasure, except in bed. Sad but true. In fact, despite the rhetoric of fitness, health, and beauty, there is a strong current of distaste for the body within the broader society. We may dutifully change our physicality (through exercise, training, diet, or surgery) to fit some particular ideal, but there is very little delight in or curiosity about the body's subtle workings. But why is this the case?

The answer may lie in our unspoken beliefs about the human body. There are two main cultural models of the body in western society, and they powerfully shape attitudes to our physical being. The first is derived from Early Christianity, although it had its roots in the ideas of Plato. In this model, the body and the soul/mind were seen as distinctly separate, and actively opposed. The 'higher functions' of thought, imagination and conscience resided in the soul/mind, while the body was seen as inherently sinful, untrustworthy and brutish, and operated as an active impediment to the soul/mind's development. It required discipline, punishment and strict control in order to prevent it from returning to a state of lazy bestiality and so damaging the soul's capacity for union with God. Not only was the body separate from the mind, it was distinctly inferior.

This concept was reinvented by the French philosopher Descartes during the Enlightenment; he retained the earlier idea about the mind/body split, while deleting the religious dimension. He also kept the idea of the body's innate inferiority, and its problematic nature. This sense of the fundamental inferiority and untrustworthiness of the body still permeates our society, manifesting in many different ways.

For performers, this attitude affects *how* we work with the body. Irrespective of style, many training practices emphasise discipline, rigour and transcendence of discomfort, and elevate these concepts to ideals. What is won through difficult endeavour is seen as worthwhile, while what comes easily is devalued. This was clearly evident in the 'no pain, no gain' ideology which came to the fore in the 1980s, alongside the boom in the fitness industry, but it has more subtle manifestations in the fundamental belief that the only way to 'train' a body is via focus, control and relentless effort. Hard work is good, while discomfort is often welcomed as a sign of positive change. The early Christian idea of punishing the body is still with us.

In addition, pleasure in body use is seen as a form of naughty self-indulgence – you might have the occasional fun 'game' in class, but it is seen as separate from the serious work of training. Interestingly, students often refer to my processes as 'games'. They are not; they are very precise and targeted exercises. But because I require the element of pleasure to be present, the students shift the work into the 'game' category. They are somehow uneasy with the idea of 'serious pleasure'. Yet pleasure is a necessary performing skill; how can a performer be playful and creative with a body that is seen as requiring harsh control, and that feels like a painful duty? There is a contradiction here between the actual requirements of performing and the unspoken cultural belief that influences the process of training.

The second key cultural attitude to the body reflects nineteenth century engineering principles. With the advance of scientific thinking after the Renaissance, involving the rediscovery of classical principles of methodical inquiry, there was a more accurate understanding of how the body actually functioned; how the blood flowed, how the muscles operated, and so on. In the nineteenth century this became allied to the ideology of advancement via industrialisation. From this 'Engineering' viewpoint, the body was seen as a series of mechanical functions, of levers, pulleys and pumps, which could be rendered more efficient via the intelligent control of the mind. Again, the mind (which had usurped the position of the soul as the seat of self/intelligence) was seen as fundamentally separate and superior; this time as the driver in the control box, supervising the smooth running of the inanimate machinery. But there was still a split between body and mind, and the mind continued to be the superior partner.

In terms of training, this ideology helped ensure that bodywork techniques respected the actual anatomical structures and functioning of the body, which is valuable and essential. But it also contains the unspoken idea that the body itself is an inert structure, requiring external manipulation and control.

This perspective also led to another unhelpful concept for performer training – the unexamined use of the word 'Movement' to define all aspects of physical engagement. This linguistic description frames the body as a passive object moved by the mind in accordance with consciously chosen patterns.

This philosophy of conscious control and patterned manipulation of the anatomy has shaped dance training, and is of clear use in this context, but it is not directly relevant to other performing styles. The aim of a dancer is to 'move well' within the patterns of the given dance style, but other performers do not have this as a prime objective. Singers and actors may occasionally need to 'move well' (be able to dance or use stylised gesture) but fundamentally their broad aim is connected physical life, whereby the body is capable of revealing thought, feeling, and reactions, plus the ability to transform according to the demand of character. This is not the same as 'moving well'.

In addition, the use of the term 'Movement' reinforces the cultural attitude of separation between the body and the other aspects of the performer (mind, emotions, and voice). In terms of actor training (compared to dancers) this creates a problem, which is further reinforced by the separation of Movement from Voice and Acting in most drama school syllabuses. While there are some very good reasons for discrete classes (such as the provision of sessions of technical detail), there is a risk of actively impeding the development of connected physical life, which is what actors need.

This cultural inheritance of division and disdain for the body is still very much with us, and affects every aspect of our engagement with process. It elevates pain and distrusts ease, it creates an unwillingness to trust the body, and it discourages full investigation and ownership. In all aspects of our work we must fight to discard this outworn and inaccurate philosophy. Avoid dualism. Forget hierarchy. Instead, try to view the human body with respect and pleasure. Never forget that the body and the mind are in fact a single, dynamic unit.

LACK OF PERMISSION

I have already discussed the process of socialisation, and indicated how all-pervasive it can be. One of mechanisms of this process takes the form of inner 'voices' that comment and assess our actions as they unfold. In everyday life, we are hardly aware of them, but they have a huge impact on what we allow ourselves to do. They sometimes encourage us to be more efficient ('Come on now. Just sit down and do the work. Get it over with') or even encouraging ('Keep going, not long now'), but many other inner voices judge us harshly and even withhold permission. They emerge very strongly when we are exploring or improvising in a creative situation. There are three main families of voices that tend to appear.

The Voice of Instinct:
The inner 'Yes' I have referred to so often; the resonance that occurs when a moment is real and connected. This voice tends to be in the present tense and has a limited vocabulary. It says things like 'Yes! Go go go go go!' or 'Nearly, nearly . . .' or 'Yuck! Bullshit.' We listen for this when we are in the process of working.

The Voice of Assessment:

The part of us that is honest about what is happening: which moment is real, and which one is banal. This observes and monitors, but does not comment or intervene while the work is taking place. After the work is finished, it examines what has occurred, deciding what worked and what didn't, what began to work and then fell apart, what was virtually a waste of time except for that one interesting moment. Once it has assessed the various elements, it may also frame the parameters for the next task, e.g. 'Last time I tried it this way with some interesting results. Let's see what happens if I try it that way.'

The Voice of Judgement:

It tends to say things like 'Will this work?' 'I did this last time, I'd better do something different now' 'Is this what she wants?' 'I hope this is right' 'I really don't think this is any good' 'Look at what he is doing! He is so much better/worse than me!' and so on. It tends to be located outside the present moment (in the past, or in the future), or in terms of an imaginary critic, or comparisons with others. Many performers actually prevent themselves from exploring because of these voices. They say to themselves 'It won't work' or 'It isn't very interesting' and then withdraw from the process without ever having made a concrete offer. How do you know it won't work until you try it? Maybe it will work. Maybe it won't. Maybe most of it will be an embarrassing disaster, except for one moment, but that one moment is worth pursuing. Because these voices occur during the process of exploration and impede the work, they are a complete waste of time.

While working, we only listen for the first two voices.

FEAR AND DOUBT

Two of the strongest impediments to any kind of exploration are fear and doubt. But how can you stop them? How can you get rid of them? The answer is, you can't. Don't waste your time trying, and certainly never wait until you are fully confident before you start working. If you wait for confidence before beginning, you'll wait for ever.

What you need is to encourage some other qualities which can balance and eventually outweigh the negative ones. Two of the most useful are humour and curiosity. The dialogue goes something like this:

DOUBT: It's not going to work
CURIOSITY: Who knows? Let's see what happens.
FEAR: I'm going to look like an idiot.
HUMOUR: So what's new?

Remember that most of the performing skills you need (except those to do with extending our physical and vocal range, and demands of style) are simply retrieving what we knew as a child. Play, curiosity, a need to be aware of the outside world (because we didn't know how it operated), a willingness to be excited by the richness of our imagination. And since this is simply a matter of recalling something we know how to do, and indeed have already done successfully, it isn't particularly difficult. It's more a matter of giving permission.

LACK OF TIME

People often get scared off by difficulty when working. The word 'difficult' can mean 'impossible' or it can mean 'arduous'. We automatically tend to assume that the first meaning is true; that if we find something difficult, it will be impossible to achieve. But remember, you were once a child learning how to walk. This was extremely difficult in the sense of arduous, requiring months of hard work, frustration and lots of bumps. But it was far from impossible, since we all got there in the end. Indeed, if humanity gave up on walking simply because it was difficult and tiring, and not immediately successful, we would still be conducting our lives from the floor.

When we don't trust in our ability to engage with difficulty, it can lead to two outcomes. Firstly, if we don't get something right straight away, we abandon the task. We decide we haven't 'got what it takes' to succeed. Alternatively, we rush to an acceptable solution, rather than taking the time to investigate fully, in depth. We do work that is 'good enough' rather than excellent. In either case, we don't give ourselves enough time to explore properly, to engage fully, and then to find the most effective solution. We may never achieve our desired goal, but we must give ourselves the time to see whether it is truly impossible or merely arduous.

There are two kinds of time we need. Firstly, the time to let things unfold to their natural extent. We sometimes stop impulses before they have gone the full distance emotionally, or have completed their natural trajectory. There is a natural rhythm of development and completion. When improvising, just keep moving forwards with whatever you are doing, developing the moment. Let 'it' become more itself, till 'it' ends you, not the other way round. The natural end point of an impulse is usually further than the conscious mind imagines. Don't think 'Maybe I should end it here', or 'This must look boring. I'd better change' – these are examples of negative voices. As you work, just keep gently reminding yourself to 'Stay with it', till the impulse comes to its natural end. At that moment, you are likely to receive your clear sensation of pleasurable completion. You might be surprised to discover how far you can actually travel with a single impulse, and what it can lead you to. Sometimes, letting things unfold completely involves hard physical work and sweaty bodies, but no big effort of will or emotional crisis.

Secondly, we all require enough time to learn and explore. We need to see that you don't have to get it right first time. You can take the time to experiment, fail, try again, fail, get it right for a split second and then lose it, try again, and so on. One proviso: 'taking your time' doesn't mean spending hours mentally preparing yourself, or waiting for the muse to descend. It means physically engaging with the work, for as long or as often as it needs. Doing it in your body, on the floor.

MAINTAINING CONCENTRATION

Concentration is not a single, unchanging state that we have to grip with both hands and force ourselves to maintain. Like impulse, the natural pattern is a series of waves; in and out and in and out again. We are focused for a while, and then we lose it. We are fully inside the moment, fully engaged, and then, after a certain time, we find the work slipping away from us. Our brain may start commenting, or thinking about the next cup of coffee. Like a wave, our engagement rises and then falls away.

If we stop working when our concentration first departs, we can be left feeling defeated and even start to question our ability. But this downswing is inevitable; it is simply the natural end of the first wave of exploration. If we can find a way to stay inside the work, there inevitably will be another upswing, leading us further and deeper. When improvising, the first wave usually represents our 'party tricks'; the things we already know how to do successfully. But by the third or fourth wave, we are heading into genuinely unfamiliar territory, discovering new ways of being and working.

It is very important to recognise this wave pattern, since otherwise we feel that we ourselves are at fault when we cannot maintain a constant state of total concentration. When the first wave ends, all you need to do is to stay inside the work, ready and alert to catch the next wave and ride that one until it runs out. And so on, again and again. This is why the exercise 'Staying Out There' in the chapter on 'Impulse and Response' is so important.

THE LINE

When we start working or improvising, we sometimes feel as if we come up against an invisible line drawn on the floor. We can go so far and no further. This line is simply the demands of social reality. In daily life we walk, start getting puffed and then stop. We talk to a friend; things start getting a bit too personal, so we back off. We are considering our own lives; it starts to feel slightly uncomfortable, so we drop that train of thought and do something else. But this is precisely what we shouldn't do as performers. When we start to get the body working, we keep going in order to explore. In a dialogue, we say the unsayable and don't apologise. In private soliloquy, we follow and reveal the full depth of our confusion. So when you are working and you sense that 'line', simply remind yourself that this is your 'public behaviour pattern' making an unwanted appearance. It doesn't really belong here, and it's getting in the way. Just step over the line and keep going.

You may then hit a second line, which is your personal resistance to going into certain areas, but that is different from social resistance. As you continue working as a performer, that line of personal resistance moves back until you are comfortable exploring and using a huge range of responses.

WORKING FROM THE RIGHT PLACE

I have often noticed the drastic transformation that some young performers undergo when faced with strong or complex material, such as acting Shakespeare. Before the session starts, they will be rampaging around the studio, yelling at each other, teasing, chasing, laughing. They start to work, and suddenly all that energy is gone. Their bodies either slump or become rigid, their voices become less lively and connected, and they look like as if they are trying to crawl inside themselves and disappear. They focus all their attention inwards when they start 'acting'. In doing so, they become less interesting than they are in daily life (and for performance, you should be at least as interesting as you are in ordinary interaction, and preferably more so). What they have done is to confuse focusing and concentration with mental and physical de-energising. Without energy, you can't act.

This confusion leads many performers to begin their work from a counterproductive place. Before engaging in an improvisation, they calmly try to centre themselves, standing still and driving their legs into the earth. Or they may try to consciously relax the body, aiming for a state of full muscular looseness. Then they start concentrating on the task ahead, focusing their intentions very seriously. At this point the body may start to tense up. Becoming aware of this, they refocus on 'relaxing', sometimes accompanied by shaking out the hands, and then they concentrate even more seriously.

However, most of this actually makes it harder to respond freely and dynamically to the demands of performance. More difficult to perform, rather than easier.

Since good performance is actually more dynamic and variable than daily life, the performer must be similarly more than ordinarily alive. The key concept to pursue here is 'available'. Contrary to what you might think, the actor's state of physical readiness is not fully relaxed. It isn't tightly held or rigid, but neither is it totally floppy or loose. The body has no excess tension, no muscle that is working more than it needs to, but it is not asleep either. While you wish to minimise unnecessary muscle tension (hence the shaking out of hands), you do not aim for a state of passive relaxation. Instead, you aim to be physically 'available'. The body should be alive and active, ready to go anywhere. Like a leopard in hunting mode, motionless while watching and waiting, but able to attack in an instant.

In addition, you do not want a mental state of narrow concentration. You do not want a tight determination to 'get it right', or any similar style of harsh-willed focus. Your concentration needs to be easy and open, rather than based on any kind of drive or tension. But neither should you try to close out the world, and retreat into calm inner repose. Performance is active, not passive, and requires greater connection of yourself to the world around you, rather than emotional detachment. While you may include meditation as part of your training process, you do not meditate while performing. The mental dimension of preparation needs an open, active focus, a state of gentle curiosity about what might happen, rather than either determination or detachment.

Start your work from a place of physical ease and openness, combined with mental alertness and inner receptivity. Both the mind and the body are awake, ready to respond in an instant. The engine is running. Nothing is happening yet, but you are ready to go anywhere, at a moment's notice. Your body is alive but easy, and your senses are alert and tuned to the world around you. You are emotionally uncommitted (i.e. you have left any daily worries at the door of the studio) but know that you are available to let whatever happens affect and change you.

Through training, this alert state should eventually become be your natural starting point. In the meantime, here is an exercise that energises the body and then uses that energy to launch the work.

Exercise – Starting to Work

When you get ready to improvise or explore, don't stand in your usual 'getting ready to act' position. Instead, start by thinking about the parameters of the task, get them clear in your head, and once you are satisfied that you know what your objective is, put it out of your mind. Then start running and jumping around the space quite freely for about thirty seconds. Just move for the fun of it, without getting too serious or dedicated. Then suddenly stop in a frozen position. Find a normal in-breath, and then launch straight into your improvisation, using the out-breath to carry you into action. Do not shift your body back to your habitual starting position. Do not remind yourself of the task. Do not attempt to focus your concentration. Just start.

As well as riding the energy of your body's activity straight into the task, this exercise prevents you from retreating back into your fear and doubt, or into an overly intellectualised approach to the improvisation. Instead of stopping your natural flow of physical energy in order to start performing, you are using this flow to support your work.

An even simpler way to keep yourself physically and emotionally available is to just start working from a different starting position. Since the body and the inner realms are direct reflections of each other, always beginning in the same posture or stance will tend to lead you down the same emotional path each time. This is fine when you want to do this (and indeed is positively helpful on occasion; see 'Hooks' in the next section), but if you are trying to explore new territory, your habitual starting posture will limit you. So just change it. If you normally stand tall with your weight evenly distributed, twist your torso and put most of your weight on one foot. Or look upwards. Or start by leaning against the wall, rather than placing yourself in the centre of the room. It doesn't really matter what you change, but change something.

INNER ENERGY

When you watch a good actor, you get the feeling that there is 'somebody home'. There is 'a light on inside' at every moment, in every part and at all times. You also feel that anything could happen; there is a sense of unpredictability, even danger. We call this 'stage presence', but it is not particularly mysterious. An actor who has stage presence has a rich inner landscape coupled with physical ease and readiness.

Nearly seven hundred years ago, the Japanese Noh theatre was codified into a distinct performing style by an actor called Motokiyo Zeami (1363-1443). He also articulated many of the requirements of good acting in the treatises he wrote. One of his key concepts was 'the rule of seven-tenths'. In the book *The Mirror Held to the Flower*, he said: 'What is felt by the heart is ten, what appears in movement seven.' In other words, after years of training, the skilled actor can ease back the physical form of expression, while keeping the inner dimension at the maximum. Young performers often do the opposite; they maximise their physical display while the interior may be quite empty and arid. In adapting Zeami's concept for western theatrical performers, I would suggest maintaining the outer expressiveness of your action as precisely as you can, but ensuring that your inner life is even more vibrant. (By the way, I would recommend Zeami's treatises to any practitioner. His writing style is a little opaque, but his concepts and approach are worth the effort of pursuing. An excellent translation is *On the*

Art of the Noh Drama by J. Thomas Rimer and Yamazaki Masakazu, Princeton University Press.)

Exercise – Running Inside

Run as fast as you can for twenty to thirty seconds. Then freeze. Just stop the body exactly where it is for about fifteen seconds. Not a tense, held position, merely a cessation of movement, like hitting the pause button on a video. Then start running again. Keep going strongly. Freeze again. Then run once more. And a third stop. But this time when you stop, imagine that you are still running inside. Faster. Faster. But keep the body still and calm. Then release again into the run.

You will sense the inner life when you stop for the third time. The idea of 'running inside' gives you a focus for your inner energy, so that the calm, physical stillness remains energised. You stay 'switched on' when you freeze, rather than disengaging your mind when you stop the body. You may also notice that when you start running again, you go into action more directly and powerfully. This is because you have 'kept the engine running' even though the body is still.

Run again as fast as you can, then freeze once more with the inside still going a hundred miles an hour. Then come out of the freeze and stand naturally (without losing the inner running) and just walk easily around the space.

You can feel that the inside is equally vibrant whether you are running flat out, standing motionless or moving in an easy, relaxed manner. The inner dimension is the same and equally alive, irrespective of the outward form of the action.

This inner aliveness is central to every form of performing. It doesn't matter whether you are doing the most personal, minimal work for the camera or raging all over the space in a ferocious movement piece, the inner vibrancy is always present. Even when you are just standing there 'doing nothing'. In this exercise, the inner dimension is the sensation of running, but it can be anything. In a real performance, it is the demand of the moment as given in the text or by your director/choreographer. But whatever you use, it must be alive and vibrant. Keep the heart at ten.

PLAYFULNESS

Many directors and teachers say the same thing in rehearsal: 'Have fun', 'Just play', 'Enjoy yourself out there', 'Don't get too serious', 'Free it up'. They are all referring to the same phenomenon: the energy (and ease) that the actors contact when they allow themselves the pleasure of 'playing'. This is very important, since tension and seriousness are often closely linked. The more seriously you approach the work, the narrower and tighter your concentration becomes. And the muscles tend to follow the same pattern. When you become tense either physically or mentally, you move further away from your instinct and ability to respond.

But when you are having problems, or feeling frustrated with a particular scene, the last thing you want to hear is 'Just have fun!' It is very hard to refocus your mind suddenly into joy and humour. But you can easily change your body.

Exercise – The Sillies
This lasts about fifteen seconds. Run about the room, making as big a fool of yourself as possible. Quickly, crazily. Leap all over the place, wave your arms, pull faces, squeal like an animal, do rude gestures, be as inelegant as you can possibly manage. Silly, fast lunacy. Then stop, take a natural in-breath and start working.

You can use the 'Sillies' whenever you feel you are getting stuck, physically, emotionally or mentally. It looks ridiculous, but it works. In fact, many actors instinctively use a version of the 'Sillies' to loosen themselves up when they feel their process is getting blocked; they will run around the room, or shake out their whole body. This works, but it becomes even more effective when you add the dimension of humour. Making a fool of yourself prevents preciousness and reduces fear of failure. You have just made a complete public idiot of yourself, so what is there to worry about?

NOT KNOWING

As a performer, it is vital to work from a place of 'not knowing' – almost from a sense of discomfort, where you choose to wait for an impulse to arise rather than quickly coming up with an easy response. In ordinary daily life, this place of discomfort can feel (and be) quite dangerous, since it means you don't know what to do in a particular situation. You have no answers, no clear responses to get you out of trouble. But the same state of 'discomfort' is wonderful when exploring; it means you have relinquished glib reactions and are genuinely investigating the possibilities of the situation. This is what it means to 'take risks'.

It helps to remind yourself that what may be dangerous in a public context might be essential to good performance. The streets are full of strangers whose motivations may be obscure, and getting it wrong may carry a high price. But a rehearsal room is not a particularly dangerous place, and everyone in it is trying to create a worthwhile piece of work. You are all collaborating in a shared endeavour, and you all know that what you are doing isn't 'really real' (although it may be very true).

The discomfort of not knowing links to the fear of getting it wrong. But this implies that there is a 'right' interpretation somewhere. As if this model exists out there in space, and that your work consists of constructing something that resembles it as closely as possible. In fact, as you work with impulse and resonance, you realize that there are hundreds of 'right' impulses. The job is to select and refine the one that is most appropriate for the particular task, or performance demand. And this process of selection needs to involve the body. It can seem intellectually correct to go for version A, but once you follow it on to the floor, you realise that it is inauthentic.

But beware. Just because something feels 'right' on the floor doesn't necessarily mean that you have found the most useful interpretation. You can provide a moment of great authenticity that your body recognizes as truthful, but which is inappropriate for the specific interpretation being developed. Or, as I once told some actors, 'great scene, wrong play'. Their work was real, interesting, fascinating to watch, but not for the version of the play I was directing. But that is half the fun of directing; having actors who can make extreme and diverse offers while remaining authentic and human. Then it is simply a question of selecting and refining various choices.

A simple note: don't do each other's work. It is the performer's job to be creative, to make offers, to bring material to the table. It is the director's job to stimulate, select and shape the material. Too many performers censor their work before it has even appeared because they are not sure it is the kind of material required. Don't worry. Let the director decide. In the same way, directors should let performers get on with their work. Set parameters, define the goals, clarify the tasks, shape the outcome by all means. But don't impose the details of your own personal performing style on them. At best you will get a pale copy of yourself; at worst, a group of unhappy, uncreative, unresponsive serfs.

Chapter 8
LEARNING AND TEACHING

I hate the words 'Learning' and 'Teaching'. For me they bring up memories of my school days, which I utterly detested. So it's ironic that a large part of my life has revolved around learning how to be a creative practitioner, and teaching these skills to various groups of students.

Despite the negative connotations, it is worth examining these concepts in some detail, since (hopefully) we are all engaged in learning throughout our lives. And most of us also teach – ourselves, our children, as well as students in a more formal learning context. But this is not a chapter on teaching methodologies; plenty of books and courses approach this subject with great thoroughness. Rather, I want to highlight a few areas where subtle problems exist, and where simple changes can make a difference. I'm sure that anyone who has ever been a student or a teacher could add thousands more examples.

THE PROBLEM PACKAGE

In terms of learning (for both teacher and student), there are three basic principles, which I allude to constantly throughout this book. Firstly, *everything is connected*. Thought, reactions, dreams, memory, emotions, the imagination, in fact everything we place under the title 'mind' is one integrated system within the body. Secondly, because everything is integrated, *nothing is neutral*. Every physical action and reaction you undertake will have an inner resonance. Thirdly, *everything is embedded in culture*. Our actions and reactions, our thoughts and feelings are experienced, processed and judged according to social context and the appropriate personal narrative ('Who I am').

And these three concepts are tangled together. Recently I was teaching a session on the Elizabethan body to a group of young actors. We explored the physical realities, the actual environment at that time, the psychological priorities, and the sociological structures in order to sense what body patterns dominated at that time in history. As they walked and sat, found their use of time and space, discovered which parts of their anatomy opened up and which parts became restricted, I asked how they felt. Most answered with words like 'strong', 'open', 'tall' and so on. The usual kind of answers good students give movement teachers. I went on:

'How do you feel emotionally, as you move around inside that body?'
'Powerful.'
'Dangerous.'
'In control.'
So far so good. But one girl replied (with admirable honesty):
'Arrogant.'
'And how do you feel about feeling arrogant?'
'I hate it!'
'Why?'
'People will think I'm a stuck-up bitch!'

And there you have the whole package. The actor changed her physical pattern and body use, which then had an impact on her inner landscape; she felt new and strong emotions. She then assessed what those emotions meant in her current social context, and assigned them the label of 'stuck-up bitch'. And since this label would not be popular in her youth context, she felt uncomfortable with the new reality. In other words, changing her body changed her feelings, which were then judged as valid or invalid according to her current social framework.

Now the tricky bit – how can this understanding help us learn and make choices in a clearer and more chosen way? How do we use this knowledge to facilitate learning, rather than impede it?

EVERYTHING IS CONNECTED

Starting with the first principle, 'Everything is connected', there is a clear tactic: make the work concrete. Don't think about whatever you want to acquire, or discuss it – do it. This holds whether you want to acquire a deeper understanding of the text, or an integrated transformation into another character, or a grasp of a difficult theoretical concept. Find a way to make it concrete.

Because the body is the prime site for emotion, as well as being the location of action and reaction, acquisition of new material is most effective when it takes place in the body in real time and real space. It is quite hard (though not impossible) to change the body by thinking. It is easy to change the body by acting directly on it. Conversely, while the mind can change itself by thinking, it can also be directly accessed via the body. In other words, direct physical experience is an efficient mode of learning and transformation of both the body and the inner landscape.

For example, I worked on a production of *Much Ado About Nothing* for the Royal Shakespeare Company, where the director wanted the actors to develop a stronger sense of hierarchy and social position. Instead of discussing this issue, I asked the actors to position themselves in a single line across the room according to who had power over whom. I asked questions like; 'Who do you depend on for physical survival? Who could have you killed or thrown out to starve? Who, when push comes to shove, has to follow your orders, whether they like it or not?' After much shuffling about and argument ('No! You're not above me! I'm your superior officer! I give the orders here!') the actors finally arranged themselves to everyone's satisfaction. There were a few surprised faces. I then asked them to look down the line, and note who was inferior to them. Next, they were asked to look up the line at the people upon whose good opinion their survival depended.

Of course, all of this could have been done via discussion, but it was actually quicker to do it physically, since everybody was involved at the same time. It also had a more profound effect on the actors since they could literally see and feel their place in the social hierarchy.

In addition, excessive discussion can be a defence against creative exploration. The key fact to remember is that performance is a concrete act – your body moves and utters sounds in time and space. So your process should reflect that reality.

NOTHING IS NEUTRAL

As I mentioned earlier, when you want to alter a physical pattern in the body, it helps to find a positive, pleasurable association or image. As a learner of a new technique, you need to find genuine pleasure of some kind in that specific moment. Maybe an amusing image, maybe a positive memory, maybe an acknowledgment of the sensual pleasure of the action, maybe pride in mastery. It doesn't matter what you use, as long as it is conscious and positive. As a teacher, you need to encourage the students in this process. By the way, this is different from general fun or enjoyment; it is very specific. The students are not simply bouncing around in a cheerful way – they are finding a unique positive association which links to that precise skill or technique.

And remember, if a new pattern has negative associations, there will be very little desire to repeat it enough to become habitual, and there will be no sense of ownership. Negative associations can range from boredom, to duty, to fear, to a sense of being coerced, to feeling judged. And they get in the way of real learning. (Which links to another problem: people sometimes confuse experiencing with learning. Experiencing an exercise or a technique means that you have encountered it once and understood its logic. Learning means that you have repeated it so often that you can reproduce its function at will. It is no longer something you have met once and found interesting; it is something you own, that you have claimed and can easily repeat, whenever and wherever required. Ownership comes from repetition – remember how long it took you to become relaxed as a driver? Use the fact that 'nothing is neutral' to promote repetition, via the use of positive association.)

This concept of 'Nothing is Neutral' also the underlies the experiential 'Method' approach, where through dressing, eating, and working as the character you gradually transform yourself, and gain insight into the character's psychology. It may even go as far as the character 'taking over' your body. This is not a false perception, since through these techniques you are reprogramming the mind via the body. And why, if you do not understand the technique, it can be very hard to drop your role. The character's patterns have literally taken over your physical reality, reactions and responses.

Actors who work experientially are often accused of being neurotic or precious when they claim that they found it difficult to return to themselves after the performance. But they aren't being silly; the physical patterning of the character is literally reshaping their mental configuration. There's no need to panic or worry about being possessed by your role; you simply use the same mechanism to undo the patterning. At the end of the filming or play, you deliberately break the physical matrix of the character by moving in a different way (e.g. walking faster or slower, blinking the eyes furiously, etc.) In this way the mind/body link serves to undo the imposed patterning. In addition, if you consciously return to your own physical reality (your favourite chair, your comfortable shoes, even your every-night glass of beer), you reignite the older programme. Again the key is to work physically – it is a direct path to the brain.

There is a line in Shakespeare's play *Coriolanus* where the title character refuses to perform the physical action of kneeling, for fear that doing so will change his emotional profile. He says, in Act 3 scene 2:

CORIOLANUS: . . . I will not do't
Lest I surcease to honour mine own truth,

And, by my body's action, teach my mind
A most inherent baseness.

Shakespeare clearly understood that there was a link between body
action and psychology.

EVERYTHING IS EMBEDDED IN CULTURE

One of the problems young actors and singers face (more frequently
than dancers, it seems) comes from clinging to their sense of who
they are in the daily, social world. Students often fear making fools
of themselves, or doing embarrassing actions, or looking
incompetent. They also fear that going into behavioural patterns
that are outside their normal socialised persona might be somehow
dangerous or diminish the integrity of their personality. But in
thinking this way, they are working from the wrong place.

This situation arises through unclear thinking. When we talk
about our 'self', we are generally pretty fuzzy. What is our 'true'
self? Is it our conscious idea of who we are? Or is it our persona (the
self that enables successful functioning in a particular social
context)?

In fact, there are many aspects to the self: the persona (social
presentation), the intimate self (shared with close friends and
family), the private self (what we know and think but do not expose
to anyone). The sum of these three aspects is the personality - the
person we know exists. But there is one further aspect; the self that
we do *not* know exists. This is our hidden unconscious, which
makes itself most evident when we dream at night. In fact, your
actual, true self is the sum of all of the public, private, and
unconscious processes. And it is with this self we work as creative
beings.

When young actors work, they often locate themselves in their
persona, and try to react from that place. Which is virtually
impossible, since this is not the totality of the individual. It is too
small. It is also the place where difficult interactions and feelings are

carefully managed so as not to endanger our place within our social group. Therefore, it is by definition a place of deliberately limited emotions, which is not helpful to any performer who wants to reveal the depth and complexity of the human situation. To solve this problem, it can be useful to make an explicit separation between the operating arena of real life and that of the creative space.

THE WORLD OF PERFORMANCE

In social situations there are unspoken rules and tactics for managing behaviour and response, but these are not the same rules that promote success in creating vibrant, authentic, and interesting performances. For example, in a real-life social situation where I am being watched by strangers, I will try to avoid revealing anything too private or personal. But in performance I must strive to do the exact opposite; I must be private in public, and permit aspects that are normally hidden to emerge. In the same way, if I am at a party and someone accidentally (or deliberately) 'pushes my buttons', I will try to manage my impulses, and attempt to disengage the emotions and reactions that are arising. But when rehearsing a scene, if a co-actor 'pushes the character's buttons', I am grateful and delighted, and curious to see where this might lead. Once we are clear that these are two separate worlds, with different sets of rules, it is much easier to understand how to work more effectively.

Simple choices can help keep the two worlds separate. For example, since you do not want to remind yourself of your habitual social persona while you are training or rehearsing, you should wear special clothes for working in. In addition, choose outfits that do not need management (they don't require hitching up, or tucking in), since these gestures belong to daily clothes in daily life. They shouldn't distract you (hair in the eyes), or remind you of the familiar social world and its values (jewellery, watches). And they should provide greater physical freedom than the clothes you wear in daily life, since performing requires far more energy and range.

When working, you are a different person, in a different world, doing a different job. And you want to select a costume that will reinforce that role.

The main thing to remember is that when we work, we are not trying to change our personalities or replace our current persona with a better model. This would be impractical as well as inappropriate. Instead, we simply discover two quite different sets of 'correct behaviours' which are applied to two very different contexts.

GENERAL HINTS FOR LEARNING

Although I recommend getting onto your feet as quickly as possible, I am not saying that there should be no intellectual research or exploration when working on the performing process. Quite the opposite. But rather than viewing it as an activity of the mind, it is more useful to view it as a kind of 'feeding' of the entire entity, through the senses as well as the intellect. In other words, make your research concrete.

We will look at how directors can 'feed' their productions in the next section, but as individual artists, we have a responsibility to feed ourselves on a daily basis. Even when we are not working. Everything we do, see, touch, smell, taste, speak, feel, and utter provides the material we draw upon in our creative work. And we never know when we will need it.

Fortunately it isn't difficult to refresh our system. But please remember the key idea – make it concrete. Reading a new book or watching a new film or performance is stimulus on one level, but it isn't the same as direct physical experience. We need to let our bodies walk down a new path to the studio, taste new foods, encounter new environments. It isn't difficult, but it does require conscious decision; left to itself, the organism will simply follow the programme already laid down. And we will remain stuck in our habits.

LEARNING VERSUS DOING

Unfortunately, there is no magic wand in real learning. You have to physically experience, then repeat and claim through practice. But when you come to actually do the job, you basically forget about all of this. You've done it. It's in your body. Now you can just relax and enjoy doing the task. Solid learning is what gives you the confidence to play. And remember, the core business of performing is repeatability. Every night on stage you must be able to repeat and reproduce a vivid performance. When filming, you must be able to repeat a moment of great sensitivity again and again, until the director has all the takes that he or she wants.

Students sometimes ask me, 'How do you concentrate on all the important things, like breath, and alignment, and staying open, etc., when you are actually performing?' The answer is simple: you don't. You work very hard in training, and then shift your focus away from the skill processes when rehearsing. And you rarely think about technical adjustments when performing, unless you sense that something is going wrong. Then you use your learned skills to recalibrate the work.

In fact, there are three stages in performance process. The first is preparation of the performer. This is the focus of most training – getting the body, the voice, the emotions and the imagination, ready and available for work. The second stage is application to task – focusing on the text, the score or the choreography of that show. Rehearsing to uncover what is happening, and getting it clear and strong. Finally there is performance itself, where you reveal the work to the audience.

It is important to understand the distinctions of each stage, since they demand different processes from the performer. And you must be able to let go of earlier stages as you move on. When you are in preparation mode, you don't over-analyse how you will use the exercises in performance. Then, when you are involved with application to task (i.e. rehearsing), you focus on clarifying the performance. You don't worry too much about your technical skills. And in performance you let go of the rehearsal process, and trust that the work you have done will unfold on the stage.

Think of your training as a tool kit. At first, you have to learn what tools you possess and how to use them. Then how to maintain them. Then when to use them. Finally, you put them away until needed. In fact, having a good tool kit and knowing how to use it is what leads to the magical goal of confidence.

Many years ago, I attended sculpture classes in order to improve my mask-making skills. I no longer make masks, but another lesson I learned at the time is still with me; the importance of tools. During his course, the teacher Mike Leman introduced me to an extensive range of chisels, gouges, mallets, electric saws, and various gauges of sandpaper, all of which were used for woodcarving. Initially I thought that I only required a single chisel and mallet (sculpture à la Hollywood), and all these different tools, and different sizes of the same tool, seemed excessive and unnecessarily expensive. But I very quickly learned the opposite. The right tool for the task helped enormously, and made the work quicker and easier. You don't use a fine chisel to cut a block of wood in half, nor do you use a chainsaw to do detailed contouring.

Mike also imparted technical hints, such as carving *with* the grain of the wood (I had been hacking away at various angles), and letting the tool do most of the work (this is the advantage of the right tool). Also practical habits, such as sharpening the chisels and gouges on a regular basis, so that you are never carving with a semi-blunt tool, and how to actually sharpen the blades – the method for sharpening a hemi-spherical gouge isn't self-evident to a beginner.

But the most useful tool was intangible; what he gave me was the art of seeing things three-dimensionally. I began the course working with clay, and Mike would not permit me to move onto wood carving until I learned to see in three dimensions. Needless to say, I had no idea what he was talking about; I thought I *was* seeing in three dimensions. Doesn't everybody? Then one day I realised that the piece I was working on was strangely flat. When I looked at it from the front, it was OK; all the shapes were where I wanted them to be. But when I turned it sideways, it lacked depth and dimension. So I worked on it from the side for a while, but of course that

nt angle, which I then had to redo. Which then
revise the side angle, and so on. I worked for a while
oving from angle to angle, and then realised that none of
gles was truly separate; they all flowed into and from each
. There could be clear point-to-point connection, or more
sotle links using implied space, but every point on the surface was
joined to every other point, and the eye could travel easily between
them. After this discovery, I was promoted to wood.

Until I acquired the sculptor's eye, I could not progress. It was an
essential tool, and yet I had no idea that such a thing existed.

For a performer, the equivalent tool is honest perception. If you
cannot define the problem exactly, you cannot select the
appropriate technical tool to help you solve it. Too often people just
throw pre-learnt answers at a problem in the hope that one of them
might miraculously stick. This rarely works, because most pre-
learnt or passed-on solutions are the response to a different
situation. The world constantly changes and no two situations are
identical. We have to be able to see exactly what we are dealing
with, here and now, before we can create the best response.

For teachers this is a critical area. For example, you prepare a
class, well designed and informative, but when you get in front of
the students you sense that it just isn't working. At this point young
teachers either blame themselves ('I can't teach'), or the exercise ('It
isn't a good exercise after all') or the students ('They're hopeless).
In fact none of these responses is accurate or useful. What is
happening is a mismatch between the material and the students at
that moment in time. The exercise might be wonderful at another
point in their training, or even another point in the day. Or with
another group.

Rather than seeking who or what to blame, step back, look at the
situation honestly, and work out what is actually going on. In
extreme cases (which are fortunately very rare), don't be afraid to
stop the class and ask the students what is happening. Obviously,
there are contexts where this is inappropriate, but it can prove very
enlightening, as long as you keep it focused on the here-and-now of
work in the room. I can honestly say that many of my exercises were

developed in this way. What I had planned to do wasn't working, so I had to find an alternative approach. Not yet another exercise from my repertoire, but a genuinely fresh process that attempted to address the specific problem in front of me at that moment. Teachers are allowed to be as creative as any other artist.

The whole point of training is to be able (eventually) to forget it. The control and range you develop in class and in your personal practice becomes so embedded in the body that it becomes automatic. You do the basic preparation work; you learn the skills of body, voice, imagination and emotional availability; then you practise them until you find ease and effortless accessibility. In other words, your body and voice can be trusted to do their jobs, and you know you can access your inner landscape without fear or hesitation. You are now ready to start investigating the material (play, choreography, score) with your fellow performers and your director.

PART 3

PUTTING IT INTO PRACTICE

Chapter 9
GETTING TO WORK

Hopefully by now your body is beginning to come alive, you are sensing the connection between your inner life and physical action, and you are starting to feel the confidence and delight that comes with true ownership. Your body is vibrant, hungry to explore, ready to communicate.

Now, what do we do with it?

We start to use it for creation and performance. And to do this, we must shift into a collective mode. There is only so far you can go on your own, since communication tends to require the presence of other people. A company of actors or dancers working together on performance material. A film team collaborating and combining their skills.

We start with group preparatory process, then move on to responding work, focusing on the relationship between two or more individuals. The next chapter then explores some aspects of character work, mainly using text-based material, since it demands total integration of language and voice with the physical and emotional life. If you are working in a non-text style (such as physical theatre, or dance), the work is still useful since the basic principles remain valid. Just adapt it to your own material.

As always, some exercises will be useful while others may be irrelevant to your needs. Choose what seems helpful, but never hesitate to discard anything that seems obscure, inappropriate or excessively unwieldy. This book is about exploration, not theology. There are no 'right' answers here, or universal recipes for instant success. Everyone is unique, everyone learns in their own way, everyone has the right to adapt the material to their own needs. But always remember the pleasure principle. If it isn't fun on some level or another, why bother?

WARMING UP

I don't really like the term 'warming up'. It suggests a process of mechanically heating the muscles, and has overtones of obligation and duty, something you know you ought to do rather than want to do. And you often see this in action in companies before rehearsal. In one corner, you have the 'goodies' virtuously stretching, running and generally being visibly athletic. In the other corner (or more commonly the green room), the 'baddies' are finishing their final coffee and chat before easing inconspicuously into the rehearsal room. The two groups regard each other with a certain disdain. The 'goodies' judge the 'baddies' as unprofessional. The 'baddies' regard the 'goodies' as over-conscientious prigs. Even before the rehearsal commences, the company is divided.

Sometimes companies avoid this division by instituting a compulsory group warm-up which is led by one or other member. But even these tend to be joyless duties, terminated as soon as is practicable. All of this is unnecessary and impedes the working process. It occurs because people have not understood the deep function of a warm-up, which is transformation.

When you arrive for your rehearsal, or performance, or whatever, you are your daily self. You have your daily body, your daily feelings, your social voice and your social responses. Through the warm-up, you gradually shed this persona and transform into a performer, a being who is hungry to engage with the work at the highest level. This is what a warm-up must be designed to achieve.

A good warm-up requires great honesty. You have to be frank with yourself about where you are before you begin, and where you know you need to be when you terminate. If you know you need to be sprightly and full of life in your performance, but you actually feel like death, both of these facts need to be acknowledged. It is through doing the warm-up that you transform yourself from a state of 'death' to a state of 'sprightly liveliness'. But too often, people either avoid doing warm-ups when they feel drained, or alternatively they only do exercises that they like and find easy and undemanding. In both cases, the function of warm-up as a tool for transformation has been ignored. A warm-up is not something you 'ought' to do, or a way of reconfirming your favourite physical activities, but something you want to do in order to work effectively. And it is flexible, able to adapt to changes in you, and the different demands of the work. While a certain level of ritual is useful (for example, many people always start their warm-ups with exactly the same actions, as this helps them to shift their concentration away from the outside world and refocuses them on the work), it must remain flexible and responsive to the specific demands of the task. And it must adapt to where you are on any given day.

The basic structure of a warm-up should be: mobilisation, stretching, task-specific work, launch.

Mobilisation is undemanding movement work that engages the entire body. You want all of the major muscle groups to come alive, to get the lungs breathing more deeply, and to get the blood to begin flowing through the tissues. Mobilisation is active, but doesn't involve strong stretching or acrobatics, or any other kind of demanding activity. That comes later, after the muscles have been stretched. Easy swinging of shoulders and legs, reaching up and about with your arms, wriggling your torso around, or less demanding yoga stretches such as the 'Sun Salute' are all useful here. Low-impact running is also helpful. The key things to remember are: nothing fast, nothing hard and nothing abrupt and sudden.

Once the body has been generally mobilised (and this takes about ten to fifteen minutes), you move on to stretching. Again, working the entire body, not just your favourite bits. I like to begin this with 'Playtime for Hips/Shoulders'. This exercise has the advantage of starting to engage the concentration as well as gently opening up key joints. Indeed, any kind of stretch/flexibility work should be used as an opportunity to connect the breath and mind to the physicality.

The key thing to remember when stretching in a warm-up is that you are not doing a training session. You do not do developmental stretching at this time. The aim is to prepare you for work, not to focus on long-term change in your physicality. So it is just basic stretching, with the aim of making the muscles more flexible and responsive to demand. You work the whole body, but you are also aware of the forthcoming task. If you know you will be standing around for a long period of time, you should pay a great deal of attention to the lower back, hamstrings and calf muscles. If you will be working acrobatically, you must be truly certain that the entire spinal column and shoulders are totally free. Again, the duration of your stretching will depend on the nature of the forthcoming work; ten to fifteen minutes for straight acting, fifteen to twenty-five for dance or anything more demanding physically.

Then you move to task-specific work. These are exercises which focus on enhancing the particular qualities needed in the forth-coming work. If you are doing fast comedy, this requires sharp, speedy responses to co-actors. So you may choose to play partnered games that promote this skill. If you are working on a play set in a particular period, you may decide to respond physically to music from that world, or even practise a dance from that period. Sometimes this work can be quite technical, linking voice to body to intention. Sometimes it can be improvisatory. It doesn't matter, as long as it enhances your ability to connect to the specific demands of the work.

Finally, the launch. This tends to follow naturally from the previous section. It is a matter of carrying the task-specific work up to the moment for the work to begin. If you are doing a class, this might mean bringing your mind and body together, ready and hungry to experience what the class offers. In which case, you would do focusing work. If you are rehearsing, it might be bringing your attention to the character you are playing and the words you will be speaking. If performing, you might want to start moving around the space totally in character, gradually working your way up to the moment just prior to your entry.

Task-specific work combined with the launch can last from ten to twenty minutes. By this calculation a basic warm-up for relatively undemanding work lasts thirty minutes (ten minutes for mobilisation, ten for stretching and ten for the final stage). A more demanding style of performance (dance, physical theatre, musical theatre, farce, tragedy) will take longer, maybe as long as an hour. The exact timing is less important than the recognition that full transformation has taken place, and that you are now truly ready to work.

You can see that a good warm-up has a rhythm. It starts slowly and simply, gradually getting more demanding physically and mentally, and then channels itself towards the forthcoming task. As well as ensuring that you can work safely, it enables you to leave behind your daily self. It also acts as a springboard, launching you easily into the work. It is important to respect this rhythm and not just bounce from exercise to exercise in a haphazard manner. In particular, follow the momentum of the body. Start gently, then become increasingly active as well as increasingly focused. Too often, I see actors jumping around frantically for five minutes before lying on the ground for ten minutes to work on their breathing. By the time they come to their feet again, they are half-asleep, and essentially have to start the warm-up all over again.

Find ways to incorporate breathing and voice exercises into your physical process, so that they link with body work rather than interrupt it. In addition, exercises that integrate voice with action are very useful since they reinforce the essential unity of the body. At the end of any warm-up, you should be alive, alert, with a body that is ready to go.

In addition, a well-planned warm-up transforms an actor psychologically, and focuses them on the specific work of that day's rehearsal. This operates by recognising and employing the interconnection of the mind and body. Many years ago I was working in Australia with Gregorii Ditiakovski, a director from the Maly Theatre (St. Petersburg) on a production of *A Doll's House*. Each morning he would tell me exactly which creative impulse he wanted the actors to use in that day's rehearsal, and I would lead the warm-up in such a way as to encourage that precise outcome. Once it was emotional availability, the next day it was clarity of perception, while on a third day it was attention to moment-by-moment unfolding of the situation. As a director, he understood the connection between body experience and inner response, and also knew how to use the power of a warm-up to transform the actors in precise mental and emotional ways. In addition, he permitted no break between the warm-up and the start of rehearsals.

In terms of your ongoing training work (preparation of instrument as versus application to task), you should incorporate a warm-up into your programme, prior to starting the more demanding technical work. It will make it easier and safer, and help you learn more effectively. Most training programmes have a warm-up built in to the process, but if you feel (either physically or mentally) that you need something more, come early to the class and warm up in your own way.

On the technical level, when designing any kind of warm-up (or training) programme for yourself or other people, you should be careful about which exercises you include. Many exercises that are in current use are actively harmful or counterproductive, or only appropriate for a highly trained body. Just because somebody somewhere has taught you an exercise doesn't mean that it is automatically safe or valid. Bad practice is handed on as easily as good practice. For example, some people still use (or teach) head circles as a way of releasing neck tension. This exercise is actively unhelpful since the anatomical design of the neck vertebrae does not accommodate full circling. That 'crunching' sensation you sometimes get when you force the neck past the angle at the back diagonal is the sound of bones trying to rearrange themselves. Not useful in any way. Head drops (chin towards chest) or half-circles (from right profile down to head dropped forwards and then up to left profile) are far safer and more effective.

Many other harmful or unproductive exercises are frequently taught. Detailing these would require another book, and indeed there are such books on the market – usually found under the heading of 'Sports Medicine' rather than 'Performing Arts'. I have found the following ones helpful, although others are undoubtedly available:

Stop Exercise Danger by Donovan, McNamara and Gianoli. Published by Wellness Australia, ISBN: 1 875139 03 6. This is an easy book to follow and gives clear advice on which exercises are potentially hazardous and why they should be avoided, as well as offering safe alternatives. Highly recommended.

Athletic Ability and the Anatomy of Motion by Wirhed. Published by Wolfe Medical Publications, ISBN: 0 7234 1540 4. A complete technical guide to body use which explains exactly how and why certain exercises are dangerous or ineffective. For example, why you should do sit-ups with bent legs rather than straight ones. Geared more to teachers than the general readership, but worth persisting with.

Chapter 10
CONNECTING TO OTHERS

Just as our upbringing has taught us to withhold or redirect the passage of impulse through our body, it has similarly blocked the natural response to the actions of other people. For example, you are sitting on a beach enjoying your solitude, when a stranger arrives and sits right down beside you-too close. You feel uncomfortable, your body tenses up, you may shift a little to the side, you redirect your gaze away from the incomer's direction, you focus all your attention on your book. What your body is doing is screaming at you is 'GET UP AND MOVE AWAY!', but that would be impolite, so you stay there, squirming with unease.

As performers, however, we need to be aware of these flickers of genuine physical response to the reality of others, and to be able to pick them up and follow them through into our own actions. To sense what that person makes our body want to do, and then simply to do it. Completely. Without hesitation or apology. In this way, we create a believable, dynamic physical relationship between real, responsive individuals.

And so we start working to increase our body's ability to respond fully to the actions of others. In this way we discover whether the character needs to be close to the other in order to say the line with ease and authenticity, or very far away; whether to touch the other's arm, or to avoid contact. Without this direct physical response to the impact of others, you end up acting in a bubble, focused only on how you have decided to deliver your own lines, aware of your co-performer only as something that gives you your cue to act.

The basic relationship in performance is partnership. Partnership between the writer and the director, the director (or choreographer) and the entire creative team, among the performers, and betwee the performers and the audience. They are all co-operating to achieve the maximum impact of the work.

There are many styles of partnership within the broad field of performance, but for the moment I will only focus on 'equal' and 'unequal', within the work of the performer. In a certain sense, all performing requires an equal partnership; as professionals, we should all give equally generously and respond equally well in order to create the best possible work. However, inside the performance, the characters we incarnate will not be equally 'equal'. Some will have greater power while others are minor roles whose main function is to respond to the chief protagonists. In addition, the responsibility for driving the scene changes constantly. We have to be able to shift between the functions of leader (initiator) and follower (responder) as the action unfolds. And, as co-professionals, we sometimes serve each other, working together to clarify problems or elucidate deeper levels of action.

EQUAL PARTNERSHIP (DIALOGUE)

The fundamental relationship with others is dialogue; an equal exchange of human impulse, where neither partner leads and both respond.

Exercise – Action/Response

Two people work together. Each one aims to respond to the other. No planning. No leader. Person A initiates the exercise by doing a simple action, a single gesture, such as turning the body away, lifting the head, moving to another part of the room. It doesn't matter what you do; the action itself isn't important. Person B watches this action, letting it impact on him or her. B then responds with another simple action, sitting down, shifting weight, grabbing A. This is not a planned movement, rather a direct response arising out of the impact of A's first action. B's action now impacts on A, who responds with another simple action, and so on. A, B, A, B . . . As in a game of tennis, what you do depends on what your partner gives you. It is a kind of instinctive dialogue; a 'conversation' on a direct human level.

This is the same kind of 'Listening to the Body and Responding' work you did earlier, but instead of 'responding' to the room, you respond to another human being, who in turn responds to you.

The important thing with this exercise is not to plan your response, or consciously choreograph your move. Keep it simple and direct. Don't be interesting – be human. The key thought is 'How does that make me feel?' You look for the impact of the other person's action on you. It is not 'What do I want to do to them?' You don't focus on your own actions, you focus on your reactions, and then these lead directly to your response. The key feeling is 'receptive'; staying open to what is happening to you in the moment. The other person's action somehow 'hits' you and bounces you into a response. You permit the impact to carry you into a simple action, which in turn impacts on your partner.

You can do this exercise either choreographically or emotionally. 'Choreographically' means that the prime focus is on the movements of the body. Person A raises the leg, person B replies by flexing the back. 'Emotionally' means that you are using simple human actions which have direct emotional impact on your partner, such as turning away, or walking to another part of the room, or gently touching the other's face.

In neither case do you perform 'charades', miming a thought or a word, or use verbal gestures, like beckoning with your hand in order to say 'come here'. If you are using the emotional style and you want your partner to 'come here', you just walk over to them, grab them, and propel them to where you want them to be. Or you can try (the minute you pull, they may resist, in which case the conversation takes another turn). But this work is direct and non-verbal. Even the physical patterns should be non-verbal.

It sometimes takes a little while to get the hang of this exercise; to permit unconstructed responses to the actions of the other. In the beginning, people often try to be excessively 'interesting', or to do complex movements. Keep it simple and direct: single gestures, simple shifts of weight, nothing too rich with meaning. And certainly nothing that looks planned or enacted.

It is also very easy to become focused on controlling the other person, trying to shape their response, or to insist that they follow your path. Instead, focus on opening up, letting yourself feel the true impact of the other person's action as it affects you. You don't think 'What shall I do?' or 'They should do this'. Instead, you think 'What is happening in me now?' or even more simply, 'I see that', and then letting the impact of what you see alter you.

The final pitfall in this exercise is feeling that you have to do something all the time. Sometimes it takes a while for the impact of your partner's action to produce a true response. Don't be afraid to wait. And never feel you ought to construct something if nothing seems to be happening. Leave it. Even a lack of response is a 'response' for your partner. Your blankness still provides something that can impact on him or her.

Which brings me to a question I am very often asked. 'What do you do if you are working hard at being open to your partner, but he or she gives you nothing back?' The obvious reply is that such a thing should never happen among good performers. Nonetheless, it does occasionally occur. The bottom line is that whatever is happening between you on stage is real. It is what the audience sees, and what you must work with. You have to use what you are actually given by your partner; not what you want to be given, or what you think you ought to be given. What is out there is what you work with. It looks completely unreal to the audience if actor A is blocking actor B's offers, yet B acts as if she or he is getting a genuine response (unless this is specifically written into the script). If you make an offer and get no reaction, this lack of response affects you and alters the way you proceed (just as it would in real life). Maybe you have to change tactics, or allow the character to find a stronger need to get through to the other.

It isn't a perfect way to proceed as performers, but at least the action will look believable to the audience. Don't pretend it isn't happening, and don't waste time trying to convince your partner that they are in the wrong. Use what you are being given. Focus on your own responses, not your co-performer's deficiencies.

This next exercise carries the principles of responding into combined verbal and physical action. Too often, we see physical action stuck on top of the line; word plus gesture, rather than a single impulse that propels the actor into speech and action simultaneously. It uses a very simple 'script' of two words, but the key element is to link your word directly to your physical action. You move and speak simultaneously.

On the surface, this exercise has an unequal power relationship. Partner A is attempting to change partner B, while B merely responds. But on the deeper level, there is full equality, since B's response actually changes A. As you do this exercise, remain aware that you are both equally active and equally responsive.

Exercise – Please/Maybe

Person A has one word: 'Please'. Person B has one word: 'Maybe'. A's intention is to convince B, using this word together with a clear 'tactic'. Tactics could include teasing, seducing, convincing, insisting, asking for sympathy, begging or clarifying. With this single, clear tactic (no changing in midstream, however much you may want to), you make a simultaneous physical and verbal action. If you are using 'teasing' as your tactic, you might tickle actor B's ribs while clucking the words 'please, please, please'. The key thing is to release the sound and the action at exactly the same moment, and to finish them at the same moment. Not one and then the other.

The other important element is to 'stay out there' with the offer. By this, I mean, when you have finished your tickle and your 'please', don't take your hand away or shift your gaze. You have made your offer, so now stay where you are and wait for the response.

Actor B has one word, 'maybe', but he or she can choose to interpret this as either a 'yes' or a 'no', depending on preference. Again the 'maybe' is spoken at the same moment as a physical acceptance or rejection of A's tactic. For example, if B is mentally saying 'yes' to A's teasing, B's response could be a naughty 'maybe' accompanied by tickling A in return. If B is mentally saying 'no' to the teasing, the 'maybe' could be harshly spoken while B removes A's hands from his/her ribs.

Now the ball is back in A's court. Irrespective of whether she/he has received a 'yes' or a 'no', A renews the chosen tactic at a higher level, but modifies it according to whether the other person is becoming more persuadable or more resistant. It is fairly easy to stick with your tactic if you sense that B is beginning to agree. It is working and B simply needs more convincing. But if A senses that the 'maybe' is actually a 'no', it becomes tempting to change course and try another tactic. Don't. Stick with the original tactic ('teasing') and try harder (go for the soles of B's feet).

Continue this exchange of 'please' and 'maybe', building on your partner's response, developing the offer and response, until the exchange just comes to a natural halt. Then stay there for a moment or so, and then begin the game again with a new tactic (maybe 'insisting B understands').

One of the aims of the exercise is to take the game of offer/ response to its natural (as opposed to social) limit. The game will automatically end itself when A receives the final capitulation ('maybe' as 'Yes, I totally give in') or the absolute refusal ('maybe' as 'No, no way! Finished!'). These points lie well beyond the level of daily chit-chat. As one of my students pointed out, it is more like a child negotiating with a parent; only the definitive 'yes' or 'no' will end the dialogue. It is very important to continue the game until it naturally ends itself, not to make a decision to end it, or to change tactic in midstream.

If you are person B, permit yourself to yield and if necessary to be defeated. The aim is not to resist in order to win, but to develop the exchange all the way to its natural conclusion. Be honest. But equally, don't be too polite. If you want to leave, just get up and go.

A also ignores the pressure to be polite. A sticks to his or her tactic, even if normally 'it isn't polite to insist'. Don't withdraw the offer or dilute it in any way. Instead, leave the other actor with an interesting 'problem' to solve. In particular, sustain your physical offers. Quite often, A will grab B's shoulders while saying 'please' but will then release the grip when the words end. Don't. Maintain your grip on B's body as you wait for a response. The physical reality of your hands gives B something concrete to work with.

In the same way, B must allow the physical offer to happen fully. Quite often, B will brush A's hands away as they begin to reach forward. This prevents A from completing the offer. Let A grip your shoulders and say 'please, please, please'. When he or she is satisfied that the offer is complete (they have done the best they can in that moment), A will stop and watch to see what reply B will give. At that point, B can wrench A's hands away and say 'maybe'.

This isn't to say that the exercise proceeds slowly. Rather, that both actors work to ensure that the exchange of offer and response is given the space to grow and develop.

You will soon see that this exercise is proceeding on two levels. Character B is blocking character A on the surface by not immediately saying 'yes'. That is the character level. But on the 'working' level, performer B is supporting A by allowing the work to grow and develop. The 'maybe' is not a block, it actually advances the scene and allows it to move beyond the limits of normal social interchange. Although the power nexus between the characters is unequal, the performers' relationship is an equal partnership.

When you are rehearsing a script, this kind of impulse work can help uncover the subtext within the scene. We frequently encounter subtext as we work; the surface of the words floats along, but underneath you sense something else going on. The character may be talking about the weather, but what he or she really wants is to romantically engage with the other.

Uncovering the subtext is part of rehearsal, but we don't always do it in enough specific physical detail. In order to embody the subtext, it must move from being an abstract concept ('romantically engage') into a concrete action. Knowing that your character 'wants to romantically engage' isn't as clear as 'wants to touch the hair' or 'wants to embrace'. 'Romantically engage' is hard to play because it is too broad and generalised; your body doesn't know how precisely to manifest this concept. It doesn't know where to begin, so you have to bring it into focus. You are talking about the weather, but as you look at the other person, you become aware that your hand wants to reach forward and stroke that lock of hair, or your arms want to slide round the other's waist and bring the body close. Or to place your lips on your partner's. These are concrete, physical and very specific.

Knowing your character's physical impulse is to kiss the other person also produces a very different gesture pattern from knowing you want to feel your hands against his or her back. If you play a scene out fully following physical impulse (i.e. let the body do the touching and embracing), your body starts to understand what is going on during the speech. Once you have played it out, you can go back to just standing there and talking about the weather. But this time, your body knows the specific details of what is happening. It is also a very good way of checking that you truly understand and 'own' your character's inner reality. Most of the indefinite twitching and arm-waving gestures are caused by a lack of precise awareness of exactly what the body wants to do in that moment.

You can also use this kind of physical response work in rehearsal to elucidate group alliances, or even as a directing tool. A number of years ago I worked on *Richard III* with a friend called Rodney Bolt, and we used this approach.

In Act 1, scene 3, most of the key figures (Richard, Elizabeth, Buckingham, Margaret) are on stage together, along with members of the court. Each main character challenges and argues with various other characters on a range of topics. We gave the following note to every actor in the scene; listen to whoever is speaking now. Within the world of the play, is your character on their side, or against them, or neutral and uninvolved? Whenever you feel your alliances being activated (e.g. when Margaret starts attacking Elizabeth), move either towards or away from those protagonists. Or if you are neutral, stay where you are. Respond appropriately. If you were playing either Lord Rivers or Lord Grey and therefore Elizabeth was your sister, you might walk across the stage in order to stand right next to her, shoulder to shoulder, glaring at Margaret. If you were simply a courtier who liked Elizabeth, you might simply shift your weight slightly towards her. If you were someone who had no opinion about either protagonist, you might stay put, or even step prudently back out of the arena. And if you positively disliked Elizabeth, you might drift over to Margaret's side of the stage.

But then Margaret starts attacking Richard and all the alliances shift again.

The same process occurs with the issues being raised. As well as knowing where their character's allegiances lay, we asked the actors to sense whether the particular topic/issue the protagonist is discussing touched them personally, or involved them in any way. For example, when Margaret goes through the list of deaths that have occurred, do any of them matter to you? Does the death of the child Rutland (referred to by Margaret as a 'peevish brat') touch you in a way that the death of a king does not? Or vice versa.

When you are rehearsing a scene and hear a phrase that impacts on your character, let the body react. Maybe you find yourself turning away, or simply tightening your lips, or suddenly paying more attention to what she or he will say next, because now it matters; now it really concerns your character.

Of course, in order to do this, you must truly understand your character and the world of the play. Only in this way can it look real, and feel natural. In the reality of our daily lives we know where we stand on every person and issue around us. We may have no strong opinion (be neutral), but we know we have no strong opinion. If performance is going to have the same richness and complexity as real life, it must have the same degree of knowledge underpinning every moment.

This is all part of your preparation as an actor. But this kind of work allows you to get that knowledge out of your brain and on to the stage, moment by moment.

How far and how large these reactions need to be is a matter for the director. In *Richard III*, we wanted a very clean look to the scene, so we asked the actors to channel each of their reactions into one single, well-defined move. Maybe a large move across the space, maybe a tiny shift, but only one. And only when they were truly 'impacted' by what was said. When they were not specifically reacting, we asked them to remain still, in a state of attentive awareness. From the audience's perspective, the stage was quiet but charged, with small reactions occurring here and there, plus the occasional larger one. But sometimes (for example, on the description of a murdered child as a 'peevish brat') virtually everyone on the stage responded, which in turn affected Margaret's next phrase.

UNEQUAL PARTNERSHIP (WHO DRIVES?)

In dramatic situations, as in life, we are in the middle of a web of constantly shifting power relations. This occurs even in ordinary conversation. You are at a dinner party and certain topics arise as you eat, chat and argue. On the question of international trade, Mr X is an authority and everyone defers to him, permitting him to speak his monologue, which is only occasionally interrupted by intelligent questions or requests for further enlightenment. But when the topic shifts to education, someone else takes the lead, and Mr X abdicates. Sometimes you will have two authorities and a tussle takes place, with the rest of the guests silently, or not so silently, aligning themselves with one or the other protagonist. These kinds of shifting alliances occur everywhere, though we do not always define them as power relationships.

Understanding power relations and how they alter and adapt is essential to character-based acting, although it is still useful for other performing styles. It is perhaps better to rechristen them as 'drives', as in 'Which character is driving the scene now?' or 'Which performer is driving the action?' It is easy to confuse 'power' with ideas of emotion (strong, angry, energetic), or with statements of clear intent ('I am in charge here'). A character may be very energetic and utterly confident in asserting their power, within the world of the play, and yet be following rather than driving the scene. In the same way, a performer who is doing very little

167

physically may still be providing the stimulus for his or her co-performers.

We can clearly see the power exchanges in the following scene from *Richard III* (Act 4, scene 4). The character driving the exchange at any given moment has his/her words in capitals.

RICHARD: BE ELOQUENT IN MY BEHALF TO HER.

ELIZABETH: An honest tale speeds best being plainly told.

RICHARD: THEN PLAINLY TO HER TELL MY LOVING TALE.

ELIZABETH : Plain and not honest is too harsh a style.

RICHARD : YOUR REASONS ARE TOO SHALLOW AND TOO QUICK.

ELIZABETH : O no, my reasons are too deep and dead:

TOO DEEP AND DEAD, POOR INFANTS, IN THEIR GRAVES.

RICHARD : HARP NOT ON THAT STRING, MADAM; THAT IS PAST.

ELIZABETH : Harp on it still shall I, till heartstrings break.

RICHARD : NOW BY MY GEORGE, MY GARTER AND MY CROWN –

ELIZABETH : Profaned, dishonoured, and the third usurped.

RICHARD : I SWEAR –

ELIZABETH : By nothing, for this is no oath:

THY GEORGE, PROFANED, HATH LOST HIS HOLY HONOUR;

THY GARTER, BLEMISHED, PAWNED HIS KNIGHTLY VIRTUE;

THY CROWN, USURPED, DISGRACED HIS KINGLY GLORY.

IF SOMETHING YOU WOULDST SWEAR TO BE BELIEVED,

SWEAR THEN BY SOMETHING THOU HAST NOT WRONGED.

RICHARD : Now, by the world –

ELIZABETH : IT IS FULL OF THY FOUL WRONGS.

RICHARD : My father's death –

ELIZABETH : THY LIFE HATH IT DISHONOURED.

RICHARD : Then by myself –

ELIZABETH : THY SELF IS SELF MISUSED.

RICHARD : Why then, by God –

ELIZABETH : GOD'S WRONG IS MOST OF ALL.

In the beginning, Richard is driving the scene and Elizabeth is responding to his statements. She lets him finish his impulse, and then answers it. But she briefly wrests control of the scene from him with the line 'Too deep and dead, poor infants, in their graves'. He responds to her for one line, and then regains control with the line 'Harp not on that string' and continues to 'Now, by my George, my garter, and my crown –'. But instead of following and answering his completed phrase (as she did in the beginning), Elizabeth cuts right through and interrupts him in the middle of his line. And then, after a brief tussle, she pushes him aside with the line 'By nothing, for this is no oath.' She takes control and drives the scene, forcing him to respond to her challenge.

When I talk about who drives the scene, I am not talking about the subject matter or the character. I am talking about which actor, through their character and their lines, is making the 'offer' and which actor is focused on 'responding' appropriately. The surface meaning of the words is no guide. A line like 'Then plainly to her tell my loving tale' employs soft and gentle vocabulary, but is utterly ruthless in its determination to drive the scene. In the same way, the final lines from Elizabeth could be seen as 'responses' to Richard, since her words are replies to his offers, but she has not abdicated the drive. The very fact that she never permits him to complete an offer makes this clear. But analysing the written text is not as effective a tool for uncovering drives as the body.

To discover the pattern of 'Who drives?' within a scene, do the following exercise.

Exercise – Space and Power

Two actors work together on a scene, preferably one involving exchanges of short lines rather than alternating monologues (a game of tennis, rather than 'you do your turn, and then I'll do mine'). The Richard/Elizabeth scene is a good example, but there are hundreds of others. I often use the exchanges from various Beckett plays when teaching this exercise.

If you don't know the text, then hold the book in your hands. Or even better, use 'ghosts' (see later section). Partner A begins, standing about five feet away from B, facing them. As A speaks the phrase, she/he tunes in to the body and senses if there is an active feel there. Are you trying to do something to B? Are you 'pushing' at your partner with your words? If so, take a step towards them as you speak.

B then speaks his/her line. A's 'push' has affected you. What do you want to do in reponse? As you speak, are you 'pushing back' at your partner? Maybe not. Instead, you may feel a desire to retreat, to get away from them. In which case, step back one pace as you speak. Occasionally you will feel a need to stand firm, neither retreating nor pushing. If so, stand still where you are.

What emerges is a dance of power, with one person advancing pace by pace while the other retreats. And then it reverses. Or it goes back and forth for a while. Or occasionally one person literally drives the other around the stage for some considerable time (as does Elizabeth, when she finally takes control of the scene with the line, 'Thy George usurped . . .')

WORKING TOGETHER

In a sense, the use of language always implies the presence of an 'other'. We use words in order to transfer our inner reality into the mind of someone else, or to influence them in some way. When working, we need the presence of the 'other' in order to find our impulse to communicate, and to discover how it shapes itself.

While I have suggested a number of ways for the performer to connect with and own the writer's language, and how to move from text into speech, none of these deals with interpretation (how you actually say the line). That comes out of the precise interaction between the characters in the moment. The other person's reaction affects you, and your response to their reaction is what determines the interpretation. How you say your phrase depends on what you see and hear in front of you. Not on some decision you have made in the privacy of your own home.

This is fairly straightforward when you have a 'tennis-match'style dialogue, but what happens when you have a long monologue, or even worse, a true soliloquy?

Nobody actually talks to themselves in real life. They talk to God ('Please, please don't tell me I've wiped that document off the computer'), or to objects that have been endowed with human characteristics ('Come on, boil, you bastard'). Or there is a conversation between two aspects of the self ('Really! You've just got to get yourself better organised'). Or they imagine that a specific individual is present and address their words to him or her ('Well, you always said I'd go mad').

It is the same when an actor is alone on stage. All of the above possibilities exist, along with the real presence of the audience. Actors shouldn't think of directing their words into empty air. Instead they should be very specific about who they are talking to. There is a line in *The Bacchae* by Euripides: 'Run, fleet hounds of madness, to the mountains, run!' The chorus is not 'being generally dramatic and expressive' (as, unfortunately, bad Greek tragedy too often is). They are giving very specific instructions to a particular group of entities. They know who they are talking to and what they are saying.

When you are working on monologue, I recommend that you use a co-performer as partner. They can either take the role of the actual other in the scene (the person to whom you are directing your monologue), or you can create an imaginary other. In either case, your partner acts as a 'reaction giver', actively listening to you, and, through their responses, encouraging you to keep reaching in for the next thought.

Remember that few people talk for the delight of noise-making. You usually want something from your other. It might be action. You might want them to leave, or to come and hold you, or to lend you some money. Or what you want them to do might lie in the mental realms. You might want them to comprehend what is happening, to sympathise with your situation, or to realise what they have done and feel dreadful about it. You have an objective, but the objective lies in the response of the listener. You keep talking until you have achieved that objective, or until it is clear that continuing to speak is useless, because the other is impervious. But while the other is undecided, or wavering, you will keep reaching in

171

for more thoughts, more phrases, more tactics, in an attempt to win through to them. You need these words, and the response of the other is what drives this ongoing necessity.

Your partner listens and encourages you to keep going through the speech, either through questioning and challenging, or by registering confusion or non-acceptance of what is being said.

This monologue from *A Midsummer Night's Dream* (Act 1, scene 1) shows how the 'reactor' works. The unspoken responses that might encourage Helena to keep speaking are in capitals.

HELENA: Call you me fair? /WHAT?/ That fair again unsay! /WHY?/ Demetrius loves your fair; /OH COME ON/ O Happy fair! /WHAT DO YOU MEAN?/ Your eyes are like lode-stars /REALLY?/ and your tongue's sweet air more tuneable than lark to shepherd's ear, /??/ when wheat is green, /??/ when hawthorn buds appear. /ANYTHING ELSE? /Sickness is catching/ WHAT ARE YOU TALKING ABOUT?/ . . . And so on.

The reactor can actually use words like these as long as their interjections aren't too long or interesting. The aim is to encourage the language impulse in the speaker, not to interrupt it or send it in another direction. But it is usually better to use body language: a blank look, a bored sigh, a sharpening of your gaze, a puzzled lift of the shoulders. Again, don't get too carried away with your own creativity. In this exercise, you are not an equal partner; you are assisting your partner to find the need to keep talking. You offer mild resistance to what they are saying, so that they have to reach inwards to find more words, moment by moment. But not so much resistance that the true response of the speaker would be to shut up because there would be no point in continuing to talk. You are resistant, but not impervious.

This is none the less a real dialogue. As a reactor you actually listen to the speaker, and if a particular phrase isn't clear, you make them say it again until it makes sense, just as you would in real life ('I'm sorry, could you repeat that?'). Similarly, if you don't believe that the phrase comes from the truth of that person's reality, you do not permit them to proceed until what they are saying rings true.

You must believe it when you hear it. Not necessarily agree with it, but be convinced that the speaker knows what he or she is talking about. Again, just as we do in real life ('What exactly are you trying to say here?').

In sense, the listener is operating on two levels: as a character driving another character to find more words, and as an actor driving a co-actor to remain connected and authentic.

In the same way, the speaker doesn't just push through the speech, ignoring the interruptions, aiming to get the next phrase out as quickly as possible. The speaker watches the effect of the words on the listener, and it is the incomprehension or resistance that provokes the need to find more words, or to ensure that you actually speak a clearer and more connected truth. A single phrase may need to be repeated three or more times before you move on to the next. Or it may be fine. It is the listening, and demanding authenticity, that matter here.

In addition, the exact nature of the listener's reaction affects the speaker. If the listener laughs at what you are saying, that impacts on you and modifies the way in which you speak the next phrase. Or a sympathetic look reaches you, and softens your insistent tone. The listener's reactions are real; use them to propel you on through the speech, moment by moment.

This is where the earlier work on 'Connecting to Text' fits in. If the actor doesn't understand what the words mean, or doesn't 'own' these words and phrases fully, it is very hard to speak with conviction and authenticity, or to adapt your communication according to the reaction of others. You have to know exactly what you are saying before you can reveal this certain knowledge to the listener, in whatever way is most effective. In a sense, you always reveal what you know to be true. This fact, that reaction, those precise thoughts. You do not attempt to convince anyone that the words mean 'something generally significant'.

This brings me to an important point: I have already mentioned that the physical gesture pattern of head forward/eyes pushing/ hands reaching forward (also known as 'goose/goggle/grapefruit') is unhelpful. In fact, its psychological profile is that of pleading. A person using that pattern in dialogue is begging for something from the other, perhaps understanding or agreement. It tends to occur when the actor (rather than the character) is 'pleading' to be believed. The actor's mouth is delivering the phrase 'I am sad', but the actor's body is saying 'I am sad, really, truly. Please believe me. Please.' The best way to eliminate this pattern is for the actor to deeply connect to the exact truth of what they are saying, so that they speak from total certainty rather than the need to convince. In which case, the phrase becomes 'I am sad' (words), 'Here it is. This is it' (body), and because the actor is fully revealing a felt and authentic truth, rather than pleading or attempting to convince, the body realigns itself with the core feeling. The body then reveals the truth of the character's sadness, not the actor's need to be believed.

These exercises all stress the importance of responding; of letting your impulse arise as a consequence of your partner's action. But in order to sense how you need to act with your co-performer, you need to be able to see them. Your body also needs to be free to respond in any way appropriate. It can do neither if you are holding a book in your hands. Constantly looking down to get your next line disconnects you from your partner and what is happening between you. It also requires that you read 'text' and then turn it into 'speech' as you go along. You are asking your brain and body to jump between two modes of operation. All of this impedes the organic process.

But you have to use the words of the text, and these are written down. What can you do? You could learn all of your lines prior to rehearsal (without imposing an interpretation), and discover how they need to be said when working on the floor. Or you could use a 'ghost' (I have based this approach on the work of Kim Durban, a colleague in Australia).

Exercise – Using Ghosts

Performer A (who is playing character A) has a 'ghost'. The ghost holds the text and follows the performer around the space. The text has been divided into phrases by performer A. In other words, performer A has taken the 'text' and turned it into sayable units by whatever system works best for him or her, before handing it to the ghost. Performer B also has a ghost.

The performers tune to each other. They start to sense what is happening between them. They look at each other. Ghost A whispers the first phrase into performer A's ear. When performer A feels the necessity to use language to connect with performer B, he or she speaks that phrase in whichever way rings true in the moment. The body also follows impulse. That phrase and action then impact on performer B, who responds appropriately, following their replying impulse and using the line that ghost B has whispered. And so on.

There is no particular time frame. Some phrases pile on top of each other, and the ghost has to work hard to keep up. At other times, the performer may choose to wait, while the impulse coalesces into the need for speech. In which case, the ghost waits and doesn't prompt. If the performer needs the lines to come more quickly, or they need to hear the phrase again, they signal with the hand without disturbing the relation with the other actor. This latter point is crucial.

The whole idea behind using ghosts is to avoid interrupting the connection between the two performers. Looking to your ghost for a prompt, or requesting a line with your voice, is counter-productive. It may be impolite to beckon someone sharply with your hand, or to click your fingers, but in terms of respecting the dramatic situation, it is the most effective solution.

It may take a while to get into the swing of this, especially for the ghosts. It can be hard work to keep your eyes on the text, follow your performer round the space, recognise their signals and speak the phrases without giving your own interpretation.

NEGOTIATING THE WORK

Using impulse makes it easier to act, since you simply follow the response as it arises, rather than constructing an unwieldy edifice which you hope will convey the correct meaning to the audience. But the key to good responding is remaining in a place of constant alertness and sensitivity to the moment. You can't switch off for a second. You have to work to remain in the place where 'work can happen to you'. You also have to be able to relinquish the socially correct patterns of responding to others, and allow yourself to be 'impolite'. Performance isn't the same as a dinner party, even though they both involve entertaining a group of strangers.

However, this isn't a licence to egotistically batter or grope our fellow actors. We are always respectful towards other performers, and are very generous and careful in our work together. But at the same time, our work mustn't become tepid or excessively polite. In the daily world, unmodified physical contact can lead to genuinely uncomfortable or even dangerous situations. Our social rules exist to ease and safeguard our contact with other people. While they are useful and necessary in our ordinary reality, performance does not live in ordinary reality. It is 'extra-ordinary', and inhabits the realm of the unspoken impulses, things we cannot say, or feelings we hesitate to acknowledge publicly. Since it is a performer's job to speak the unspeakable, to be private in public, to reveal what is normally hidden, they must to be able to respond to the actions of another person in an authentic, 'impolite' manner.

So how do we reconcile these two seemingly incompatible needs: the need to be fully authentic, and the need to respect our co-actors?

First, don't confuse 'generosity' with 'politeness'. Actors are not polite when working. They may be polite to each other in the coffee bar or the street, but in the rehearsal room they are never polite. 'Polite' exists in the daily world of normal social relationships, where it is very useful. But in theatre, polite work is usually banal and boring. But the opposite of 'polite' in terms of actors working together is not 'horrible, aggressive, insensitive'; it is 'generous, sensitive, playful, responsive'.

The key word here is 'responsive'. As long as we stay completely open to our fellow performer, and respond to what is happening between us, we can negotiate even the most uncomfortable material with generosity and respect.

When I teach this work, I always set up a few basic rules before we begin. Some of them are so obvious that they hardly seem worth mentioning, but I've found that it is often useful to state the obvious out loud. That way, we all know what we are doing.

First Rule:

When improvising, you never do anything that could be physically harmful. Scenes involving violence or combat need to be choreographed under supervision.

Second Rule:

Any part of the body that is normally covered by a swimming costume is off limits. Again, scenes involving sexual material are best choreographed under supervision.

This rule is not the result of squeamishness or prudery. Rather the reverse: once everyone knows which areas are out of bounds, it gives them the freedom to engage everywhere else. You don't have to stop and think 'Is it OK to do this?' or 'Should she be doing that?' You don't have to think about setting your own limits to your work. Once the boundaries are clear, you can relax and just get on with it.

Third Rule:

Take full responsibility for your offers. It's no good offering a passionate kiss to your co-actor and then getting defensive when they lick your face. You might fall about laughing, but you can't say 'No, No! That wasn't what I wanted at all!'

This is how we negotiate strong material, through offer and counter-offer. If we take the example of the first exercise, we can see how this operates. Your partner makes a strong offer by embracing you, and you can accept or refuse this offer. If you accept, you might rest your head on your partner's shoulder. And the action continues from there. If you refuse the initial offer, you might extricate yourself from the embrace. And your partner must accept whichever response you choose and work with that, since it is the consequence of the initial offer. No one should insist on imposing an offer on another person. This isn't to say that your partner cannot attempt to embrace you again after your initial refusal, but the re-offer must be a response to your refusal and be modified accordingly. There is no sense of controlling the other person, only of responding.

Fourth Rule:

Do what 'is required in the moment', not what 'you want'. There is a difference in feel between 'Yes, this is exactly what is needed here' and 'I think this might be fun/interesting/dramatic/show my skill to the public'. In the first case, you are focused on the work and what is happening in the performing situation. In the second case, you are focused on your own 'self' and your own opinion of what will look impressive. This can lead to accidents, insensitive performing and what we all recognise as self-indulgent work.

We can even carry this responding work into our daily life. For example, you are trying to convince a stranger of the correctness of your chosen course of action. You are becoming very passionate and insistent. Your voice rises and you become physically agitated. At which point, your listener starts to feel slightly uncomfortable and leans back in his or her chair as if to put a little more distance between the pair of you (the mouth may be saying 'Yes, yes. I do agree', but the body manifests discomfort). Your body, in turn, registers this shift, but in most cases it does so subconsciously. Because you haven't become consciously aware of the listener's reaction, you ignore it and continue your oration unchanged. Or, if you have half-registered the reaction of shrinking back, it might prompt you to become even more insistent. At which point, the listener's body retreats even further. You very often see this kind of 'push/retreat/push harder/retreat further' pattern in social situations.

But if you allow yourself to become more consciously aware of your listener's reaction, you can allow it to change you and then modify your speech accordingly. You register the lean-back, you become aware that you are 'pushing' at the other, not allowing him or her enough space, so you retreat slightly. You speak less forcefully, or relax your body, or even make a joke to shift the tone of the communication. You adapt yourself in order to make the listener feel more comfortable in the situation. But you can only do this if you are truly aware of the other.

Chapter 11 CHARACTER

In any style of performance there are three key elements: connection, transformation and communication. Or, to put it more simply, you mean what you say, you are who you say you are, and the audience receives what you intend them to. If you are playing Hamlet, the audience believes that you are a prince dealing with the consequences of your father's murder. If you are Giselle, they believe that you are the ghost of a betrayed girl, revealing the nature of love and death. Sometimes you use words to tell the story, sometimes a heightened and stylised vocabulary of movement. But the fundamentals remain.

And transformation is essential; to become 'other', a person with a different life, family, job, position. A different history, an alternative existence, another set of relationships and responsibilities. All of this is implied by 'character'.

I'm not keen on the word 'character'. It is too close to the word 'caricature' and can lead to the idea that a character is a simplification of a human being. This implies that 'becoming a character' is a matter of changing a few details, adding some mannerisms, but remaining essentially unchanged inside. In fact the real process of embodying another human being is one of full transformation; of temporarily relinquishing your own self in order to become someone else. Someone who is just as complex, contradictory and interesting as you are.

Now, all of this could sound quite pretentious or worrying, if we didn't understand the role of persona. When I say 'relinquish your self', I am talking about the general persona you have built up in response to your specific social culture. The way you present your body, the way you dress, your voice and accent, your accepted social manners. Not your biology or basic essence. In fact, I find it useful to think of character in terms of 'Who would I have become if I had been born into that family, that culture, and had experienced that kind of life?' You are still working with your genetically inherited body, your brain and mindset, and fundamental predispositions. But you see what kind of persona would emerge from the changed circumstances. 'You' become transformed into an 'other' you.

We actually practise a version of this in real life. Who we are with, or where we are, affects which aspects of ourselves we manifest. If you are spending time with your grandparents, or going mad at an all-night party, or trying to impress a potential employer, your behaviour, costume and choice of vocabulary will be different. Each situation calls forth a different persona. Character work simply carries this process further, allowing the transformation to be more complete and consistent.

There are three main areas of persona that we need to consider when looking at transformation: physical presentation, emotional and mental patterns, and relations to the outside world and the people in it. Of course, in practice these tend to link and fuse. How we walk and sit reflects our mindset, and in turn affects how other people judge us and how they relate to us.

When working on a specific character/persona, I recommend a threefold approach. Firstly, bring forward the parts of yourself that are relevant to the character. Then put aside the parts of yourself that are irrelevant. Finally, fill in any missing elements through research and investigation. And this process applies equally to the areas of physicality, inner life and response to the world.

For example; if a modern woman were playing a genuinely devout woman living in a world structured by hierarchical religion (such as Mary Proctor in *The Crucible* by Arthur Miller), she might have to travel a considerable distance away from her normal persona. In physical terms, she would relinquish her relaxed and open body habits (which are a reflection of a twentieth-century upbringing), but would retain her energy and physical control. In emotional terms, she would have to relinquish her occasionally cynical edge and direct speaking habits, but bring forward her certainty and determination. In terms of the space around her, she would have to start seeing objects as less disposable, since everything would have been handmade and difficult to replace. The home would be a place of safety in an alien land, a land full of dangers and only recently settled. As for other people, she would set aside her own willingness to offer opinions, but bring forward a memory of trust in authority. Finally, through reading, historical research, talking to women in that kind of situation, imagination and empathy, she would fill in the gaps. She would then seek to fuse all of these elements into a living, breathing, thinking, feeling, responding whole.

So, how do we begin?

You can work in two ways: from the inside out, or from the outside in. Both are effective, as long as you remember to look for the place of connection between these two realities. To use an inner impulse in order to discover the outward patterns of action. Or to observe and embody an alien way of being and reacting in order to gain insight into that person's inner landscape. In practice, you will often find yourself alternating between the two approaches. Use whatever works for you.

Once again, the core is the body. And following the imperative to make our process concrete, we look for opportunities to get our research and insight into the flesh itself. It is not enough to mentally comprehend a character; we must embody it, making it real and tangible in time and space. And once it has become concrete, the world around can see it and respond. Work that remains abstract, existing only within our thoughts, cannot develop organically. It lacks the dimension offered by direct, physical experience, and the immediate feedback of the world and other performers to inform our choices and decisions.

PHYSICAL METHODS

There are already many books on body work for character, and a variety of approaches. Some of the more commonly employed include Laban analysis, animal work, Lecoq's ideas of elements and materials, and imitation of someone else (role-modelling). Use whichever methods suit the role and your individual way of working. What all these approaches share is a detailed understanding of the dynamics of physical presentation, and although they may analyse and approach the process from slightly different angles, there is an overlap of insight. They basically utilise an outside-in approach. Either you do detailed observation of a prototype (an animal, or a specific human individual) and then reproduce these observations on your own body, or you select a concept (a slower rhythm, a 'gliding' dynamic) and alter your body accordingly. In either case, the starting point is changing your physicality.

Key areas to focus on include the following:

Rhythm/Dynamic:
What speeds and rhythms the character uses. (Laban work. Also, indirectly, Lecoq's element/materials approach.)

Shape/Outline:
The general form of the body. Which parts 'lead' when walking.

Weight:
The sense of upwardness/downpulling in the body. How heavy or light or 'bouncy' the person seems to be.

Texture:
How dense/soft/crisp/floppy the flesh itself is. Does the body seem made of clay, or oil, or steel, or smoke? (Lecoq's work on materials.)

Space:
How expansive/direct/indirect the person is in action. Do they seem to be moving inwards, or outwards? Do they seem to take up a lot of space, or very little? Do they move directly to what they want, or do they corkscrew themselves into the chair when they sit?

Flow:
Whether the person stops and starts, or whether their actions flow smoothly from one to another. (Laban is good for these last two).

I would add certain other factors:

Inner Rhythm:
How fast/slow the inner machine seems to be running. How fast they seem to think. The heartbeat.

The Gaze:
How the person looks at the world.

Zones of Tension/Relaxation:
Which parts of the body are held and which released.

Angles:
Are the key joints of the body (hips, neck, pelvis, elbows, etc.) generally held at a particular angle?

Touch:
How do the hands connect with objects?

Duration:
How long is any particular action or position sustained? How frequently does the body need to shift?

You can probably find other factors. It doesn't really matter which system you use, or if you use all of them together. What matters is training the eye to see what is there, and having a framework that allows you to transform what you have observed into a physical manifestation. For instance, if you are using an animal as a prototype for a character (as you need to for certain plays, such as Ben Jonson's *Volpone*, or for the style of Commedia dell'Arte), you use this framework in order to 'see' clearly and accurately. You look for the weight, rhythm, shape, etc., but also look at how the creature places its paw on the ground, how long it stays in one place, how rapidly it shifts between stillness and action. Using a detailed framework for observation makes the analysis easier and more specific. It also helps you avoid cliché and facile emotional identification.

Too often when we observe other beings, we interpret their actions sentimentally and superficially. The lion is proud. Well, no, actually it isn't. It walks with a heavy, relaxed lope and alternates long periods of rest with short periods of higher inner-rhythm alertness (stalking), followed occasionally by high-activity running incorporating an extension of the body frame (running attack). But if you expect to see a 'proud' lion, that is probably the only thing you will see. Keep things open. See things as clearly as you can, without preconception or sentimentality, and analyse what you observe as precisely as possible. A clear framework makes this process easier.

Once you have isolated the key elements from your prototype, place those observations into your own body and then see what they offer to you. Recreate the specific 'lion' pattern of action in your own body and you will probably discover something much more complex than simple pride.

This is the important second stage of the 'outside-in' approach; letting the elements you have observed seep into your inner world. As you start to embody your observations, you may become aware that changing your rhythm, as well as affecting body use, might also shift your emotions to another place. Altering the sharpness of your gaze or holding your focus for longer changes how people react to you and may also shift your mental process.

Pursue this link; see what kind of inner response the physical pattern evokes. Find out who lives inside this skin. How that entity thinks, feels and views the world. What are the urgencies, the hesitations, the priorities? If you don't undertake this second stage, you cannot truly transform into 'another'. The character seems to be 'pasted on top' of your body, and the audience can see you working, telling them that 'the character is like this'. The audience should not see the actor working. They should only see the character living, feeling and responding in a natural and authentic way. You do not show the audience the character; you simply are that person.

Exercise – Copying a Role Model.

Work with a partner (preferably of the same gender; cross-gender work requires additional attention). Partner A is the role model, and partner B works to copy them. Partner A walks around the room, sits, lies, does what feels natural. Quite often, A feels very self-conscious in the beginning. This is fine; let the body be embarrassed and don't try to act 'normal' or cover up in any way. It takes a while to settle in. Partner B walks with Partner A, without talking to them, observing and echoing A's patterns. Partner B looks for the weight, the rhythm, the shape, the drive, of A's body. B also focuses on inner rhythm, zones of tension and release, angles of the head/neck, hips, shoulders and feet. Other factors are the habitual resting positions of the mouth, hands and feet.

As B gets more familiar with A's pattern, B starts to watch for more subtle factors: how often A shifts position, how sharply this change happens, where in the room A prefers to go, how long they stay in one place, whether they really rest when they stop moving or if there is ongoing activity in the feet, hands or eyes. What is the gaze? Sharp, sustained, or hesitant? And check the smile – not only how the mouth forms, but also how frequently the smile occurs and how long it is sustained. A smile is a very important part of the persona's public presentation.

Also notice what you have to eliminate from your own body in order to reflect your partner's physicality. Perhaps you tighten the neck, while their neck remains relaxed. Perhaps they very seldom gesture, while you have an impulse to shift every five seconds.

If you are doing this exercise in a large group, you can also observe the social dynamics. All of the As can speak to each other (though not to any of the Bs). As A moves in and out of contact with other As, the Bs observe how often their A approaches other people, where in the group they place themselves (close to others, or keeping a certain distance, in the centre, or at the edge), whether they initiate contact or wait to respond, how long they stay there.

If it feels right, B can also echo the voice and speech patterns of A, paying particular attention to the energy, volume, pitch, range and accent. The laugh is also useful; its quality, but also its frequency.

This stage of the exercise can take up to forty-five minutes (a minimum of twenty minutes is suggested). The exercise is not parody or caricature; in those styles, a few habits or traits are selected and then amplified. A true transformation requires the maximum information; as many patterns and details as possible. Hence the need for a longer duration.

In the second part of the exercise, the Bs 'become' A by placing everything they have observed into their own body. They become A in as much detail as they can manage. Then the As go and sit and watch 'themselves'.

The final part can be tricky. The Bs must resist the urge to play for comedy or to overstate certain characteristics (parody). They must strive to retain as many details as possible. This can be hard work, especially when you have to do less than you normally do, or you have to radically alter your rhythms. But persist, and gradually a real person starts to emerge.

Then let this information link to the interior. See the world through these new eyes. React to what A reacts to. Be as active or inactive as A prefers. As you continue, you may find your own thoughts and impulses moving in new directions. You find an inner life that corresponds to this transformed body. In this way, you create a real and fully rounded portrait of the other, rather than a cartoon that only emphasises certain characteristics.

When you are working on a specific character, you should consider this approach. If you are playing a librarian, go to a library and observe. And don't just observe 'librarians-in-general'; choose a particular individual and use them as a role model. Or adapt the approach. If you are playing a lawyer in a play set in the nineteenth century, you obviously will be unable to use a real role model. But you can spend time in the courts, or in the bars near the courts, in order to gain some insight. Find a few details that can deepen your understanding and assist transformation.

REMEMBERING THE CHARACTER

Once you get a sense of the character's body, you need to find a system that allows you to return to that physical matrix at will, without needing to re-create your initial process every time. You need to find 'hooks' to hang your work on.

If you are working from a role model, the 'hooks' are clear. The details you have observed are your anchor, and you can return to them at will whenever you feel your body slipping back into your own patterns. But sometimes we don't have the opportunity, or the time, to undertake such detailed work – in which case, we use a simpler approach to the physical life of the character, using three main 'hooks'. These are stance, walk and gesture.

Everyone has a typical stance – a way of situating their feet, distributing their weight and placing their hands that is easy and habitual. Obviously, we all change our stance as events unroll and we react to different people, but we do tend to have a 'home territory' to which we return without thinking. The same process applies to our habitual sitting position.

When you work on embodying another person, find their comfortable baseline stances. One for standing, and one for sitting in a chair. It will prevent that horrible 'What do I do with my hands while I am standing/sitting here, listening to everyone else?' feeling. You know what to do. Return to your resting position, including where you place your hands.

It is the same with walking. We all have a typical rhythm, a typical length of stride, a typical placement of the foot on the ground, and so on. Again, it is always responsive and adaptable, but there is a basic walk.

Exercise – Stance, Sitting, Walking

Start standing in the centre of the space, and begin speaking some of the text (if using a written play), but don't worry about interpretation. As you speak, try to sense the rhythms, energy, weight and attack of the language. Keep speaking and begin to become the body that corresponds to your words and voice. Become the body for which this is the inevitable and right language. Find the standing position which feels 'nice'. How wide apart are your feet? Turned in or out? Is your weight equally distributed, or more forward or back? On one or both feet? What is the angle of the spine and head? Is your flesh heavy and clay-like, or brittle like crystal? What is the particular quality of your gaze? Are your hands in your pockets, hanging loosely by your side, or clasped together in front of you? And so on. Then do the same process for sitting.

Next, start walking. How abruptly does the body depart? How long is the stride? How fast? Jerky, or smooth? How often do you change direction? Find a walk that corresponds to the feel of the words you are speaking.

It is important to do this work while speaking the lines of the text if you are in a scripted performance. The voice emanates from the body. So does the language structure. You have to find a body that corresponds not only to the logic of the text, but also to its rhythms and energy. If you find the right body, the words become easier to speak. In particular, play around with rhythm; sometimes speeding up the body makes the words effortless to articulate. Or try slowing down a little. The key thing here is to sense which physical pattern makes it easier to actually speak. You might have previously decided in your head that the character has a slow rhythm, yet when you start speaking from that slow body, the words become an effort. Find a better physical reality, one that fits the words and makes them easier to speak.

Similarly, you need to clarify the voice's energy; how much strength and emphasis it uses, and how long or short its verbal impulses are. Short, blunt sentences, using monosyllabic words? Or long, meandering peregrinations employing obscure and complex language and many descriptive phrases? Look for the exact physical pattern that is required by the words. Move your body till it fits the language, not vice versa.

In real life, the voice (and its energy and music) is a direct reflection of the body. This is why voice and body must be fully integrated when you create a character. Not movement plus voice. Somebody who uses a lot of words without hesitation in a single sentence is likely have a speedy inner rhythm. That person is thinking and forming communication quickly and directly, without requiring periods of reflection. Many pauses in the text, or short phrases that stop and start, or change direction, indicate a different physical and mental reality.

Try to integrate whatever language pattern the writer has provided, by speaking and searching within the body. Do so until the voice and the body become one single entity; an entity that likes and enjoys the exact language that the author has provided.

The fourth useful 'hook' for character is 'release gesture'. We all have a physical pattern or habit which allows the body to release tension, usually without us being aware of what we are doing. This tends to occur when we are under some kind of inner pressure (either positive or negative). You find the situation amusing, and you tilt the head downwards. You are nervous, and your foot starts tapping, or you grip your hands more tightly. Or you smile inanely. Indeed, a lot of the twitching that occurs on stage is the actor's own release gesture trying to take over. The performer's body attempts to manifest the inner tension and reverts to the actor's own habits, instead of the character's. By the way, a 'gesture' doesn't necessarily imply movements of the hands alone. The release gesture can be a toss of the head, a shift of weight from foot to foot, or a subtle lengthening of the back.

Exercise – Release Gesture

Once you have found a stance, a sitting position, and a walk that feels good and enables you to speak more easily, and with greater inner life and connection, choose a moment in the script at which the character is under some kind of pressure. Stand up and start speaking, and allow the character to get emotional. Then, by trial and error, find a gesture that helps the person release their emotion. Remember to experiment with the whole body, not just the hands. Keep exploring till you find something that feels right and links to the words and the voice. Stick to one or two gestures only, and define them clearly.

In performance, you keep these four elements flexible. The stance is not the only way you stand, and you will adapt the walk to the urgency of the situation. You will most certainly not get stuck repeating the same release gesture at every opportunity. That would be as unhelpful and distracting as undefined twitching. Your work must always respond to the ever-changing circumstances of the performance. What these three elements give you is a departure point; a series of 'hooks' that you use to remind yourself of the physical reality of the person you are playing. It sometimes helps to trigger them prior to your first entry, and then to forget about them as you respond to the action. If at any time you feel you are inappropriately returning to your own physical reality during the show, you can use the hooks to reconnect to the character.

COSTUME

I am frequently bewildered by the attitudes of actors and directors towards costume, since it is a major component of a character's physical presentation. While the designer has prime responsibility for the visual world of the performance, the actor should try to integrate those choices into their character as early as possible in the rehearsal process.

A costume is not fancy dress; it is how the character feels

comfortable presenting themselves in public. What you choose to wear, which colours, how casual or formal you like to be, whether you dress to fit in or stand out; all of these are very strong reflections of your persona. For this reason, you should think very carefully about how your character would dress, right down to the smallest detail. How would they wear their hair? How much make-up? Which shoes? What colour tie? After all, it isn't really a costume; it is how the character feels 'right' in public. It is how they are happy to be seen by other people in their world.

More than that, other people see your choices and draw certain conclusions from this information. They will also feel more or less close to you, according to how your decisions mesh with their own. You recognise members of your own costume 'tribe'.

If you cannot work with your complete costume from the beginning of rehearsal, talk to the designer so that you can find a working equivalent – something that has the same feel and look. In this way, your character's persona will be visually established in the eyes of your co-actors; they can see who you are, and this will clarify their responses to you. In a sense, it is an ongoing contradiction to rehearse a historical play while wearing a T-shirt and trainers. You might say you are 'bound by the conventions of nineteenth-century France', but your body feels no constriction. In the same way, your co-actor hears you talking about how restricted your life is, but sees a modern woman. Raid your wardrobe. Wear a high collar and tie to rehearsal, or a corset and long skirt. It might not be perfect, but every detail helps. It is much easier to be organic when what you feel is in line with what you say, and what your co-actors see reinforces what they hear.

Rehearsing in costume (or its equivalent) has other advantages. If you get used to wearing a corset, or carrying a sword, it becomes a natural part of you – just as it would be for the real person living that life. And, as the costume becomes a part of you, it starts to become a positive aspect of the performance, rather than an impediment. How an eighteenth-century lady handles a fan expresses her emotions, but a twenty-first-century woman can't do this easily unless her hands are truly comfortable with the fan and the object becomes a natural extension of the body.

Even in a non-classical performance, this remains true. Many years ago, I worked on a physical theatre piece, where my performing partner and I decided to work in high heels. This decision was taken on visual grounds; we wanted a certain look to the piece. But as we started working, rehearsing in the heels, we discovered an unexpected sound dimension. A percussive effect which eventually became central to the piece. We would never have found this if we had waited until the dress rehearsal to wear the shoes.

This brings me to the importance of shoes. The kind of shoes you wear affects your entire posture and body use. Therefore, you should rehearse in the style of shoes you will be wearing in performance, since it takes a while for the body to adjust to a different distribution of weight, and then even longer for this to become easy and effortless. If your character wears high heels, and your normal footwear is trainers, you will have to give your body time to learn how to handle them. Not just to clarify the character, but also to prevent injury.

FEEDING

As part of the research component of your character work, you will investigate the world of the play. Its history, its politics, its specific culture. Too often, this research remains purely intellectual. You read and observe and take notes, but the information stays inside your head or your notebook. Instead, try to find ways to make this research more concrete and physical. Engage the senses. Cook and eat the food from that culture. Listen to the music. Even use perfume or spices to give a scent dimension to the world of the play.

In the film *The Little Shop of Horrors*, the ever-growing monstrous vegetable made a constant demand on its owner. In increasingly deep tones it urged:

'FEED ME!'

Those words should be engraved over the doorway of every

school, theatre, and rehearsal room in the world, since no creative practitioner can operate creatively in the absence of nutritious feeding. In productions, it is part of the director's job to feed their performers well.

In too many productions, the director provides the actors with a few theatre games (which are disconnected from the meat of the production, and are usually thrown in to bond the team, or simply because the director feels that this is the correct way to start rehearsals). Or there is a 'research' phase, which too often consists of bringing in an outside expert to talk, or showing a video, or taping up a few photos or articles on the studio wall. While these tactics are certainly a step in the right direction, and better than nothing at all, they are thin sustenance for a hungry performer. Why? Because the research material is passive and intellectual rather than physical, and whatever physical material is provided is disconnected to the specific demands of the production.

Remembering the principle that concepts are best acquired via concrete experience, feeding should be physical, sensory, and directly linked to the life of the performance. This is something the director Peter Brook understood very well.

Wherever possible Brook physically transported his actors to the 'world of the play'. For *The Mahabharata*, the actors travelled to India to encounter the country and its people directly, meeting various artists, writers and priests who could offer insights into the text itself, and its contexts. In the same way, they went to Morocco as preparation for the 2004 production of *Tierno Bokar*. For work that is based in European culture, a parallel process took place; preparation for *The Man Who* required the actors to spend extensive periods in the Salpetriere hospital in Paris, observing individuals with various forms of brain dysfunction.

The unusual element in this process is that the entire company takes itself out into the 'territory of the play', rather than bringing the 'world of the play' into the rehearsal room. In many contemporary productions, the director or the dramaturg selects relevant research material, which is then brought to the cast, while experts might be invited to the rehearsal room to address the assembled company. In this case, the actors remain in the known territory of their rehearsal room, while knowledge is selected and brought to them. For Brook's actors, abandoning their own familiar territory and entering the 'terrain of knowledge' themselves changes their relationship to the material.

In this way, the volume of knowledge available to the performers became far greater, and much less packaged. It allowed the experience of each actor to be unique and individual. The actors shared the overall experience, and whatever was offered to the company as a whole, but what each of them encountered away from the group depended on their own choices, and the element of chance.

Working in this way also provides material that is not simply intellectual; it is also sensory. Food, drink, odours, sounds all play a role in feeding the inner richness of the characters and the world of the play, and in stimulating the performers. By using the body's sense mechanism, non-verbal 'information' can reach the brain directly.

While few companies have the resources to transport the entire cast to the 'world of the play' (or indeed the world of the play may no longer exist in the current geographic reality), it is possible to utilise the second idea of sensory input. On a simple level, if you are doing a Chekhov play, keep a samovar in the rehearsal room, so that the actors can drink real Russian tea during rehearsal. This provides 'taste' information, while the scent of the tea will also gently alter the atmosphere. Listening to music or dancing the dances from the period or world of the play can fulfil a similar function.

Brook employed a slightly different 'feeding' process for the production of *The Ik*. This 1975 production was based on an anthropological study by Colin Turnbull. The Ik were a tribe in northern Uganda who had suffered extreme hardship and starvation as the result of a forced relocation of their community. Brook's production involved no theatrical artifice; no special design concept or lighting plot. The same logic prevailed with the actors; they did not use make-up to change their appearance, and wore their own ordinary, European-style clothes in the actual performance. The believability of the characters depended entirely on the actors' skills in physical transformation. To assist in this process, Turnbulls' photographs of the actual villagers were used.

The actors were asked to exactly imitate the photos. The precise position of their bodies. The feet, the arm, the angle of the head. They created a direct imitation, and asked themselves how they felt in that position. What inner sensation was evoked by that specific physical reality? Then they extended the exercise into the time dimension. They had to enact what happened before the moment in the photo, and discover how to arrive at that precise position. And then the moment after the photo; how to move from that place, and where it took them.

What is interesting about this process is that it was directly physical; they did not simply look at the photos and attempt to imagine what it must have been like to be in that situation. They placed their bodies in the actual shape of the reality. By using this approach, Brook also recognised the power of the body's link to inner life.

But there is a third important point here: it was very, very specific. The actors were required to reproduce every single detail in the photos – the angle in the head, the tension in the neck, the twist in the hips. Not a generalised sketch of human suffering, or the clichéd image of a starving villager. But the exact, multifaceted manifestation of their reality in physical terms.

LEVELS OF INVESTMENT

All actors know that understanding the world of the play is centrally important. But what sometimes gets forgotten is that each 'world' includes a specific social universe with its own rules and priorities, and its own requirements for success and survival. And these can be be very far from our own. If we fail to understand this, we cannot accurately incarnate a character from that world, and we will fail to understand their unique emotional drives.

Logically we understand this phenomenon, but our comprehension must be transmuted into an equivalent current-day term. We must uncover the levels of emotional investment for the character in each idea or situation. Too often, actors speak words about a matter of life and death within the world of the performance, but it feels to the audience as if they are discussing whose turn it is to do the shopping. This generally occurs because the level of investment in that subject has changed over time; it mattered at that time, but it isn't strongly relevant any more.

A good example is the theme of risk-taking. Many plays set in the nineteenth century or earlier investigate risk-taking through the idea of sexual or social transgression. (A good example is *The Lady of the Camellias* by Alexandre Dumas.) But sex then and sex now are totally different in terms of danger and consequences. The fundamental human urge is the same, but the degree of commitment required and the implications of acting on the urge are different.

Prior to the twentieth century, there was no cure for venereal disease, no sure contraception and a high death rate in pregnancy and childbirth. Socially, there was no state-provided safety net. If you were poor and became excluded from your family and community as a result of breaking the rules, you could literally end up dead. So, any woman who decided to have sex with a man outside marriage was taking a huge risk. Literally, a matter of life and death. And an actor who plays such a role must be aware that the level of personal investment required to reflect the enormity of the decision accurately is very high. An actor cannot rely on personal (western, twenty-first-century) experience as a guide, since most sex now is relatively safe, and most of us will survive it without too much trouble. Instead, the actor must find a higher level of personal investment (e.g. imagining that they have decided to have unprotected sex with someone who is openly HIV positive) in order to gain a true sense of what the role requires.

Too often, period plays lack the rawness of human pain and confusion, simply because there is insufficient understanding of what that specific world required, enforced and punished.

PUTTING IT TOGETHER

You have done the work. You have drawn as much information as possible from the text, researched the world of the play and the situation of the character, found a real-life prototype which you have used as a role model, discovered aspects of the character's life that you can empathise with, or imaginatively created a link between the role and yourself. What do you need next?

Answer: time to physically integrate your character, for their actions and reactions to saturate your body and mind.

Exercise – Integrating the Body
In the evening, or at the weekend, when you are alone in the privacy of your home, set aside about four hours. A period when you won't be disturbed. Place the physical choices you have made into your body and go about your daily life. Get dressed in an equivalent of your costume, eat breakfast, wash the dishes, read, clean the house. Ordinary, daily activities, but done in the body of your character, maintaining their physical reality. See what colours 'you' would wear. What music 'you' would listen to. Classical? Jazz? Heavy metal? What would 'you' drink? Tea? Coffee? Vodka? And how? Does the tea need to be served in a cup and saucer, or slurped out of a heavy mug? As the time passes, the character's patterns, habits and perceptions will become easy to maintain, almost automatic. In this way, your body will absorb the reality of this alternative persona. The character's physicality becomes a natural way of being, moving and responding. Not something you work hard to remember and sustain.

In addition, the character's body now has history. It has lived and breathed, eaten food, handled objects. It has existed in time and concrete reality, rather than as an abstract concept in the imagination.

EMOTIONAL LIFE

As I mentioned earlier, everyone's physicality is shaped by culture, family and personal experience, with the body continuing to carry the imprint of those factors in the form of patterns. If the genetic being that is 'you' had lived an alternative life, the body patterns would be different. And the same process would occur in your emotional life. Emotions that 'you' find difficult to express, 'the alternative you' might find straightforward. And vice versa. But they are still 'your' emotions. 'You' are still you, but a different 'you' who has developed along another path, with all the rich interior life (and the contradictions) that you have as a person. But with an alternate interior life, and different contradictions.

In terms of the emotional life of a character, you cannot simply 'be yourself', following your habitual emotional responses. But neither should you struggle to construct something totally outside your experience. Rather, you should connect with your own emotional core and then modify the patterns of emotional expression to suit the character's history and reality. Remember, everyone has a rich emotional life and knows the taste of anger, joy, frustration and fear. And, as I mentioned earlier, what differs from person to person is the pattern of expression; which factors trigger the emotion, how far it goes, how long it lives, how easily it emerges and the action it leads you to take.

The text itself gives you information about the emotional life of a character. Not only stated facts – what the character says about themselves, or what other people say about them – but more subtle factors. See what kind of words the character uses (swear words? prayers? long words? lots of phrases with 'I' in them?) How easily and directly do they speak? Do they continue on a single theme for a long time, or do they stop and start, or change topic frequently? What do they often speak about? What do they never speak about? Who do they never speak to? Do they speak easily in public, or only in a one-to-one situation? All of this will give you a sense of where and how they are blocked, which emotions are easy or difficult for them to manifest, and under which circumstances.

You can use the earlier 'Wall' exercise to get a sense of alternative emotional patterning for a character.

Exercise – Emotional Matrix and Character

Go to the wall. Generate an emotion in the same way as you did in the chapter on 'Emotion'. See where it wants to go in the body. Once you are satisfied that you have connected to most of your channels, reinforce them. The heaviness of the feeling now becomes the normal weight of your body; the sense of expansiveness is now your permanent relationship to space; your rhythm now becomes your habitual speed in daily life. Once you have integrated these patterns into the body, throw away the initial emotion and replace it with a sensation of calm neutrality. You feel fine, no particular worries, but no vast passions either. Just fine. But not in your own body. And then go about the task again. As that person. Look at the world through their eyes. Touch your coat with their hands. Breathe with their lungs.

If you are doing this in a group, allow yourself to observe the others through the gaze of the character. Don't interact or speak to them; simply notice what you feel about them. Whether they make you comfortable or not. Whether they irritate you or not.

What we have done here is to turn the emotional patterns into habit. You are a character who may have experienced great fear, or certainty, or despair in his or her life, and this has become incorporated into the physical patterning. But in the present moment, that emotion is not actively engaged. As you go about the task, you get a sense of how that person relates to the world around. How direct they are. Where they feel comfortable. What matters to them. What happens if something goes wrong when they are doing the task.

As you experiment with the various emotional bodies, you may start to sense that although your basic mood is calm, certain other emotions are quite near the surface. You can sense that it wouldn't take a lot to tip that person over into anger, or that even small difficulties with the buttons on your coat can confirm that that life is tough for 'you'. Equally, other bodies hardly notice problems, or if they do, it isn't anything that bothers them.

You can apply this work directly to certain characters – for example, Leontes in *A Winter's Tale*. At the beginning of the play, Leontes is certain that his jealous suspicions about his wife's infidelity are correct. Then follows the death of his son and the supposed death of his wife and infant daughter, and the realisation that his unfounded jealousy has caused these events. Sixteen years later, we see him again. You could use 'grief/despair' as a physical shaping device, to clarify his emotional journey during those sixteen years.

Next, we can explore how a person whose body has been imprinted with a different emotional matrix experiences their moment-to-moment feelings.

Exercise – Character and Emotion

Go back to the wall. Generate emotion A (for example: 'despair'). Lock it in as character. Then release the emotion. Just as you did in the last exercise.

Then, instead of just feeling calm/unbothered, generate a second strong emotion such as 'joy'. You become a despair person experiencing joy in the here and now. Permit this emotion to find its own channels through the despair-shaped body. Try not to revert to your own body's way of experiencing joy.

For example, when you yourself experience despair, your breathing might become slow and shallow, located in the upper chest; and when you experience joy, your breathing may drop down into the abdomen and become deep and slightly fast. But what happens when you channel joy through the despair body instead of your own? Perhaps the breath speeds up, but remains high in the chest, and shallow. In other words, the rhythm changes but not the placement or depth. And suddenly you may feel an urge to burst into tears. You are using your own real experience of joy, but the way it is expressed belongs to that 'despair-shaped' person, not 'you'. The feeling is real but it lives in a body that has a different pattern of emotional expression. Stick with the challenge of finding what this new body requires. Once you are person A feeling emotion B, go about your task again and see what happens.

As you do this exercise, you must embrace and wrestle with contradictions. You may feel a strong desire just to release the joy in its normal way. Don't. Stay with the struggle to maintain both the character body and the emotional reality. Then you will see which emotions can and cannot pass easily into this body. Also, which emotions slide sideways into another form. Or simply cannot express themselves at all.

This emotional patterning work can have many applications. A useful one is in status work.

Exercise – Status
Divide the group into two halves. Group A will go to the wall and call up 'certainty', while group B calls up 'fear/doubt/hesitancy'. They shape their bodies according to these two emotions and then go about their tasks. Each person is independent, aware of the others but not looking for contact. Like a crowd at a railway station. Gradually certain patterns emerge. For example, the 'certainty' people tend to become more dominant in the space, going where they like, when they like. The other group tends to hesitate more and reacts quickly when someone comes close. This is just one of the many manifestations. Focus on maintaining your 'fear' body or your 'certainty' body and allowing it to respond to the situation. Don't try to show the emotion, or to play your status. Staying open and responsive allows many subtle patterns to emerge.

This is a direct experience of differing status. After all, a 'high-status' person is a member of the group that is socially in charge. They make the rules. They know what needs to happen. They are 'certain'. Low-status people are more dependent. They follow the rules others create. Their success, their livelihood and maybe even their lives depend on responding accurately to imposed demands. There is a different emotional necessity.

RELATIONSHIP TO THE WORLD

Several of the previous exercises have touched on this area already, but it is worth clarifying its importance. No individual lives in isolation; we all exist in a concrete world, and in the centre of a web of human connection. Every character responds to time, space, objects and other people in different ways. That is why I always use the idea of a 'task' as a focusing device for emotions. It forces your body to engage with the physical world. Once you have a task, the emotion moves from the abstract realm of thought and memory and enters the concrete territory of the body, which then interacts with tangible reality. What you feel becomes visible; how you shift a chair reveals what is happening inside you.

It is the same with human relations. For example, no person has a single, unvarying way of speaking. Depending on how well they know someone, how close they are, what kind of relationship they have (personal, family, professional, etc.), they will use different words, various degrees of politeness, tone of voice, levels of honesty and openness. So, when you play a character, you look for the particular nature of the relationships with each other character, and you see how that affects the voice. The words are there in the text, but how you say them will not be identical in every scene with every character; who you are speaking to will affect how you speak. In addition, the presence of others will have an effect. How you speak to person A in private will be different from how you speak to them in the presence of person B, or in the presence of persons B, C and D.

There are many other factors that change in the same way; whether you sit or stand in a certain character's presence, how close you will approach them, whether you relax or become more formal when they appear, whether you become more or less attentive to the situation, etc. When you rehearse, the essential is to stay tuned to your body, and to allow it to change and respond according to the presence and actions of each other character.

This next exercise allows you to explore the area of interpersonal responses in an improvisational setting (it is a variant of 'hot-seating', a common character exercise which is normally done solo, where your character sits in a chair and replies to questions about his or her life). You can do this work with a character you have 'role-modelled' from the real world (someone you have observed in great detail and have now become), or a character from a play (where you have done the research in order to fully embody them). The key thing is to go all the way with this process, changing your body, costume, voice patterns and emotional matrix.

Exercise – Public Opinion Interview

The performers do their character work before the session, coming fully prepared and dressed. They must look like real people, not like performers, so no stage make-up, weird costumes or wigs. If they walked through the streets of London, they would not stand out any more than anyone else (which actually gives you great freedom).

The leader/director sets up the following scenario. Four to seven people have been chosen at random from the community to come in and give their opinions on a number of social issues. They do not know each other or anything about each other. They enter the room and find chairs arranged in a semicircle, facing the leader (now taking the role of interviewer). The interviewer asks a number of questions on relevant topics, starting with easy factual information (jobs, attitude to public transport) and gradually leading the discussion into more charged territory, e.g. the role of religion, homosexuality, immigration. The characters give their opinions, but also allow themselves to respond and react to the actions and opinions of others.

Listening and watching becomes as important as speaking. Alliances start to form on certain issues; inner judgements are made about the others; attraction, repulsion, interest and boredom start to manifest in an organic way.

As I mentioned above, the characters arrive in full and detailed costume. If the characters are from a historical play, you can either set the interview in that period world and adapt the questions accordingly, or you can update it. This involves asking the actors to find a modern-day equivalent; as if the director had decided to set *Hamlet* in current-day London. This has certain advantages, since it forces the actors to think deeply about the character and prevents them from oversimplifying. When you know the character must be as believable as someone you pass in the street, you can't get away with caricature.

There are many more exercises and approaches you can use for character work, but the main tools are personal identification, research, observation, imagination and empathy. By employing all of these, you can create a believable person who is fully alive, yet not limited by the particular focus of your own personal experience. A rich and complex being who is completely integrated into your body and mind.

One final thought on character. Never judge your character and then attempt to play that judgement. Never say to yourself 'Arturo Ui is based on Hitler, therefore I will play him evilly', or 'Ophelia dies mad, therefore I will play her madly.' They are real people; difficult, complex, contradictory, as are all humans. And we must embrace these factors rather than allowing judgement to oversimplify and flatten the performance. Yoshi Oida once said that you should put your characters on a pedestal, believing that they are more interesting than you are yourself. And then you should strive to encompass their richness. You shed your own skin for a while and slip inside theirs.

Now you have finished rehearsing. Your words are fully integrated, you are the embodiment of your role, you know how you feel about the other characters. You have done your research and filled yourself with the world of the play till you dream it. You have listened again and again to the music, finding your timing. You have worked until that movement is absolutely precise, and you have got the entire journey clear in your mind and body. And once you have done all this, you forget it. Just go on, trust the work you have done, relax and play.

With an audience. Whether they are in a theatre, a cinema, a circus tent, or the street. Without them, the work is pointless. After all, no performer or creator works purely for their own personal satisfaction. The challenge is to pass ideas, themes and experiences into the minds and bodies of the watchers, so that they may be changed by the experience. Perhaps not any dramatic volte-face or blinding illumination: just to make them laugh is sufficient. But whatever the nature of the change we want the audience to undergo, we definitely want them to experience something real.

PART 4

CREATING MEANING

Chapter 12 THE AUDIENCE

The response of the audience is the final stage of the creative process. The transmission of ideas begins with the writer, passes on to the director or choreographer, and is then manifested physically by the performers. Then the audience takes over. Out of what we offer them, they create meaning and interpretation.

A man wanders slowly across the stage. He walks, pauses occasionally and then starts walking again. A few steps here, a few steps there. Suddenly, a woman rushes in and collapses into a chair. As an audience, we observe these ordinary actions, yet at the same time we sense that something else is happening, something is going on inside the performer. The man is doing more than simply getting from A to B. The woman is not just relaxing. And we begin to interpret what we see. Perhaps the man is considering his situation, working out what to do next. The woman is exhausted from running; there is danger outside, but now she is safe.

The actions themselves are straightforward – walk across the stage, sit in the chair – but in themselves they say very little to an audience. It is how you do these actions that creates the emotional dimension that we call 'physical acting'. In your mind, replay the same actions in another way: the man throws his body across the stage, the woman crisply strides to the chair, stops for a moment, and then carefully lowers her body on to the seat. A completely different drama, a different set of stories.

In both film and stage performances, the audience constantly creates interpretations about what it is seeing, based on visual information. Everything the actor does is observed, and a meaning is constructed for the action. As an audience, we are usually unaware of this process; an onlooker is unlikely to say to herself, 'Oh, the actor is walking slightly faster than normal, and is carrying excess tension in the shoulders, therefore I interpret that he has made a decision to undertake a slightly distasteful action.' Nonetheless, this process of interpretation happens all the time, in real life as well as on the screen or stage. It isn't a purely analytical, intellectual process; the body is also involved.

This is particularly clear in performing situations. Next time you watch the Olympics on television, or see a fantastic piece of flamenco or a fierce game of tennis, observe what happens to your own body. You will find that it is very slightly mimicking the action you are watching. As the sprinter nears the finishing line, your body is reaching for the tape. As the footballer lines up the crucial kick of the match, you hold your breath, and when the ball goes into the net, you release the tension with a yell. The same thing happens on stage during a good piece of theatre. It is as if the performer's body is creating the 'large' movement, and the onlooker's body echoes this with a 'small' version of the same reality. The actor is wrestling with thought and feeling, and the watcher echoes the breathing and muscular tension that consumes the performer's body. The audience is literally 'moved' by what they see. Breathtaking theatre actually takes their breath away.

The mechanism behind this process has recently been uncovered by researchers; it involves something called mirror neurons, which exist within the human brain. When person A does an action such as raising a cup, a particular sequence of neuron firing occurs within their brain. When person B watches this action, the same sequence of firing is repeated in their own brain as well. This is a very recent discovery, and not all of the implications are clear, but it appears that mirror neurons may be a mechanism of empathy. We watch another person, we see a particular physical manifestation, it triggers the same firing pattern in our brain, including the emotional resonances of the person's action, and so we get a sense of what the other is feeling. (If you want to follow this further, look for the names of Marco Iacoboni, or Giacomo Rizzolatti, who are two of the major researchers in this field.)

The implications of this discovery for performing are huge. It isn't telepathy: mirror neurons operate via observation of *physical* states and actions. Therefore, the audience can only feel what the *bodies* of the performers are manifesting. If these are imprecise or contradictory, the inner reality of the audience will remain equally confused. In addition, if actors have 'dead' bodies that do not permit physical manifestation of living emotion, thought and response, the audience will not be able to enter the drama empathically. And without empathic identification, they cannot experience that extraordinary sense of release and transformation that is the ultimate power of theatre. The mystery of catharsis.

Performers have always sensed this invisible thread of connection between actor and audience, but thanks to advances in neuroscience, it is no longer a mysterious, mystical process. Nonetheless, it does require that the actor be fully present in their body, inhabiting and, most, importantly, manifesting the experience of the moment. Whatever the performer feels must be given concrete and visible form, otherwise transmission cannot happen.

We know the body is central to transmission of experiences, and now we understand why. But the body itself operates within a broader framework of communication.

MEANING

When creating meaning for an audience, there are four main factors: time, space, physical environment (the set, props, and costume), and the bodies of the performers. It is the dynamic relation between concrete objects and human bodies operating in time and within the empty air of space that enables performance to unfold.

We have already looked at some aspects of the theatre space and use of props in the chapter on 'Responding', and will continue examining it, and the element of time in this section. But, before we do that, there is still one further aspect of the body itself that needs exploration – the body in relationship to the observer.

THE BODY IN RELATIONSHIP TO OTHERS

Someone stands in front of us. We look at them. They look back at us. On the surface this would seem to be a fairly direct and uncomplicated relationship. But in fact, a great deal is conveyed by subtle details. What is the angle of their body? Where are their arms? And their shoulders?

In relationship work, the chest and abdomen area are very important, since, in terms of our animal natures, this area is our 'soft underbelly'. Subconsciously, we feel that it is our most personal and vulnerable area and we hesitate to expose it to potential attack. If we face someone directly, and we keep this area fully and easily open, we communicate certain possibilities, such as 'I don't fear you', 'You are no threat', or 'I trust you', 'I like you', 'I am totally comfortable in this situation.' If we cross our arms across the belly or chest, we are protecting ourselves in some way. Hunching our shoulders, or ducking our head is similarly self-protective.

And if we angle the body away from another person, it similarly changes the relationship. Perhaps we are not comfortable being totally direct and open with that individual, or perhaps our prime attention has been caught by something else, in which case our torso will reorient itself towards that object. Our head might stay where it is, but there is no longer full engagement with the onlooker.

In terms of anatomy, the head is 'perception' (it turns to see something of potential interest), and the body is 'engagement' (if what we see is engaging enough, the body will turn to join the head; if not, the head will turn back to rejoin the body). The flavour of the engagement can be virtually anything (we might be angry, or amused, or filled with desire), but the fact of engagement is manifested in where we angle our bellies.

And the audience reads this very clearly. If the performer is completely unblocked in the shoulders, chest and abdomen, and keeps the entire torso open and oriented to the audience, the audience will sense that the performer is comfortable in this direct relationship. That somehow the performer likes and trusts the audience, and wants to be 'in partnership' with them. And their bodies are likely to pick up and echo this pattern. They open and relax, and feel they can trust the performer to take them on a journey. This pattern is used where the performer is in an explicit relationship with the audience, such as stand up comedy. People working in this style should avoid hunching over or closing their torso in with nervousness or fear, since they are contradicting the relationship they want.

If performers angle their torso away from the audience, a different kind of relationship is created – one that is less direct. This is commonly seen in dance, and fourth-wall-style drama, where the audience is an observer, rather than a participant. In these styles, there may be moments of direct audience address (in which case the torso orients to the audience), but most of the time the focus of engagement is elsewhere, usually on the other characters in the scene.

The various angles of the torso create differing degrees of interpersonal engagement between people, but this is not enough to clarify meaning. Like the other tangible element (objects), these need to be embedded in the invisible structure of time and space. It is very easy to ignore these latter two elements (especially during training, when we tend to focus on the person and their individual body), yet they are central to the creation of meaning.

TIME

Time has several aspects, and one of the most important for performers is rhythm.

We all live in a rhythmic world, from the slow progression of the sun from horizon to horizon to the speeding of cars down the highway. We are surrounded by rhythm at every minute of the day. And not only in the outside world; the body itself is full of rhythms. The steady pulse of the heart, the in-and-out of breath, the stop–start–go rhythm of impulse. And broader rhythmic experiences: languorous mornings in bed, a panicky rush out the door, steady sweeps of the vacuum cleaner across the carpet. The human body also uses rhythm as one of its prime means of communication.

Especially of emotional communication. Think about the example I gave at the beginning of the chapter, where the man wanders across the stage while the woman runs. It is the particular rhythm of the action that conveys the inner reality.

Exercise – Rhythm and Inner Reality

Get a chair, put it in the centre of the space, and place a folded sheet of blank paper on the seat. Your script is as follows. See the paper from a distance, approach the chair, stop beside the chair, pick up the paper, sit in the chair, unfold the paper, read it, fold it again, stand up, put the paper back on the seat of the chair, leave. This is the sequence you follow. Do not change it or add any further elements. It is like a script; you follow it without adding any new writing.

Now be aware of the rhythmic possibilities within that script. You could run to the chair, pick up the letter very slowly, sit down at a normal pace, unfold it sharply, read it equally sharply, fold it incredibly slowly, rise normally, place the letter down fairly slowly, and leave, walking slightly faster than normal. Or else you could slowly approach the chair, grab the letter, sit down sharply, open it normally and so on. Any combination of rhythms. Do the script one way, then try it again with a different range of rhythms. And then play with a third version. You always follow the same script, but how you perform it moment by moment is different.

When doing this exercise, be aware that each 'phrase' in the script is a separate unit. Don't run the sitting, unfolding, reading, standing into each other at the same pace, unless that is what you have specifically chosen to do. Keep each element separate and give each one a particular rhythm. Try to use a broad spectrum of different rhythms, not just basic fast or slow, and mix them up. Not only fast – slow – fast – slow – fast, though this is a possible pattern.

The two factors here are the speeds of the individual phrases and the length of the pauses between them. You can sit down fast, then immediately open the letter, or you can sit down fast and then pause for a long time before beginning to unfold the paper. The point of the exercise is to see what happens when you do the same scenario at different speeds and with different-sized gaps.

Don't try to tell a story, or start the exercise with a clear emotional objective in mind. You know the script and you are curious to see what happens to your inner process as the different rhythms impact on the body. You remain connected, however, ready to be affected and changed by the action, not attempting to maintain any imposed idea of neutrality.

When watching this exercise, the audience learns a great deal. Provided that the actors remain connected, the audience will automatically create a storyline for what they see. The man is worried, the letter contains bad news, or that the woman realises that she might be too late, and needs to rush out. The audience even 'write' the words that they imagine are on the letter (which is, of course, a blank sheet of paper). You can see very clearly in this exercise how the four elements (tangible objects – the paper and the chair – human body, time, and space) coalesce to create narrative.

In a real sense, rhythm is emotion. Inexperienced performers sometimes make the mistake of believing that facial expression or gesture is the carrier of emotion to the audience, but this is misplaced effort. It is rhythm – how quickly or how slowly you do the actions, and how long you wait between them – that is the prime conveyor of thought and feeling. For this reason, all performers need to develop a greater sensitivity to rhythm. They need to become aware of the incredible range of rhythms available to them (from 'as fast as you can' to 'as slow as you dare'), and also alert to the subtle differences between two similar rhythm patterns.

Exercise – Tuning to Rhythm

The continuum of available rhythm runs from 'as fast as you can' to incredibly fast, to very very fast, to very fast, to fast, to normal, to slow, to very slow, to very very slow, to incredibly slow, to 'as slow as you dare'. These include, but also go well beyond, the rhythms we use in ordinary life.

Take a simple action, such as walking or running, sitting down, or tucking in your shirt. Do it very, very, slowly. Does it evoke a feeling, or remind you of anything? Is there some kind of inner echo, a flash of memory, an image? Take the same action and do it again very, very fast. See what alters. Keep repeating the action, using as many different rhythms as you can.

As you work, pay attention to the rhythms that are just slightly 'off' your normal pattern. The fast way of brushing your hair that is just slightly faster than your normal 'fast'. Change rhythm when you want, and play with different actions, but never try to be too interesting. You are investigating rhythm and its impact and connection, not trying to be creatively expressive. Keep the actions simple and tangible. If you want to explore the action of drinking water, get a real bottle of real water – don't use mime.

When doing rhythm work, I don't employ music. Not because I dislike it, but because it is too easy (and fun) to dance to the rhythms rather than sense the inner reality they evoke.

TIME AND PERFORMANCE

Some of our performance problems arise from the fact that it does not exist in real time. Most plays recount the events of a week or a year and then compress them into two hours. Or some styles (such as dance or performance art) seem to exist in 'no-time', an indefinite, clock-free world. And even in those rare performances where the action takes place in real time (the events are set in an identical timeframe to the performance), it is still an un-real reality. More things happen in those two hours than in any normal period of 120 minutes.

This has huge implications for how we manage our performance, since our everyday experience of time does not support the demands of the dramatic context. We need to adapt and adjust our actions so they read as 'true' within this compressed and intensified time frame.

Emotional Mobility:

Real life is rarely dramatic; most of the time it is simply ordinary. During the course of a typical day, we encounter a number of emotional experiences – some powerful, some habitual, some fleeting and potent, but most of them are fairly humdrum. Familiar monotony interspersed with flashes of drama. We wake up and our thoughts may be banal and practical; we shower, then decide what to eat for breakfast. Then there's a brief moment of panic as we realise we are running late. Then long periods of bored inattention as we travel to work, occasionally interrupted by flashes of irritation at the person sitting next to us. Then more vague thoughts and feelings as we get ready to work. Then suddenly a phone call from a close friend, delighting us with good news. Then back to just getting on with business. The emotional script for such a scene might go something like this: 'um, um, um, um, um, PANIC, um, um, um, um, um, um, um, IRRITATION, um, um, um, um, um, um, um, DELIGHT, um, um, um, um, um'. And so on. Occasional dramatic moments separated by long periods of emotional static.

But dramatic writing is all dramatic moments, with few ordinary humdrum passages. In performance, the same script would tend to go something like: 'um, um, PANIC, um, um, IRRITATION, um, MORE IRRITATION, um, um, DELIGHT, DELIGHT, DELIGHT. Um, um . . .' In the world of performance, more things happen, and go further, faster than in real life.

Performers need great inner flexibility and mobility, so that they can shift and respond to the quicksilver demands of performance. They should have the ability to shift rapidly and directly from thought to thought, from emotion to emotion, and from one impulse to the next. More quickly and more completely than they would in daily life. They must be very light on their mental and emotional 'feet'. This is why performers need to practise accessing their emotions, thoughts, and imagination during training; they need the skill of quick and easy connections. Plus the ability to turn things on and off at will.

In the chapter on 'What Stops us Working', there are exercises to promote the basic actor state of energised alertness, which makes it easier to access and maintain the necessary fluidity of action and response. In fact, lack of energy is the single biggest block to emotional freedom in rehearsal. If you are working from a place of boredom, or half-hearted engagement, it is difficult to locate a vivid inner landscape. Get your energy up, by running or jumping about, preferably using a positive image (such as running on a beach in Bali). Then you will find it easier to connect with whatever you need.

But there is no point being alert and ready to shift if you have no idea where you need to shift to. Mental and emotional mobility can only occur when there is the clear understanding of exactly where you are going within the performance, and the frequency of change. (Sensing this will indicate how energised your performance needs to be. A fast-shifting role indicates that you need to enter an extremely heightened state of clarity and alertness. Speed requires energy.) You have to be clear about where and how far you have to change.

Normally, when you analyse a text or structure a work, you look for consistencies and reappearing themes. I would suggest that you also look for changes and 'hinges'; places where the character or the action alters direction. The earlier work on 'Points of View' is useful here, and helps you avoid any kind of fixed state when doing long speeches. You don't need to overemphasise these shifts in viewpoint when actually performing; you still have your through-line, or objective (or whatever technical framework you prefer using). But you become aware that this objective is multifaceted, and shouldn't be played on a single, unchanging note.

In the same way, we need to sense the mutability of the whole play (not just a single speech). How each scene starts from a different reality, how the entry of each new performer alters the action on the stage.

Although most staged performances take place over a short period of time, with few interruptions (typically one to three hours, with one or two intervals), the work itself tends to be structured into a procession of scenes, each of which represents a significant change or development from the previous one. Sometimes this is formalised into acts and scenes, as found in scripted text, or it may simply be an informal division of the choreography or structure. Irrespective of whether the scene is given that formal title or not, this method of articulating the changes that occur within the performing time frame finds its reflection in the rehearsal structure. We all (dancers, actors, performance artists) tend to work on one scene in depth and get it right (or at least 'better') before we move on to the next one.

But when it comes to performing, we run these scenes up against each other in rapid succession, and there is no time to re-create the rehearsal process that enabled the right scene to emerge organically. Instead, we must find ways of retrieving our work quickly but accurately. This is where the earlier idea of 'hooks' can be useful. They work for character, as we've already seen, but they also offer a means of physically connecting to change.

Hooks:

We have already encountered the use of hooks in the section on character, but they are equally useful for retrieving key moments. When rehearsing or improvising, we often discover moments that are absolutely right. Romeo sees Juliet for the first time, and the actor truly experiences a sense of dazed elation. It is all there. But too often that moment passes and we find it difficult to retrieve. We then either blame ourselves or start working harder and more seriously, neither of which will be particularly effective. Instead, try the following. At the exact moment that something is working (or more practically, after the rehearsal), notice the physical sensations. The tightness in your pelvis, the exact quality of your gaze, where in the room you were standing, what you were touching, how fast you were thinking.

You are not trying to re-create the entire emotional response itself, but rather the exact physical reality associated with it. By connecting to a specific physical reality that is associated with the inner place you wish to retrieve, you create a 'hook' that can help you.

Find effective 'hooks' for key moments of change, especially your entry, or re-entry on to the stage. In linear, time-based performance, quite a lot happens to characters while they are offstage. They may have aged a few years, or simply have discovered their dog has run away. But they will rarely re-enter in the same reality as when they departed from the previous scene. The actor may only have spent a minute or two in the wings, but the character has had life-changing experiences. Maybe huge, maybe banal, but something has happened. And these must inform the character before they set foot on the stage again.

You improvise these hidden scenes at some stage in rehearsal, creating a vibrant physical life for that reality, and noting the key hooks. Then, during the performance, in your few brief moments in the wings, you trigger the hooks and use them to launch you back into the action, carrying the changed circumstances with you.

Exercise – Finding Hooks

In rehearsal (although this is also easy enough to do at home), take some time to find out what mood or need the character has prior to each entry. Don't rush this process; you want to discover where they are, not just impose some kind of judgement on them. When it feels absolutely right and you can sense that you are eager to start speaking the opening words or doing the next action, begin noticing as many physical details as you can. The more 'hooks', the better. Remember exactly what they are. Inner rhythm, the quality of the gaze, weight placement, an odd sensation in the elbows. Some people use images, or even hold music in their head. It doesn't matter how quirky the 'hook', what matters is that it works.

When you come to performance, take a few seconds to trigger those hooks. Once they are in place, and you can sense the change they link to, enter the action and then forget about them.

As you work on the text, you start to structure your performance. You create a map of your journey through the play. You discover that you need to move from A to B to C to D. You know exactly where A and B are located emotionally and physically, and you can sense what they feel like in your body. In performance, you move clearly and decisively from point to point, from A to B to C to D. And the 'hooks' enable you to shift yourself to each of those locations, rapidly and completely. One caution: the hooks exist to help you re-create the trigger for the response; they are not intended to codify the performance. Their function is stimulus and connection, not a dead reproduction of moves.

The exercise outlined above should go some way to keeping the character dynamic, provided that the 'hooks' you use are precise and specific to this exact moment. For example, your character is excited about her birthday, and it is that excitement which propels you into the scene. Avoid thinking too far ahead. Never attempt to include what you know will happen later in the play into your preparation and 'hook'. You do not manifest the excitement of your birthday, plus the foreknowledge of tragedy and pain that you (the actor) know will occur in Act 3. One of the reasons we need to play precise moment by precise moment is that the character has no idea of what will happen next, and neither does the audience.

Yet actors sometimes make a number of decisions about the play as a whole, and then try to drive this unchanging edifice through the entire two hours. When this occurs with character, it looks quite unnatural. It isn't true to life; none of us are one single thing in every context, with every other person, at every minute of the day. We are probably five things in an hour, if not more. We change from one reality to another, from serious to funny to irritated. And we behave differently depending on who is in the room.

The problem may arise because actors forget the dimension of time and change when preparing their work. They do their research on the complexities of the person and get a broad picture of how the character fits into the play as a whole, and then they attempt to show all of this understanding, all of the time.

But 'showing all of the character all of the time' does not follow the natural pattern of audience understanding. When we encounter new people in real life, we form an initial impression which solidifies into a judgment about who they are. Then something appears out of the blue that modifies that assessment. A difficult moment arrives, and the way that person reacts either confirms our initial judgement or it surprises us by showing an unexpected facet of the individual's personality. It is the same for the audience; we meet the character, and through his or her reactions and responses, we gradually build a picture of who they are. One aspect might be dominant for several lines, but then suddenly another aspect appears, then just as suddenly disappears again. But even that momentary appearance has altered our understanding of who that person is. We also become more interested in who he or she is; we have glimpsed a hidden aspect and we now want to know more. Change is actually the process of revelation.

DEVELOPMENT

The ideas outlined above focus on the importance of dynamic change; of being able to shift rapidly and completely from moment to moment in order to reflect the compression and heightening of life used in performance. But change on its own is not enough. And change for the sake of change is counterproductive. Artificial variety is not the answer; we must find the right change at the right time. There must also be development.

Jo Ha Kyu:
In the earlier books I wrote with Yoshi Oida, we outlined the idea of Jo Ha Kyu. Although it is a concept derived from Japanese Noh theatre, it is not an exotic foreign technique. We all live in a rhythmic world, and Japanese theatre has simply articulated one of the fundamental rhythms of real life and given it a name. In theatrical terms, it is the organic rhythm of development and completion. It is the natural onward momentum of performance. To put it bluntly, Jo Ha Kyu is the rhythm of sex. You start slowly, gradually building, gradually intensifying, then becoming stronger, clearer, sharper. More, and more, and more. Until the climax is reached. And then you relax down. And then, after a time, you begin again.

This rhythm is universal, and it is embedded in each of our

bodies. I often notice when teaching exercises that are rhythmic (like stamping, or clapping), that unless I actually give a structured beat through counting or music, the movements will tend to speed up automatically. Without realising it, the students will be following Jo Ha Kyu. You can also see the same rhythm in a running race (start, speed up, tactics, more effort, faster, hit the tape, slow down, stop, walk off the field). In western culture, this form appears in music; both the crescendo and the sonata form use what the Japanese call Jo Ha Kyu. In fact, once you are attuned, you will notice it everywhere. And you will see that many fine performers or creators use it instinctively. They know somehow that it works.

The only problem with Jo Ha Kyu is that it is extremely hard to describe in words, and extremely easy to do on the floor. Talking about it may offer some limited understanding, but the physical sensation is unmistakable.

Exercise – Improvising with Jo Ha Kyu

Use simple walking as a starting point. Stand quietly for a moment, then start to walk, very slowly. Don't try to add anything artistic; just walk. You take your first step, very slowly. And then the second step is a fraction faster than the first, but still very slow. And then the third step, slightly faster again. There is no hurry to speed up, but you are aware that things are gently moving forward. Then follow that momentum, gradually accelerating. Keep following it. Don't stop and start. Just keep going, on and on, gradually getting faster and faster. At a certain point you will feel that you have no choice but to break into a run. Do it. But only when you have no other choice. If you find yourself thinking 'Maybe I should start running here', you aren't ready yet. It is a physical imperative you are following, not a logical plan. And then the run accelerates. Keep going until the body decides to stop. Again, this is not the mind saying 'I don't think I can keep going. I'd better stop'. Just continue following the rhythm until the body itself decides to end it.

Usually, you start to sense the rhythmic imperative after the first few steps. Once you have connected to it, just continue. Follow the need to keep moving onwards. Follow the momentum. The rhythm itself will carry you right to the end if you allow it to. The key to this exercise is gentle awareness. You are not trying to prove anything (which might lead you to continue longer than the organic moment in order to demonstrate your strength and determination). Nor are you limiting yourself through judgements (which might lead you to stop too early, because you think you might be getting boring, or you don't think you are strong enough to keep going). Just follow the body in a spirit of soft curiosity; start, then see how you keep moving forwards.

Jo Ha Kyu isn't simply a question of pure acceleration. It isn't the gradually increasing speed that is Jo Ha Kyu, but the sense of onward momentum. You can increase your momentum even when you slow down physically, if you keep some other aspect of your performance moving forward. You can even stand still, provided that your inner life is continuing the development. You can have as much variety as you want – from stillness to speed to languor, from physical action to pure speech, from comic mayhem to internalised vulnerability – provided that each change somehow moves the action onwards. You constantly change as required by the structure of the performance, but the change is embedded in the momentum of development.

Exercise – Jo Ha Kyu and Change

Start with a simple action like walking, and connect to the Jo Ha Kyu rhythm. When circumstances dictate, change the action (you have walked till you arrive at the wall, so you turn, lean on it and slither to the ground). Each of these changes somehow develops the action. The turn is slow, but somehow more personal than the walk. The lean is even slower, but your gaze widens to take in the whole space. The slither carries the action onwards into a moment of helpless abandon. Try to avoid deciding to change; let the circumstances dictate it. You have run out of breath, so you move more slowly (but more intently). The wall is in front of you, so you use it. The body is tired, so you move into speech. Your eyes are caught by the light, so you move out of speech into silent contemplation. Your feet get twitchy, so you move out of silent contemplation into idiotic stupidity.

The specific choice you use as the next change isn't important; what matters is that it advances the action onwards. There is a feeling of 'no retreat'; once you have begun, there is no way back. Just 'more' and 'further' and 'keep going' until you simply and inevitably end.

At a certain point, you are likely to sense that the journey has truly ended itself, usually in a climax of some sort. There is a feeling of satisfaction; you know you have taken the action to its natural and organic end, and you find yourself in a state of quiescent waiting. This is part of Jo Ha Kyu; you have completed one cycle. And the next cycle is preparing to depart from this new starting place. Wait, and when it feels right, start the whole thing again.

But again I remind you, the body is what decides when the cycle has ended, not the mind. If you find yourself saying 'Maybe this is where I should stop', you haven't reached the natural end point. Let the body decide where that point is. Quite often, the true end point is much further on than the logical mind can envisage. And when the body recognises completion, the performer usually has a clear sense of satisfaction, a kind of inner smile. The body might be dripping sweat, but there is no feeling of ground-down, dull exhaustion.

Within a single performance, there are many Jo Ha Kyu cycles. The performance as a whole has Jo Ha Kyu, as does each act and scene. In text-based work, each speech has its own Jo Ha Kyu. And even a single gesture has a subtle sense of development. Sensing these cycles is the key to performance development, both for the performer and for the audience.

The Jo Ha Kyu rhythm is universal. It is used by good performers, but it also lives in the body of every member of the audience. If you can connect to Jo Ha Kyu in your own work, you will trigger the same pattern in the onlookers. Their bodies will follow your Jo Ha Kyu towards a sensation of organic completion and satisfaction. In a sense, you are manipulating the audience's bodies, via the mirror neurons, so that their experience of the performance journey will be physically satisfying. And this occurs on a level well below that of logic and intellectual understanding. Empathy and catharsis are physically generated, and Jo Ha Kyu is central to this process.

Think about what happens if you watch a play or film. It is going along nicely, and then it seems to get stuck in the same place, not moving forward. You may find yourself saying to yourself, 'Yes, yes. Come on. I do understand. Yes, fine. Let's move on.' In this case, the development isn't happening fast enough. The Jo Ha Kyu is not moving forwards. In other cases, you are watching, saying to yourself, 'Yes, that's it! And? Yes! And? . . . ? . . . ? . . . ? . . . Oh, that's all? No more? . . . Oh.' Here, the action has moved too rapidly to its conclusion and the development has not had the time to reach an organic climax. But when the Jo Ha Kyu is properly developed, your body echoes the momentum of the action. Your words might be something like 'Yes . . . that's it . . . and . . . Yes, yes . . . and yes, that's it, yes/yes/yes!... YES!!!'

As well as being useful for performers, Jo Ha Kyu is a valuable tool for directors and writers. It provides a framework for dramatic development that is not limited to the written text or narrative structure, but instead incorporates the entire performance context.

Take the case of *Richard III*. When we were working on this play we encountered a problem: the climactic battle scene between Richard and Richmond has no words provided. The previous scene (Act 5, scene 4) is only thirteen lines long, ending with the famous cry 'A horse! A horse! My kingdom for a horse!' And scene 5 is essentially the epilogue after the death of Richard, though it begins with the stage direction 'Enter King Richard and Richmond; they fight. Richard is slain . . .' Not a lot of textual assistance there.

In terms of the overall Jo Ha Kyu of the play, this had to be a big, high-energy, intensely gripping scene, since it was the true climax of the piece. If it wasn't permitted to follow its natural momentum, the audience would not be physically and emotionally satisfied by the performance. So, despite the lack of words, we built this scene up into a large-scale battle involving most of the cast, filled with drums and ferocious action, culminating in an almost ritualistic execution of the king. Into the resultant stillness, the epilogue fell like the promise of a new beginning (which indeed is what the text indicates).

We didn't stage the scene this way in order to be tricksy or self-consciously artistic; it was the result of needing to fulfil the Jo Ha Kyu. And I suspect that Shakespeare himself did something similar; that in the original staging, there was some kind of strong, dramatic action at this point, but being non-verbal, it never made its way into the transmitted text. I feel sure of this because Shakespeare is constantly exhibiting perfect Jo Ha Kyu in his work. His work has a natural onward momentum. Beckett is the same.

Understanding Jo Ha Kyu is a great help to a director. And a director can use many other elements of the performing context to maintain dynamic connection to the audience, not just the performers' bodies. If you are directing, you may sense that something needs to change in order to maintain development, yet you are satisfied with the performers' work and would prefer not to interfere with it. In this case, try changing the lighting state, or bringing in music when the momentum is flagging. The intervention must harmonise with the action, but what you choose to do doesn't really matter, since Jo Ha Kyu is felt by the audience on an unconscious physical level. Keep their bodies aligned with Jo Ha Kyu and they will somehow feel satisfied by the production. Even if they don't entirely understand it.

SPACE

The final key element in physical communication of meaning is space. How close, or how distant your body is from an object, or the wall, or another person. The air in between is alive.

In daily life we have a clear sense of personal space, or how close we will allow strangers to approach us. This is learned (children have no sense of personal space and will quite happily clamber all over you and each other) and varies from culture to culture (some cultures keep a gap of three feet round the body as private territory; in other cultures the gap might be two feet, or even as little as one). The privacy zone can adapt itself to particular circumstances, such as when you are forced to stand squashed up against strangers in a crowded train, but it is always present in adults. We feel uncomfortable if someone comes too close. Normally, we only 'let people in' to our privacy zone if we like and trust them. Friends, family, lovers. Sometimes people will force their way into our territory, and we feel this to be insensitive or aggressive.

Space is never neutral, but it is very easy to forget this fact. When performers have a close working relationship, there is a danger that the space between them becomes too easy and personal. They like each other, lots of hugs are shared, they squeeze together in the van. As a result, the air between them has no electricity. But within the world of the play, the characters may be strangers or even enemies, in which case the air between them needs to be highly charged and difficult to cross. Sometimes the converse is true; you are working with someone you detest, but you have to let the air between you become easy and intimate. You have to let them into your private bubble.

The audience reads the relationships between the characters according to the space between them, plus the changing angles of the body. If rhythm equals emotion, space equals relationship. And the legs are the mediators of this relationship since they determine how close we stand to another, or whether we are approaching or retreating. Put this together with an awareness of time, and you have a clear unspoken 'narrative'.

Exercise – Space and Relationship

Three people work together. The prime focus is the air between the three individuals; the distance, the proximity. To change the space, you move the body, compressing or stretching the air between you. You can use running, walking and standing still, and many different rhythms. Also, turning your body away or towards the others. Slight angles of the torso, or even turning your back completely. But your prime focus isn't on what your body is doing, it is the air between you that matters. Air that is compressed or stretched or twisted, as you follow impulse.

You tune to the others, letting what you see impact on you. As you 'take them in', something wants to happen in your body. You may feel an urge to turn away or to walk towards one of the others. That is what you do. This action in turn provokes an answering impulse in both of your partners. The whole scene now comes alive, with each of you sensing what is happening between you and following impulse. You follow emotional response: how does that person walking away make you feel? And then reply with emotional impulse, perhaps to run after them. Or just turn slightly away, so you are no longer facing them directly.

Stay very simple in this work. No interesting moves, no hands, just walking at different speeds, running, standing still, and the many subtle angles of the body. Nothing more.

As you tune in to this exercise, all sorts of subtle relationships and alliances appear. Two people may end up shoulder-to-shoulder, facing the other. The pair walks forward in unison, driving the other round the space. Or one person turns slowly to face the wall, refusing to face the others. And so on.

The key factors in this exercise are to use the air between you, rather than body gestures, and to keep the focus on the legs, sensing whether to approach or retreat, how close, and at what speed. Also, let what you see happening between the three of you have 'impact', and let that impact move you. To transgress the space when required. To let someone into your personal space if it feels right, or to step straight up to their face.

The concept of trangression is important here. Remember that successful performance behaviour is often very different from successful social intercourse, and the rules and requirements are different. You must permit yourself to transgress and forget polite behaviour. In this exercise, it means shattering the normal sense of personal space. The need to transgress becomes even clearer in the second stage of the exercise.

Exercise – Follow/Resist/Provoke

I introduced these three ways of managing impulse back in Part One. We can now apply them to group work. Start the 'Space' exercise again in exactly the same way, but this time, as what you see impacts on you, there are three choices of action. You can just 'follow', as you did above; you can 'resist' ('No, I'm not going there'); or you can 'provoke' (taking the impulse and turning it into something unexpected). One person strides quickly towards you. When they are about four or five feet away from you, you may feel an impulse to leave. You can either just walk away ('follow' the impulse), or stand your ground until you are nose-to-nose ('resist'), or just before your noses touch, you can twist slightly and lean gently against the other's body ('provoke'). And so on.

Now we are ready to add voice and text.

For the following exercise, you treat any given speech purely as vocabulary; the language 'pool' of the character in this situation. I have already mentioned (in the chapter on 'Voice and Words') that everyone has a basic pool of language, a vocabulary of words and phrases that are known, owned and strung together according to the needs of the moment, and that when you feel an impulse to communicate verbally, you reach into this pool and haul up words and phrases to meet your needs. Sometimes we have a strong impulse to communicate, but as we 'reach in', there are no suitable words. In this case, we are left literally 'speechless'. But in most cases we will find something that fits, or can be adapted to our purposes. That is how you work in the following exercise. You choose a speech from some source which becomes your pool, the only words and phrases you can employ. And when you feel an impulse, but find no appropriate language, remain 'speechless' but still in contact with the impulse.

Exercise – Follow/Resist/Provoke with Text.
Choose a short speech from any source. Something you know extremely well, so that you never have to think about the words. Forget about doing it as a speech, i.e. starting at the beginning and working your way through to the end; it is simply your pool of words and phrases, into which you dip as required. You can use single words, short phrases or entire sentences. You can take them out of order, jumble them up, or repeat them as often as you like.

Start physically first. Tune in to your co-performers, sensing what is happening between you in the space. Move into follow/resist/provoke mode, still keeping your prime focus on the air between you. Do not think about what you are going to say. At a certain moment, what you see provokes a physical impulse which also desires to be heard in the air between you. You follow that impulse into action, and at the same moment you 'reach in' and find a word or phrase that enables your voice to reflect the same reality as your body. Not move, and then speak afterwards. A simultaneous body/voice impulse. Also, no forward planning. No sense that something might be interesting to say. Just this exact moment manifesting itself visually and aurally. Equally.

Then you continue, letting what you see, and now what you hear, impact on you and bounce you into a response. And so on, using your body and whatever words are available to express and communicate.

Again, don't be polite. Don't wait your turn to speak. Speak when the impulse connects to language. It is acceptable to have three people talking over the top of each other. Equally, don't feel impelled to speak if there is no impulse to move into language, or if there aren't any 'words' for you.

I love watching this exercise. It is amazing to see how words can be placed into a range of unlikely contexts and still work. Still ring true. And it doesn't matter that one person has a speech from Shakespeare while another is using a film script and a third the lyrics of a song. Somehow they manage to use these to genuinely communicate with each other. It clearly demonstrates the fact that the surface meaning of the words is only ten per cent of the communication.

So now you have clarified what you want the audience to see, and ensured that the communication is as effective as possible. Then their creative function takes over. The audience doesn't just passively swallow what we thrust at them; our actions and words echo inside their being in very individual ways, and are interpreted differently. A strong gesture reminds one person of an attack they endured, while someone who has never been in danger finds the identical action innocuous. A certain moment will recall anger in one person, while the man sitting in the next seat will find the same moment amusing, and the woman on the other side will simply be nonplussed. It is a kind of arrogance to assume we control the reactions of the audience. We must be clear and committed, and make our performance as interesting as possible, but which exact story is played inside each individual mind remains a mystery.

Chapter 13 HINTS ON STYLE AND TECHNIQUE

The world of performance is in constant change. New material emerges, while established parts of the repertoire fade. The criteria for a star performance shift, as tastes in acting alter. Entire performing styles vanish and others are born. When I began my work in theatre, mime was a major and popular style, while circus consisted of a few tired horse and clown events. Now the reverse is true. And it will change yet again. For this reason I focus on 'hints' on style, rather than a fully examined analysis of each sub-style and its requirements. But these hints do not have a sell-by date; they examine some of the key elements behind style choices, and can be adapted as performance fashion changes.

THE ROLE OF TECHNIQUE

Good performance is always rooted in some aspect of real life. When we watch it, we sense that it rings true. Even when the unfolding story is unfamiliar to us, or presented in an alien style, we still know it speaks of events and reactions we recognise from our own lives. But this doesn't mean that it is the same as normal daily reality. Performance is more than a complete and faithful representation of real life; it 'presents' reality, but within a framework that is illusion and untruth. This is one of the central paradoxes of performance. We enact a lie, which is somehow believable to us and to the audience. We pretend we live in a world that has no actual existence. We fall in love with people we may slightly dislike, or attempt to kill an enemy who is actually our best friend. And yet the lie must ring true.

This paradox finds its reflection in our acting process; we must be able to present a believable experience of passion while remaining aware of the demands of the performing context. No matter what she feels, the stage actor must ensure that every word is audible. No matter what he feels, the film actor must not go out of shot. Heat of emotion needs to be allied with technical clarity and control.

Too often, actors assume that these two facets are automatically in opposition to each other; either you have passion, or you are working in a coldly technical way. But this is a false opposition. Good acting twines these two aspects together so that they support each other. Think about your technical control as a glass and your passion as the water that fills the glass. If you have no glass, it is difficult to carry the water from the spring to the mouth; but conversely, if the glass is empty, there is nothing to transport. In the same way, a beautifully executed technical performance that is empty is fundamentally unsatisfying for an audience; they may admire the skill and dexterity, but they will not be moved. Conversely, a performance that is all passion and no structure will also fail to reach an audience. In this case, you see the actors having a rip-roaring time, but it seems to be for their own personal pleasure and not for the benefit of any onlooker. We watch them having great emotional experiences, yet we feel excluded from the process.

And this is literally true, since the actors do not have the technical awareness or control to ensure that the performance reaches the audience in a physical form that they can respond to.

Technique is most essential when the emotions and actions are wildest. To return to our earlier analogy of the glass and the water, when the water is boiling hot, a light crystal flute will shatter. You require a goblet of steel to hold the passion. Your technique should help you communicate with clarity while respecting the hugeness of the language and subject matter. You should never dismiss technique, you should welcome it.

In the same way that young performers sometimes misunderstand the function of technique, so they can get confused about how various styles of acting operate and what they require. And sometimes issues of falseness, bad acting, overacting and empty technique get muddled with questions of style. For example, young actors often associate 'small' personal styles of acting with authenticity of feeling, while anything larger in style is associated with falseness and overacting. This leads them to resist working in a larger style, since they fear becoming bad actors. In reality, there are three quite separate factors: authenticity, scale of work and style of work.

SCALE OF PERFORMANCE

When actors start working in larger spaces, they often start to worry about the size of their performance. Is it big enough? Does it read to the audience? Too often they then start to gesticulate more broadly, and act more loudly and coarsely. In a sense, they are correct in their feeling that the work has to somehow open out more to the audience in a larger space, but they do not always make the right choices about how to achieve this. They feel they need to forget the detailed work they use in the rehearsal studio, and find a new style of performing. This isn't necessary. Essentially, the same process is used in all acting. Shifting from film, to small studio, to the largest amphitheatre does not involve a radical new way of working, just a refocusing of activity. As a camera does when moving from close-up to distance shot.

Instead of big actions, they need energised actions. Instead of simplistic acting they need clear choices which are then cleanly and accurately delineated. Acting in a large space is about clarity and commitment, not 'big-ness'. Strangely enough, this also works well on camera.

CLARITY

When you work with impulse, you begin to sense the core of each moment. You feel that *this* is what is important in the relationship, or that *this* is what drives the line. Once you have uncovered the essence, you must commit to it. One hundred percent. Not for the whole scene, or even the following second, but right now *this* is what is happening . Commit fully, and then change, and commit again.

This is one of the biggest problems I observe with young actors; they do not commit strongly enough to their choices. Or they commit, and then think this is where they will stay for the next half-hour. It is tricky – committing fully, then letting go, changing to a fresh impulse, and then committing again. But it is the easiest way to create a vivid yet subtle performance. Committing to an impulse or a choice does not imply 'big-ness'. You can commit totally to passive vulnerability; nothing is very evident on the surface, but you are one hundred percent where you need to be.

Once you have found your impulse and committed to it, you have to ensure that nothing distracts. You need clarity. You need to erase whatever is not essential to the moment. In this way, the core choice stands out cleanly and clearly, and there are no intruding irrelevancies. In physical terms, this means eliminating shadow gestures and extraneous movements.

Shadow gestures are habits that the actor is unaware of, but which punctuate their performance. Typical shadow gestures are pursing the lips before speaking, tilting the head to the side when walking, or twitchy toes when speaking or listening. These actions have not been chosen by the actor and they get in the way of what is actually being communicated. They are the visual equivalent of the 'Er' and 'Um' that can occur when speaking. These are not consciously selected, and they break the clarity of the communication. The newly emerged use of 'Like' to punctuate youth conversations is also a verbal shadow.

None of these shadow gestures or words is wrong in itself; quite the reverse, they may be an important facet of the character you are portraying. But they need to be chosen rather than automatic. This next exercise allows you to explore the experience of utter simplicity.

Exercise – One Move at a Time

Start from any position. Out of where you are emotionally, allow a single action to manifest in the body. Maybe you are bored, and you slither down the wall. But that is all you do. Just slither. Not slither, and sigh, and tilt your head. Just one clear choice. Then wait where you land. Another impulse emerges, and you channel it into a single action. Maybe you extend your left leg, or your eyes tilt upwards. But not both actions. Only one.

The moves can involve the whole body (e.g. walking across the room), or almost invisible (a shift in the focus of the gaze). It doesn't matter. What is important is the clarity of the choice. And the absence of any irrelevant or distracting details.

It is the clarity of the action that makes it readable to an audience in the back row of a huge theatre, not the size. In addition, when you work with clarity the entire audience sees believable performance. Remember, the theatre might hold twelve thousand seats, but there are still people in the front row. If you do big, overly demonstrative actions it might work for the back row, but all that the front row will see is pure ham.

AUTHENTICITY

Authenticity is the direct, simple expression of feeling. From the heart, with no cover-up or apology. It can be very small, or it can become huge, but it remains a direct and honest manifestation of the moment. And authentic feelings can be very large, odd and extreme in expression. If the inner reality and the demands of the dramatic situation are extreme, then the authentic release of emotion must be equally extreme. Otherwise, it looks false.

Lack of symmetry is the measure of bad acting. If a moment is fragile and personal, it demands a fragile and personal response, and to act 'big' in this situation would be wrong. Conversely, if the moment requires a huge response in order to be true to the situation, then this is what the actor should provide; going small and inward is another case of bad acting. Bad acting occurs when the actor's response to the moment is inappropriate.

Unless you allow 'big' emotions to find a corresponding physical reality, it is hard to encompass the demands of heightened language such as Shakespeare's, or archetypal passions, as in Greek tragedy. To perform these too naturalistically (on the scale of ordinary social interaction) is inappropriate. It betrays the writing, and it betrays the nature of performance which is so often rooted in the extraordinary moment. You don't play Medea as if she is a happy Londoner with one or two small difficulties. If you do this, you reduce the text to banality. Instead of 'bringing the text down to your level', you need to move yourself 'up to the text'.

Yet 'big' does not mean crass or overblown. Quite the opposite. You must work to stay totally authentic at this pitch, and this requires great inner energy, allied with incredible control and precision of technique. Your technique will help you communicate with clarity while respecting the hugeness of the language and subject matter.

The earlier work we did on 'Connecting to Text' should support rather than limit your ability to remain authentic, whether working on large-scale or small naturalistic performance. Once you have brought the writer's words inside your body, you own them fully. Then you forget the work you have done, you forget about 'being yourself', and instead allow your character's feelings and reactions to come to life and drive you. The language follows freely and confidently, and can adapt itself to demands of style and scale.

SCALE AND PRESENTATION

Most styles of performance demand that action be linked to authenticity of feeling. The exceptions are styles where the action is 'presented' to the audience in a clearly stated way (as in a musical, or stand-up comedy, performance art or in the theatre of Brecht). But even in these cases, the action still has its origin in recognisable human response and reaction. They start from authenticity and then shape it into a 'presentation'.

'Presentational performance' is not some alien actor skill; we often use it in daily life. If you are having a conversation with someone that is rather personal, you may find yourself speaking from the heart for a few moments, then getting embarrassed and starting to send yourself up, presenting your emotions as if you are saying: 'Well, this is what this person (me) is feeling.' People constantly shift between sincerity, presentation and even performance of another person in daily life ('I felt awful, but "the show must go on". And then he said to me 'You stupid idiot! Don't you realise what you've done?'). And this variation is the basis for shifts in style of acting.

Presentational acting occurs when a performer steps slightly outside the direct experience of the moment and packages it for the audience. As if the experience is being underlined or framed in order to observe it more clearly. It is extracted from its context, and given a slightly separate life. We see this style a great deal in comedy; it is as if the actor is saying: 'Oooh, look at me now! Boy, am I nervous! Get this!' The key thing to remember is that actors have to be able to be presentational as well as authentic. And vice versa, since both are required skills. You can't even say: 'Oh, I'll only perform authentic roles, so I don't need to work on the other style.' Many characters in plays are constantly shifting between authenticity, presentation and performance in the script. Ranevskaya in Chekhov's *The Seagull* is a good example of this phenomenon.

Exercise   Playing with Scale and Presentation

Choose a specific emotion, e.g. embarrassment. Imagine that there is an audience in the room for whom you must create this reality. The audience must see the embarrassment. So you have to get it out of the brain and into the body. Start small, using a simple, naturalistic style. Once it starts to flow, keep it moving and start to make choices. Use authenticity ('Oh God! How could I have said that? Oh no! Please, please, not him!', etc.) and let it get bigger and bigger without slipping into any form that is insincere. This is playing with scale, where you take an emotion up or down in size without ever becoming false.

Then step sideways and 'present' your embarrassment. ('You want to see embarrassment? Here it is! Earth swallow me up!') Here, your focus is on making that inner core clearly visible to the onlooker, through chosen physical actions ('You want embarrassment? OK! Here's embarrassment!' Just watch this!) . In this case, the inner dimension is smaller than the outer presentation. Or rather it has been replaced by a different inner impulse; the performer's desire to skilfully package the experience.

As you do this exercise, you will start to sense what changes in you when you shift between authenticity and presentation. Also, what shifts as you work the full range of scale, from small to huge and everything in-between.

Doing this exercise should confirm that all work is rooted in human reality; variations in scale or degrees of presentation aren't anything alien that you paste on top of your naturalistic acting, or an externalised technical demonstration. While the 'presented' form usually emphasises the physical and vocal expressive pattern, it should never totally lose touch with the authentic experienced emotion. If this happens, it becomes an empty form, devoid of recognisable humanity.

STYLISATION AND PHYSICALITY

There are a number of larger-than-life styles, such as broad farce, Commedia dell'Arte, kabuki or masked theatre. It isn't within the scope of this book to go into detail on the history, origins or techniques involved in these diverse traditions, but despite the huge differences in context and execution, there is common ground between them. As is the case with 'presentational performance', the point of origin for the expressive language is authentic reality. And they follow the same fundamental process of stylisation.

All stylisation works is based on observed reality: a gesture provoked by a real feeling, or a character trait which has a specific physical manifestation. You then amplify that particular pattern to make it clearer and more distinct. The shape becomes more defined, the rhythm pattern stronger, the spatial relationship clearer, the pitch and intonation of the voice more noticeable. Then (and this is the key step which often gets missed out) you eliminate everything else. Stylisation involves removing distractions as well as enlarging the chosen forms.

Exercise – Stylisation Process

Work with a partner – one person working, the other observing. Take a simple action, e.g. walking. Your partner observes you as you repeat this action several times. Gradually, certain key elements emerge: the pace of your walk, the angle at which you hold your head, how you place your feet. Up until now, you are doing the same exercise on 'Using a Role Model' outlined in the chapter on 'Character'. Now comes the difference. Select three or four of these elements and start to enlarge them. The rhythm becomes more pronounced, the head angle more visible, the placement of the feet larger and exaggerated. Keep going until these become very pronounced, and then ditch any other elements that might distract from these principle traits. Perhaps you wiggle your head slightly when you walk, but this will interfere with the clear angle at which you have placed your skull on your neck. So eliminate it. In this way, you have created a kind of parody or caricature of the other person. A stylised version of an authentic being.

In a sense, stylisation is like a cartoon rather than a portrait. It is a clarified but recognisable version of reality, with key factors highlighted and exaggerated, and distracting details eliminated.

You can apply the process of stylisation to psychology (where the person is reduced to three or four essential characteristics which define and dominate their behaviour; this is the basis of true melodrama), to action and gesture (where real-life movements are amplified and choreographed; this appears in both Japanese Noh theatre and in western performance art); and even to vocalisation (the vocal patterns used in kabuki are basically heightened versions of normal speech rhythms and intonations).

Whichever style you choose to work in, you are always confronted with the central paradox. What you do is false, but it looks somehow real. And it is your skill in combining authentic human truth with precise technical control that will enable the audience to believe the lie you tell. And to enjoy watching you tell it.

CAMERA WORK

Until now, I have been mainly talking about theatrical performance, and the skills required to work in a large performance space. But how do you adapt your work for film or television, where even the slightest twitch is picked up by the camera? How do you minimise distracting gestures without looking dead?

In fact, the basic principles of clarity and commitment also apply here. In particular, you have to be adept at working with very small impulses, since the camera can see actions that might be invisible in a larger space. But the body does not lose its central role in performance. Impulses may need to be reduced in scale, but they still penetrate the whole body equally. You do not reduce your work to 'face' acting; this is a fallacy, based on the fact that there are a lot of head shots on film. Remember, it is the camera that chooses to focus on the face, not the actor who decides only to come alive in one part of the anatomy. In fact, the totality of the actor's body is alive. It has to be. There may be two cameras filming; one in close-up, the other framing the whole body.

In fact, the face is the part of the body that does the least overt acting. On screen, it becomes too big to allow broad expressions to look natural. The camera allows the audience to be in the most intimate relationship with the actor's face, as if it were gazing at the features from a few inches away. And if someone were that close to you, it wouldn't be natural to grimace and pout in an exaggerated way. The face is alive, but in a subtle way.

Exercise – Draining the Face

Start improvising, using any strong impulse. As you work, keep the inner dimension alive, and the body fully connected and direct. In this state, the face will join in. Fine. Let that state of connectedness establish itself. Then, keeping the body going, drain energy from the face. Don't try to be 'neutral' or stop the face responding to what is happening. Simply let it become less interesting and engaged than the mind or the body. This is quite a tricky exercise, and only to be attempted when your body is already fully alive.

Another good camera exercise is a version of the 'One Move at a Time', detailed above in the section on 'Clarity'.

Exercise – One Move at a Time for Camera

Start from where you are. Sitting, slumping against a wall, lying on the floor – it doesn't matter. Preferably, don't stand in the centre of the room in a grounded, aligned position, since this will tend to trigger theatrical-style acting. Then start to move, as feels natural in that moment. Shift your position, breathe deeply, look out of the window. But only use one body part at a time. And when you use your face, be aware that a tightening of the lips, or a refocusing of the gaze, is one single move. And potentially a very big one from the film audience's perception. Keep any movement in the face subtle. You may want to flare your nostrils - do it, but don't let it become exaggerated. You can still use big actions, like running across the room, or wrenching open the door, but keep them simple - one move at a time, not a complex multi-limb package. And the single moves in the face are small and not intrusive.

By the way, keep your use of rhythms alive when doing this exercise. 'One Move at a Time' can easily become robotic, and this happens when the performer does each action at the same speed, and with the same time gaps between actions.

The main thing with the camera is to keep your body simple and your mind alive. The camera picks up thought, therefore you need a strong inner life. In this way, the work looks organic without being overstated. The 'Acting Starfish' exercise given in the first chapter, on 'Connecting to the Body', is useful here.

Exercise – Camera Starfish

Take an impulse, anything that reflects human reality (anger, joy, boredom) and pass it into the entire body, as if every molecule of your being is saturated by the same feeling, at the exact same moment. Then reduce the scale, making the impulse virtually invisible, but virtually invisible everywhere, equally.

One of the best pieces of advice for camera acting was Zeami's idea that 'The heart moves ten-tenths, but the body only moves seven-tenths'. Keeping this in mind ensures that your inner life is always more vibrant than your external expression. Consequently, every action becomes charged and alive, even when you do very little on the surface. Your body can remain simple, clear and full of ease, without any loss of thought and intention.

CONCLUSION

And so we come to the end. The key thing to remember is that using your body is not a matter of discipline, but rather a means of engaging more fully with your self and the world around you. Of moving outside habit and system, and reclaiming the right to exist physically in new and unexpected ways.

Performing itself is fairly straightforward. It is being alive and real in front of the audience, and allowing the performance to unfold moment by moment, within the style and the context of the work. Sometimes you can just do it, easily and directly. Great. Other roles (or styles) are more difficult, so you have to work and explore and experiment, until the work falls into place. And this is where the various exercises and approaches are useful; they are tools to help you perform. But they are not the act of performing itself. Too many students think that doing a well-known exercise, or utilising a particular methodology, or dutifully applying a specific technical system will automatically ensure the quality of performance. It won't. Performing is being vibrantly alive in the moment, communicating with the audience. The methods are only suggestions to help you get there. That's all. If you are finding something real via your own process (or lack of process), don't feel that you are doing something wrong. If it works, use it.

This doesn't mean you just sit there, satisfied with what already works. Very few performers can just 'do it', every time, in every style, in every role. There are performers who essentially repeat the same performance each time they appear, and audiences often enjoy watching them. But this isn't ideal, since the performer becomes the centre of the work, rather than the reality being communicated.

Most good performers resist this, instead trying to find ways to serve and illuminate the material.

Time doesn't stand still. You change, theatre changes, new kinds of roles emerge in films, and what works for you today may not work in five years' time. So keep exploring. Try new approaches and gain more tools to help your work. Keep training and experimenting. Not to find 'the one and only answer' and then spend the rest of your life applying it to everything you undertake. But to continue to increase the depth and range of responses available to you as a human being.